DATE DUE

SOULLESS

Also by Susan Estrich

The Case for Hillary Clinton

Dangerous Offenders (with Mark Moore et al.)

Real Rape

Getting Away with Murder: How Politics Is Destroying
the Criminal Justice System

Making the Case for Yourself: A Diet Book for Smart Women

Sex and Power

How to Get into Law School

SOULLESS

ANN COULTER AND THE RIGHT-WING CHURCH OF HATE

SUSAN ESTRICH

REGAN

An Imprint of HarperCollins*Publishers*

10161726

HarperCollins books may be purchased for educational, business, or sales promotional use. For information please write: Special Markets Department, HarperCollins Publishers Inc., 10 East 53rd Street, New York, NY 10022.

For editorial inquiries, please contact Regan, 10100 Santa Monica Blvd., 10th floor, Los Angeles, CA 90067.

FIRST EDITION

Designed by PDC

Library of Congress Cataloging-in-Publication Data has been applied for.

ISBN 10: 0-06-124649-2

ISBN 13: 978-0-06-124649-4

06 07 08 09 10 PDC/RRD 10 9 8 7 6 5 4 3 2 1

To Isabel and James
With all my love, always

ACKNOWLEDGMENTS

My deepest gratitude to Dean Ed McCaffery of the U.S.C. Gould School of Law for his friendship and support; to U.S.C. President Steve Sample for simply being the best university president anywhere, and providing me an intellectual home for the past seventeen years; to Suzanne Scott, Bill Shine, and Roger Ailes, as always, for their support and friendship; to Rose Shumow, for inspiration; to my sister and brother and my friends, for putting up with me, again; to my wonderful assistant, Michelle Kim, who keeps everything together; to John O'Mahony for his editorial assistance and Amanda Urban for her idea; and especially to my students, starting with the best of the best, Marc Gilbar, for whom this is the second book in two years; Patty Eberwine, who labored long into the night on this one; and Joanne Wu, Jessica Perata, Amy Mellow, and Yem Mai, who, in the eleventh hour, were invaluable collaborators.

CONTENTS

SOULLESS

INTRODUCTION

You're writing a book about *WHO*?

WHY GIVE HER ANY MORE ATTENTION?

Because she's already gotten the attention.

The question is no longer attention.

It's time to take her on. And take on those who give her a forum.

We can have fun with it. We don't have to be mean. Meanness is what people hate. Parody, humor, wit . . . it all works. But to an end.

It's important to take her on.

She is not just a harmless entertainer, just another blowhard on the scene. She's been around for ten years. She is part of something larger. She provides the ideological muscle and the intellectual cover for a movement that is aiming for your local ballot box, and even your child's school.

I know what you're thinking. Why stoop so low? You'll pretend she isn't there. Well, then you can be certain of one thing: You'll lose. We'll lose. Not just our shirts, but our souls. Been there, done that. I worked for that candidate. If you're my age, you can remember . . .

I don't believe in ignoring the Ann Coulters. Not when they get powerful enough to command the best time spot on *Today* and the top spot on the *New York Times* bestseller lists; not when my hero Jay Leno not only invites her on, but plays softball with her.

No, when someone who trades on hate for the fun of it is doing that well you don't put your head in the sand and wait for her to go away.

There are no problems, only opportunities, we always say in politics.

Ann Coulter is a giant opportunity. She is an opportunity to ask fundamental questions about how we do politics, how we address issues, how we communicate in this culture.

The only choice in dealing with an Ann Coulter is to figure out what she's selling, and then engage and win.

I have nothing against Ann Coulter personally. Quite the contrary, we get along just fine. I respect her intelligence and ambition, which is part of the reason I am writing this book. But I believe she and others who share her tactics are doing tremendous damage to our public discourse and our way of doing politics. It's an overused expression but it's true: We're fighting for our political soul.

I used to have this idea for a television show where a bunch of people start all over the political spectrum and the challenge is to see if they can agree on something; seeing people actually try to agree might ultimately be more interesting than the cheap thrills of televised food fights, or so I thought, apparently wrongly. But one thing is clear: The person in the group who would not want the consensus, who would see it as her job to stop it, is Ann. That is her role in the discourse.

You look at every poll and what you find is a decent, moderate, tolerant nation, being torn apart by the divisive, polarizing, mean-spirited politics of a selfish few. You find that on the fundamental issues that are supposed to be tearing us apart, we're far more united than you think, and we're being divided for sport.

Ann Coulter and those who mimic her are part of that divisiveness. She doesn't just pull the whole curve to the right, as if that weren't bad enough; she pulls us down, into the sewer, into the dark side. She feeds on the worst in people, and then nurtures it. Her specialty these days is Muslim jokes. That takes courage.

Time portrays her as the laughable, lovable Ms. Right.

Wrong. But it's not just about her.

She's not just building a personal following. She's trying to inspire a political movement. It's only the next generation. That's all.

Where are you headed?

The worst thing is not to be engaged at all.

Godless, she says. . . .

How dare she?

Let it be an inspiration to us.

1.

GODLESSNESS

My book makes a stark assertion: Liberalism is a godless religion. Hello! Anyone there? I've leapt beyond calling you traitors and I am now calling you GODLESS. Apparently, everybody's cool with that. The fact that liberals are godless is not even a controversial point anymore.

—Ann Coulter

Welcome to Ann's world. And what a mean and nasty world it is. Here she is taking all the decent impulses that make Americans compassionate, hopeful, and generous—real Liberalism—and, with a total disregard for history and humanity, twisting them into the opposite of what they are.

How does she do it? An ounce of sophistry, a touch of misrepresentation, lit up with invective and some sly wit.

But she doesn't do it alone. Not even close.

She does it by using a media that's obsessed with entertainment. For them, long, blond, svelte Ann is the cutely packaged girl next door (if next door is Darien, Connecticut) who can impress the college boys by being able to talk dirty and nasty with the best of them. Venom is what she spills.

And why does she do it?

To amuse herself? So she claims: "Most of what I say I say to amuse myself and amuse my friends. I don't spend a lot of time thinking about anything beyond that."

It goes beyond amusement, of course. Well beyond.

Ann is not harmless, an amusing conversationalist. Far from it. What she succeeds in doing is dividing us against each other, polarizing us whether we want to be polarized or not (and often we do not), playing to the lowest common denominator, and not only moving the ideological line to the right, but moving it downward in the process.

Social scientists argue, using polling data, that there is no culture war. Ann needs to create one in order to destroy the possibility that a decent progressive majority might ever triumph over the forces of hate.

The book *Godless* is Ann's latest call to arms for her hordes of true believers. What makes it different than the rest of her rants is that it plays the religion card.

In politics, that's a big card to play.

Welcome to Ann's new worldview: A politicization of God.

Look at the opposition. They have no God.

Look at us. We do. God is on our side.

It's classic stuff. When all else fails, they bring in God. Remember what Lincoln said: "Sir, my concern is not whether God is on our side; my greatest concern is to be on God's side, for God is always right."

Ann's view is not Lincoln's. What's clear to everyone except Ann is that the president has failed. The war in Iraq has failed. So what do we have in Ann's world? We have God taking sides, with certain religions preferred over others. Want to guess which ones? You might not be right. And it was just Republicans and Democrats in politics last time I checked; now you have Ann putting God in the mix.

Ironic, wouldn't you say? Here we are, facing religious zealots in the Middle East, and what is the answer? We're arguing about who has God on their side—the Right or Liberals? Do we learn nothing?

First she said liberals were biased.

Then she said we really were traitors.

Now she says we're Godless.

It's a trilogy.

Slander/Treason/Godless. Ann does it all. Attack the *New York Times.* Defend Joe McCarthy. Declare God to be on your side. Of course.

If Alan Dershowitz hadn't written a book called *Chutzpah,* Ann could have done it.

This is what Ann writes: "Liberalism is a comprehensive belief system denying the Christian [and Jewish] belief in man's immortal soul. Their religion holds that there is nothing sacred about human consciousness."

No God.

The Episcopal Church "is barely even a church" in Ann's view.

I bet you guessed Episcopalians came out on top. Only at the country club.

"Everything liberals believe is in elegant opposition to basic Biblical precepts."

Nonsense!

In one sense, in the writerly way, Ann uses God as a gimmick. Religion is the spine of her new book. She admits this. She uses God as the organizing principle for her attack.

"Of course liberalism is a religion. It has its own cosmology, its own miracles, its own beliefs in the supernatural, its own churches, its own high priests, its own saints, its own total worldview, and its own explanation of the existence of the universe. In other words, liberalism contains all the attributes of what is generally known as 'religion.'"

By trying to turn liberalism into a religion, Ann makes the old attack feel fresh and clever: Hello again to Willie Horton and partial birth abortion; hello again to gay bashing and good-bye to evolution. Liberalism isn't just liberalism, it's a religion. Teachers aren't teachers, they're priests. The schools aren't schools, they're temples. Abortion isn't abortion, it's a sacrament. . . . Got it?

But God is more than a gimmick for her here. What better source of new political energy than that old standby, religious fervor, particular with a little Muslim-hating and a lot of Charles Darwin thrown in? You can hate liberalism a lot more if it's Godless, after all—and if God is on your side, not to mention signing you up to vote with the help of Reverend James C. Dobson's Focus on the Family, and telling your kid what to think in schools.

Using God is not a new idea in politics. It brings me back, most recently, to the days at the turnstile in the Houston Airport at the 1992 Republican Convention. I had gone to Houston to work for ABC News. This was the convention where Ronald Reagan would be the moderate, where Pat Robertson would give his memorable Religious Right speech, where the platform committee would fight about references to Lincoln. But before any of that happened, I got off the plane, walking very carefully, on doctor's orders, because the airport was crowded and I didn't want to bump into people. I had checked my baggage, which I never do, because I had promised my doctor not to do my Superwoman routine.

I know who you are, the woman said to me. I smiled; she didn't. *You're the baby killer.* My jaw dropped. I clung to my purse, which contained the needles and progesterone I needed to keep me pregnant.

It was that convention. By the end of the week I was in a hat and sunglasses. I didn't want the folks who were taking Lincoln out of the platform to recognize me. I didn't want any more bad karma. But I knew Clinton would win.

* * *

This is Ann's view of the world: "We believe in populating the Earth until there's standing room only and then colonizing Mars; they believe humans are in the twilight of their existence."

She writes, "Their rage against us is their rage against the Judeo-Christian tradition. I don't particularly care if liberals believe in God. In fact, I would be crestfallen to discover any liberals in heaven. [*Would you be crestfallen to discover Ann Coulter in heaven?*] So fine, rage against God, but how about being honest about it? Liberals can believe what they want to believe, but let us not flinch from identifying liberalism as the opposition party to God."

This is a religious attack. They are the party of God. We are the opposition party.

Men have died for less. That's a joke, of course. Or is it? Do you find the fact that you are Godless ultimately amusing?

If you agree to Ann's terms, you play into her hands. This is her definition of liberalism. But it's just a game—an amusement for her and her right-wing friends.

According to Ann, our (liberals') "religion holds that there is nothing sacred about human consciousness." In other words, no God.

I had to erase everything I wrote here, I got so mad. Better write nothing, my mother would have said. What can you say to hate?

Let's start from the beginning. *B'resheet.*

Liberals "love to boast that they are not religious," she writes, "which is what one would expect to hear from the state-sanctioned religion."

This is the first sentence of *Godless.* It is a sign of what is to come. With all due respect, it is gibberish.

What in the world does it mean?

For starters, does she mean "religious" as in Jewish or Christian or Muslim religious, or religious in the sense that "liberalism is a religion" religious?

And does it matter?

Most everyone I know, liberal and conservative, boasts about how religious they are, whether they are or not. Americans tell pollsters they are very religious, in higher numbers than attend church regularly.

Most everyone I know also likes to boast about his or her politics, although I've never heard anyone talk about it as a religion, much less a state-sanctioned one. This raises a separate point.

Ann used to have herself introduced as a constitutional law expert. She knows that we constitutional law experts (I actually teach the subject) are familiar with a pesky topic called the establishment clause, which is a kind of matched set—salt and pepper—with the free-exercise clause, and prohibits the establishment of any state-sanctioned religion. We liberals feel very strongly about this, actually. We *are* against state-sanctioned religions. Perhaps Ann missed that day in class. The idea is that people exercise their own religions, free from state intrusion, because the state stays out of the religion business.

Other than that, I have no idea who she thinks loves to boast that they aren't religious—and, since she gives us no citations or references for the point, there's no reason to think she does either. She's just saying it. How does she know what liberals think?

So the truth is, the first sentence of her book doesn't mean much. But if we do this for every sentence we'll get nowhere at all.

There are terrific websites (excuse me, "Nazi block watchers," as Ann and her friends call them) put together by really smart people (excuse me, "really bad people," according to Ann and Co.), that collect information, filter it, and keep track of everything Ann Coulter says and does, and every single mistake she makes, on a daily basis.

If you go to www.mediamatters.org, you'll get connected to every error Ann Coulter has ever made; it is much more up-to-date than any book could be. "Tapped," the *American Prospect* website, did a comprehensive fact-check on her last book, *Treason*. This time, to deal with this new book *Godless,* a group of smart scientists (which no one would accuse Ann of being) have created a website that thoroughly discredits her take on evolution. Turns out she didn't go back to the primary sources (remember that from high school science?).

There is something about Ann. She invites attack. The controversy she creates makes her more popular. She is made of something different than most people, certainly most women. Criticism and controversy really doesn't seem to bother her. That is how she keeps doing it. It has been a decade now. This will be her life.

She makes you so angry sometimes that you become a mirror of her. That is her power. That's why people throw pies and nitpick footnotes.

You have this sense that she's laughing at you while you're out there struggling to find answers. She makes it a point not to break a sweat. To wear a cocktail dress in the morning. The rest of us fools are trying to dig our way out of the usual holes, but Ann doesn't get her feet wet. Even when she slips up she doesn't admit it.

I come here not to bury Caesar because of her mistakes, or cover her with whipped cream pies, but to take on her political case. What's wrong with Ann, in my judgment, is not that she is sloppier than anybody else in the political world, but that she's meaner, and it does matter; not that she copies more, but that she is crueler, and it contributes to her success; not that she is stupid but that she's clever; not that she's a copycat, but that she's creatively sly; not that she's following others, but that others will follow her. Not that she isn't guilty of some of those things some of the time. . . .

I do think she's smart. What she's up to in this current book, politicizing God, points in directions where others are likely to head. God is a good idea. When the machine is broken, they'll be looking to heaven for new parts. They need to rally the troops, and she's good at it. If her red meat works, you'll see others use it.

So here's what she's selling, to spare you some of the pain—and her some of the profits.

She asks: What does liberalism believe? (We're supposed to call our-selves progressives, by the way; it polls much better.)

"As a matter of faith, liberals believe: Darwinism is a fact, people are born gay, child molesters can be rehabilitated, recycling is a virtue, and chastity is not."

That's Ann's list.

I would have thought she might have included social justice and equality, some obligation to preserve and protect the environment, ed-ucating the next generation, providing for those in need, but do I sound too liberal?

Her list is selected to serve another purpose.

For myself, I believe that Darwinism is a fact, people are born gay, child molesters often *cannot* be rehabilitated, recycling is a virtue, and so is chastity, especially when talking about my own children.

And why are gay people and child molesters getting compared in Ann's world?

It is a trick of logic, of course, and (need I add) a mean one. She wants us to say that we believe gay people are born gay—and that mo-lesters can be changed, though of course we don't believe that—so she can use it against us. So tell me, Al Rantel, my favorite openly gay con-servative talk show host, why do you laugh? Is it funny?

Ann throws clear signals to her faithful about what she's up to. I al-most missed the first one.

Godless actually opens with a quote from Romans:

1:25–26: They exchanged the truth of God for the lie, and wor-shiped and served the creation rather than the Creator. . . . There-fore, God gave them up to passions of dishonor; for their females exchanged the natural use for that which is contrary to nature.

I sent the quote to my rabbi, and this is the note he sent back to me: "My translation for Romans 1:25–26 is close but a bit different—you should include verses 24 and 27 as well as it is a unit:

24: Therefore God gave them up in the lusts of their hearts to impurity, to the dishonoring of their bodies among themselves. 25: Because they exchanged the truth about God for a lie and worshiped and served the creature rather than the Creator, who is blessed forever! Amen. 26: For this reason God gave them up to dishonorable passions. Their women exchanged natural relations for unnatural. 27: And the men likewise gave up natural relations with women and were consumed with passion for one another, men committing shameless acts with men and receiving in their own persons the due penalty for their error."

Ann left out the last line. And that last line is, according to the Independent Gay Forum, "one of the Bible verses most frequently cited by conservative, anti-gay Christians." It's Paul's Letter to Romans. Famous.

She's talking to her base here. Now why would she choose that quote, if not as a signal? And why drop the last line, if not to fool us progressives?

Of course *Godless* was not written to recruit liberals, but to rile people against them.

We "swoon in pagan admiration of Mother Earth, mystified and overawed by her power."

The "core of environmentalism is that they hate mankind."

Since we think the Earth is actually precious, we have to protect it.

Since you think it's God given, you can destroy it and get another one.

She says we reject God so we can save Tookie Williams.

I don't even know what she means. I thought Tookie Williams found God.

Tree-huggers. Tookie savers. What ridiculous pictures to draw of liberals. What is the point of this exercise?

She is turning us into cartoons.

* * *

Throughout the book, she is quick to draw inappropriate yet worrisome analogies.

Consider her effort to demolish bestselling writer Jon Krakauer—"my guess, not a Christian," she writes of him—for his criticism of George Bush and John Ashcroft in *Under the Banner of Heaven: A Story of Violent Faith.*

In chronicling the dangers of Mormon extremism, Krakauer described the Bush administration this way: "This, after all, is a country led by a born-again Christian . . . who characterizes international relations as a biblical clash between forces of good and evil. The highest law officer in the land, Attorney General John Ashcroft, is a dyed-in-the-wool follower of a fundamentalist Christian sect."

Ann writes: "If liberals are on Red Alert with one born again Christian in the cabinet of a Christian president, imagine how they would react if there were five. Between 25 and 45 percent of the population calls itself born again or evangelical Christian. Jews make up less than 2 percent of the nation's population and yet Clinton had five in the Cabinet. He appointed two to the Supreme Court. Now guess which administration is called a neoconservative conspiracy."

It's not a neoconservative conspiracy that Krakauer was (by Coulter's own description) worried about, but a theocracy, a difference that makes the comparison to Jews a bit of a stretch. None of the Jews were orthodox fundamentalists, not to my knowledge anyway.

So the comparison is off. But pointing out how overrepresented Jews are in the Cabinet is just one of those things that you know won't be good for the Jews.

Ann is also dated in her description of the Democrats as "not particularly welcoming of 'folks' who do not believe it is a Constitutional right to stick a fork in a baby's head."

You know she wants to use the line about the fork. In fact, the Democratic Senate Campaign Committee cleared the way for anti-abortion candidate Bob Casey (I'm confident on this one) to run in Pennsylvania this year, and told the pro-choice left to pipe down about it.

The party went through a transition period where it had difficulty tolerating dissent on the issue, but that period has passed, and nowhere was this played out more symbolically than in the treatment of the son of the man barred from speaking at the 1992 Convention, whose path to the nomination was cleared.

The party that has yet to come of age on the abortion issue, as it turns out, is the Republicans.

There is, of course, a long tradition of religious involvement in politics in this country, most recently in the form of the black churches in the civil rights movement. Most of us who do politics bring our religious views to our politics; as a Jew, my religion shapes everything from my position on Israel to my commitment to social justice.

But there is a difference between a religious person doing politics and bringing your religion into politics. The former is entirely appropriate; the latter is playing with fire.

Religion is about faith and absolutes; politics is about deals and compromise. It is precisely because of the certainty that faith produces that it has no business in politics. Faith does not allow for compromise.

It is one thing to bring Christian values to politics, and quite another to seek to legislate them as policy.

So warned our students, politicians, and political operatives from the Middle East and the emerging democracies of Eastern Europe, who were already facing the challenges of Islamic fundamentalists in their countries, when we met them at a conference at the Salzburg Institute a decade ago. We were supposed to be teaching them the fundamentals of democracy at the *schlauss* where the *Sound of Music* had been filmed in Austria. But when it came to the influence of religion in politics, the campaign managers and candidates in attendance had much to teach Karl Rove, Ralph Reed, and me. And it amounted to: Watch Out.

* * *

What do you think of Ann Coulter's book, I ask my friend Cal Thomas, conservative columnist, onetime Moral Majority stalwart, and every bit as conservative as Ann in his way, but different.

I haven't read it, comes the reply.

I'm not letting him off that easy. Cal and I have done TV shows together for years, and we respect each other. It is inconceivable that he would ever call me "Godless." I respect his religious views. He respects mine. We don't call each other names.

But what do you think of her as a religious spokesman? I ask.

I wasn't aware that she was a religious spokesman, he says. . . .

Where is the part of Christianity where Jesus says that the way you deal with the people who disagree with you is by calling them names, sticking your finger in their eyes, accusing them of not believing in God?

So let me say it once. Who do you think you are, Ann Coulter? How dare you?

I am not Godless. I find that offensive. It is not okay, Ann. I am protesting.

I am sad to say that I have known days when I have felt so close to God that He has almost breathed for me, helped me place one foot in front of another, put words in my mouth. I have asked Him for the strength to get me through the day, and He has taken me by the hand and led me through the valley of the shadow of death.

I am not playing victim, Ann, it is just my life: When you lose a parent when you're still in school; when your life is threatened at twenty-one; when your sister faces cancer in her thirties and your brother faces heart disease in his forties—things like that.

God has been good to Ann. But where is her grace? She has grown up with privilege. Where is her generosity of spirit? When I was in law school, the joke was that my roommate and I were so broke that she sold blood to make ends meet, but I couldn't because my blood wasn't good enough that anyone would take it. Then my dad died, and things went downhill from there. Ha ha. I prayed to God to see me through. And yes, I was also a liberal.

My mother died last spring, and again I turned to God to see me through. She had been so afraid for so much of her life, a daughter of the Depression and of the Holocaust, a witness to discrimination and disaster, so afraid that bad things could happen to her and to her children that she lived much of her life paralyzed by fear. And bad things did happen; we weathered more than our share of storms. But on the morning she died, we were all there, her three children, by her bedside. And our cantor happened to come by, and this is what we did. We sang our favorite prayers, the ones she loved, we sang in Hebrew, we praised God, Sh'ma Yisrael. And I felt like my mother was in God's hands.

I am raising my children to be Jews. We say our prayers, we try to remember to be grateful, to live our lives as our blessings. I don't advertise it. It isn't anyone's business. It is simply who I am. How ridiculous to call me Godless. How offensive. How dare you?

The very idea that Ann stands on her high horse and calls us Godless, and gets a national forum to do it, and then gets attention for it by attacking the 9/11 widows, calling them names, is so ludicrous. . . .

A religious war?

A political war?

A publicity campaign?

A modern marketing assault?

What makes this effort particularly troubling is the extent to which it debases our discourse and undermines our collective civility in the name of God.

Who is using God to make a buck? Who is using God as a battering ram, a political weapon, a debating point? Not me. Not Cal. When my mother died, Cal sent a note of condolence. God bless you, he said.

* * *

Do you let her get away with it?

Or, once and for all, do you say, enough!

Draw a line in the sand. This far and no further. This is enough. Because if we don't, there is more to come.

Here is the truth. She is the ideological wing of something much larger than herself.

Her book, recasting the political debate with God as a partisan, came out in June.

In August, Reverend Dobson's Focus on the Family announced a massive voter registration drive aimed at recruiting millions of new voters in an explicit effort to counteract President Bush's faltering poll ratings heading into the midterm elections. The plan was to set up voter registration booths right on church parking lots, although some IRS concerns have been raised.

What's significant about Reverend Dobson's plan is how sophisticated it is: It is targeted toward eight key states that are thought to hold the balance in terms of the House and Senate Republican majorities next fall.

Imagine: God, targeting.

Once you conclude that He takes sides, why not? These are only the first steps. Ann is leading the charge.

Can you stop her?

You can if you can see through her.

And that's because, when pressed, she has no real answers.

Look how Chris Matthews pins her down:

He has seen Ted Kennedy in small churches, where there is no one there to give him credit. Is she calling him Godless? Who is she calling Godless? Will she name a Godless liberal?

She will not.

He keeps pushing.

After months of taunting the media that no one has attacked her on the subject of her book, she is under attack.

She has two answers.

He must be Godless if he supports sucking a baby's brains out. These are her words. They apply if your name is Kennedy but not if your name is Giuliani.

Chris doesn't buy this.

So she says she is describing a religion and not a person.

But if it is the public religion of liberalism, and the charge is that we keep our own religions out of it, that we adhere to the establishment clause, since when does that make you Godless?

2.

WHO IS ANN COULTER?

Ann Coulter's claim to fame in the Paula Jones case was that *she* was the one who leaked to the press the president's distinguishing physical characteristic. Yes, *that* physical characteristic.

That's Ann. She was hoping to break up the negotiations that were on the verge of producing a settlement in the case, so she thought she'd undermine the trust between the two sides. So she leaked to the press the fact that the then-president had a crooked member.

That about describes her.

* * *

Who is this woman who is such a presence on television, who defines our political culture, who is capable of writing a sentence that creates a media mania and an instant bestseller?

Off camera, she is perfectly pleasant.

On television, she can be viciously hateful.

Off camera, she wants to know how she looks, and compliments others.

In print, she calls people pie-wagons and whores, as well as witches and harpies.

In an interview, she says all feminists are weak and pathetic.

To me, she complains about how hard it is to be a woman pundit, and how the boys have it so much better than we do.

Is she a mass of contradictions? Hell, no!

She has a private and a public side. But she is consistent as can be, right-wing to the core, pleasant or pumped up.

She is one of many demagogues on the right. She is the smartest of the group. Personally I get along just fine with her. Professionally I hate what she is doing to our politics. This book is about the latter. It is not personal. She has told many people: "Susan Estrich has the best legal mind at Fox." I appreciate the compliment. She's very smart. That's why it's a challenge to take her on. And a measure of my great respect. And concern.

She was the first of what Charles Taylor, in his defining Salon.com essay, called the "conservative fembots." I just call them "the Anns."

His version of the group, as of 2002, included Kellyanne Conway, Laura Ingraham, Monica Crowley, and Lisa Pinto, along with Coulter. Ann started the trash-talking blonde gang, and it grew immediately.

Coulter suggests the same thing. "Originally I was the only female with long blonde hair. Now they all have long blonde hair."

I know about them all looking alike. In the early days, I hit upon a way to drive them crazy. It started innocently enough. I called one of them the wrong name. I can't remember if it was Laura I called Ann, or Ann Kellyanne—you know what I mean. She, whoever she was, went nuts. "I'm not . . . [whoever I thought she was]," she stammered. Remember I'm in a studio in Los Angeles looking into a camera monitor, so half the time I can't even see the other people, but it didn't matter. I started doing it on purpose. Back then, I wasn't sure who would emerge from the pack, or how.

Now, to be nice, why don't we just call them all "the Anns."

Taylor describes the "conservative fembots" (or CFs) without even actually knowing their individual stories:

They are the essence of the white privileged kids at the small New England college I attended during the heyday of the early Reagan years. What characterized those kids and what characterizes the CFs is that they seem unaware that not everyone shares their privileged existence, or seem to believe that anyone who doesn't has only themselves to blame. It's a small world, after all, and the CFs are absolutely secure about their place in it and the rightness of their views.

Coulter is forty-four (although she doesn't like to talk about her age), forty-five in December 2006. She was raised in the wealthy suburbs of Connecticut in an upper-middle-class home; her mother is reportedly even more conservative than she is.

"My father was a lawyer. He was a union buster," she told *The Guardian* with pride.

She became active in conservative journalism at Cornell, where she was one of the founding editors of the *Cornell Review,* Cornell's answer to Dartmouth's famous conservative journal. According to the *New York Observer,* she enjoyed going out after work and drinking and mocking the letters they received. She went on to Michigan Law School, where she chartered a Federalist Society chapter, clerked for a year on the United States Court of Appeals for the Eighth Circuit, then worked in corporate law in New York City.

Coulter "conveys an aura of privilege, wealth and—above all—certainty," wrote John Cloud in *Time,* who had to defend himself from attacks that his cover story was too positive. Cloud's story made the point that Ann makes very few mistakes; *not so,* as the websites prove. They have found some very serious mistakes in her work, along with a score of relatively minor ones.

Such as this unfortunate gaffe where Ann changes the history of an epoch while talking to interviewer Bob McKeown on the Canadian Broadcasting Corporation's TV news program *The Fifth Estate:*

COULTER: We were on *Hannity & Colmes* and we were discussing the antiwar protestors. Canada used to be one of our most loyal friends. And vice versa. Canada sent troops to Vietnam. Was Vietnam less containable and more of a threat?

McKEOWN: Actually, Canada did not send troops to Vietnam.

COULTER: I don't think that's right.

McKEOWN: Canada did not send troops to Vietnam.

COULTER: Indochina?

McKEOWN: Canada—Second World War, of course. Korea, yes.

COULTER: I think you're wrong.

McKEOWN: No. Took a pass on Vietnam.

COULTER: I think you're wrong.

McKEOWN: No. Australia was there. Not Canada.

COULTER: I think Canada sent troops.

McKEOWN: No.

COULTER: I'll get back to you on that.

As Taylor puts it, "No one does smug like Ann Coulter." Almost nowhere else, including anywhere in academics (okay, occasionally in math and science, but never in social science) do you ever find such certainty. No one is ever as sure that they're right as a modern very conservative ideologue of a certain age and persuasion. The fact that this war in Iraq is proving them wrong has yet to penetrate fully.

You've got some very smart women in the group—Ingraham, Crowley, and Coulter, to name the three I know best. But the smugness is another thing. It comes, if you buy Taylor's thesis, from their very limited experience of life, in which people who work hard and play by the rules can get to the top, to just where they are, because they've seen it happen. So if it doesn't happen to you, it's your fault, or your limits and you should be content with what you have. You get what you deserve.

After all, the Anns know people, of every race, who have made it. Gotten the scholarship. Gotten to the top. And they're conservatives now, too, the ones they know. The others they don't know: The ones who aren't conservative and the ones who never get anywhere. They think they belong where they are and that they are entitled to be there. They believe in the American Dream, equally available. Theirs was never in doubt. Must be nice, I say.

She went from Connecticut to New York to Michigan to New York to Washington. Other than her year as a law clerk for Pasco Bowman on the Eighth Circuit, it is widely observed that she has spent her lifetime in blue states.

Ann owns condos in New York and Florida. She likes to ski in Aspen and Vail.

"I do what comes naturally," Coulter says describing herself. "I write the things that would cause belly laughter among my right-wing friends when having after-dinner liquor. I usually get up at noon, check the Drudge Report, carefully read the *Treason Times* [her affectionate nickname for the *New York Times*], do a little writing, chat with my friends until midnight, write for another three hours and then collapse into bed at 4 A.M. Book tours completely ruin this idyllic schedule."

Ann decided to be a pundit, and she became one. I talked to one lawyer who worked in the firm with her when she made the decision; she said she was going to DC to work on the Hill and then become a pundit. It was a deliberate choice.

She did not become a pundit, the way some of us have, because her experiences in politics and law were thought to be unique; or even just because she had a lot of experience; or because she had earned the right to be thought the world's expert in something. She became a pundit because she was arrogant about what she had to say and had the looks to dress her package up; or to be cruder, a big mouth and a skinny waistline.

She also became one of Paula Jones's junior lawyers in her lawsuit against President Clinton. It is sometimes described as her biggest case.

The judge ended up dismissing the suit as being without merit. By then, Ann had used the Clinton scandal to launch her career.

*   *   *

Her first book, *High Crimes and Misdemeanors: The Case Against Bill Clinton,* was published in 1998. In it, she makes her case for the impeachment of the president. I think I'll spare us all the pain of revisiting that one, although she is happy to on any occasion.

Four years later, in 2002, she followed up with *Slander: Liberal Lies about the American Right.* If you're a conservative and you want to sell books, it's generally good to include the word "liberal" in your title. It's one of those "hate" words. Ann's next three books, notably, all followed that rule (*Liberal Treachery . . . How to Talk to a Liberal . . . The Church of Liberalism . . .*). In *Slander,* she took on the mainstream media, mostly the *New York Times,* for being unfair to conservatives. Her technique of choice was counting instances of what she saw as liberal bias, using Lexis Nexis, the research tool that allows you to tabulate the number of references according to keywords. It is technically accurate in the way that statistics are, in telling you a black-and-white story with no shades of meaning, much less colors or contrasts. Does the *New York Times* sometimes report on conservatives in a way that is stilted, foreign, and even unfair? Sure. The *New York Times* is also sometimes unfair, foreign, and stilted to liberals, women, and minorities. It is also sometimes brilliant, courageous, and challenging. In *Slander,* Ann accuses liberals of calling conservatives names. Imagine such a thing. *Slander* made it to number one on the *New York Times* bestseller list for seven weeks. Being objective, it was her best book. Being honest, not much competition.

The opening paragraph of *Slander* reads as follows: "Political 'debate' in this country is insufferable. Whether conducted in Congress, on the political talk shows, or played out at dinners and cocktail parties, politics is a nasty sport. At the risk of giving away the ending: It's all liberals' fault."

Or, as Rush Limbaugh explains in his introduction to the paperback edition, "the principal contention of Ann Coulter's *Slander* . . . is that liberals argue by slandering conservatives, calling them names— usually some variation on stupid or crazy."

Can you imagine? "Stupid or crazy?" Compared to the things that Ann calls liberals? It's almost quaint. Compared to Ann's impact on political discourse, it's insignificant.

As Alessandra Stanley, the *New York Times*'s media critic, pointed out in 2006, "It may have been the case 30 years ago, but no conservative who came of age during the Reagan Revolution can credibly claim they are marginalized or unheard. When the J. K. Rowling of political invective decries what she calls the 'intolerance' of the mainstream liberal media, it's a little like the Soviet Union complaining about oppression from Finland."

Ann's book *Treason* came out a year after *Slander*. The most interesting thing about *Treason: Liberal Treachery from the Cold War to the War on Terrorism* is that she would actually choose to write it. Historians weren't overly impressed with Ann's retroactive efforts to save Senator Joseph McCarthy from the trash heap of history, nor were they taken with her analysis of the anticommunist period as a whole. No, what made *Treason* exceptional is that in 2003 you would choose to take on the topic. Why? You have to really want a fight, go looking for one, decide not to let sleeping dogs lie, and get the old salt out to rub in the wounds. What other reason to revisit this painful chapter, other than to cause more pain?

How to Talk to a Liberal (if You Must): The World According to Ann Coulter, published in 2004, was a collection of Ann's columns. Think of this book, if you wish, as *How to Talk to Ann Coulter (If You Must).*

Finally, *Godless* is Ann's fifth book, published on June 6, 2006. As if revisiting McCarthyism weren't enough, this time it's, "Let's play the religion card." Remember, times are tough for the president and the home team. Michelle Malkin had already taken on internment. What was left?

* * *

All the CF girls, "the Anns," have this thing about looks.

Ann not only believes that the others copied her hair. She believes that her looks give her advantages in public discourse. "I am emboldened by my looks to say things Republican men wouldn't." Do you doubt that she is right?

But she doesn't want you to think she is one of those wacky women with an eating disorder. Not Ann. Too thin, maybe, but anorexic?

"Anorexics never have boyfriends. . . . That's one way to know you don't have anorexia, if you have a boyfriend."

She has had a number of very public boyfriends. Why does this matter? Heaven forbid we should think she is crazy. . . .

She believes Republican women are attractive and Democratic women are pies. This is an important point. It is, for Ann, worth losing a job over.

"I don't think I've ever encountered an attractive liberal woman in my entire life." (Ouch!)

Why does she say these things?

Here she is writing from what she called the "Spawn of Satan" 2004 Democratic Convention in Boston, in the column that would get her canned from *USA Today*—with me in the background telling her that this was not like the Pentagon Papers, not worth getting canned over, there was no principle involved:

> My allies are the ones wearing crosses or American flags. The people
> sporting shirts emblazoned with the F-word are my opponents. Also,
> as always, the pretty girls and cops are on my side, most of them
> barely able to conceal their eye rolling. . . . My pretty-girl allies stick

out like a sore thumb amongst the corn-fed, no makeup, natural fiber, no-bra needing, sandal-wearing, hirsute, somewhat fragrant hippie chick pie wagons they call "women" at the Democratic National Convention.

This from the woman who accuses liberals and Democrats of using name-calling as a strategy to attack their opponents.

She showed me the column on the Sunday night before the convention opened, and I told her that USA Today, where I had worked for years, would never print it. When I asked her why she was doing it, blowing a really great opportunity with such a big paper, after complaining to me that she didn't have enough large papers printing her, just so she could make the allegation that Republican women were better looking than Democrats, she had no answer. Besides, the Democratic women at the parties we went to (she asked me if I would bring her to some parties) were quite attractive.

Another time, when we were hanging out after a joint appearance, Ann and I had a conversation about why she does what she does in terms of her guns and get-ups, not to mention the things she says.

And she who believes in the American dream and everybody can get to the top and all that, pointed out, as I know to be true, that in our world of political media, it isn't easy being a woman; that in terms of getting newspapers (for your column), and a prestigious base at a think tank and that sort of thing, the goodies go to the boys first.

If you had been eavesdropping on us, you would have thought you heard two feminists bemoaning what it takes to succeed.

Long blonde hair, short black skirt, big gun, big mouth. She really does pose with a gun on her website. (Or at least she used to.) I kid you not. Even at that, Ann has had to work hard. There was a time when, even with three bestsellers under her belt, she didn't have a newspaper large enough to be included in Lexis Nexis; nor did any of those fancy think tanks that house the Republican boys offer her a home. She has always worked from home, not necessarily by choice.

No wonder she's so conscious of her image—a girl's got to use what she's got. But does she have to be so obsessed about it?

She accused *Time,* whose cover story of her was indeed flattering, of manipulating her cover portrait. In the shot, she complained, "My feet are the size of the Atlantic Ocean and my head is the size of a tiny little ant."

Her mother, who is fighting cancer, reportedly didn't like the picture.

It is said that conservatives complained about the cover picture and liberals about the content, especially that point about her not making mistakes.

"Women like Pamela Harriman and Patricia Duff are basically Anna Nicole Smith from the waist down. Let's just call it for what it is. They're whores."

But what about her? As the first of the blondes, she is always on her covers. For *Godless,* it's a three-quarter pose in a sleeveless dress—audacious for a woman over forty. That is how she gets attention.

And yet she writes inside, "Today's worship of physical perfection is more grotesque than Hitler's notion of the Aryan."

Which doesn't stop her from skewering Cindy Sheehan: "The only sort of authority Cindy Sheehan has is the uncanny ability to demonstrate, by example, what body types should avoid wearing shorts in public."

Asked about the seeming inconsistencies—criticizing others, parading herself—by her (flattering) *Time* cover profiler, Ann responded that of course there wasn't one; she is allowed to make fun of others while flaunting her own looks and attacking the system. "The celebrity culture leads to the deification of celebrities' boneheaded opinions solely because of their physical beauty. Harmless joking about people's body types surely goes back to caveman days."

But what about how she uses herself? Doesn't that cover photo have something to do with the worship of physical perfection? Whenever I see her, I tell her she looks great, and she does. She's one of those women who, like my mother, I always think needs to hear it. No one stays that thin without trying—I don't care what you say. I have read in a number of places that men feel guilty about how attractive they find her, and that explains why they love to hate her so much. I can't say I quite understand. This is certainly not a problem women face in dealing with Ann. In that sense, we "pies" are at a certain advantage.

But while her svelte blonde looks are used to advantage, nasty doesn't begin to describe her mind when she's on the attack. When she can't take cheap shots at her opponents' looks, she disparages their patriotism, their integrity, and their honor—and finds it funny to threaten their lives.

Democrats who oppose the war in Iraq "are not only traitors, but gutless traitors." New Yorkers are cowards; they would "immediately surrender" to terrorists if their city were attacked. "Environmentalists can be dismissed as stupid girls who like birds."

Whatever anyone has ever done to her, she has done them many times better.

Katie Couric is "the affable Eva Braun of morning television." "Reporters [in 'bush league' cities] have all the venom of the big-city newspapers, combined with retard-level IQs." Gloria Steinem she describes as a "deeply ridiculous figure" who "had to sleep" with a rich liberal to support *MS. Magazine,* and she describes Senator Jim Jeffords as a "half wit."

"If you were a Democrat and wanted to win, whom would you pick?" she was asked.

"If I were a Democrat, I wouldn't have an opinion on this. I'd wait until one candidate emerged from the pack as a front-runner, then pretend I'd been supporting that candidate all along, like the sniveling, gutless little America-hater I would be if I were a Democrat."

And yes, oh yes, she wishes death to her opponents, with acid wit.

We need "somebody to put rat poisoning in [liberal Supreme Court] Justice Stevens' *crème brûlée.*" My old boss.

She could never decide whether the appropriate punishment for President Clinton was "impeachment or assassination." Ha ha.

I counted at least a dozen other times where she suggested death for an opponent.

She had this to say last August about Maxine Waters, the African American U.S. representative: "Congresswoman Maxine Waters had parachuted into Connecticut earlier in the week to campaign against [Sen. Joseph I.] Lieberman because he once expressed reservations about affirmative action, without which she would not have a job that didn't involve wearing a paper hat. Waters also considers Joe 'soft' on the issue of the CIA inventing crack cocaine and AIDS to kill all the black people in America."

And even poor Princess Diana. Apparently Ann never heard the rule of never speaking ill of the dead:

> Her children knew she's sleeping with all these men. That just seems to me, it's the definition of "not a good mother." . . . Is everyone just saying here that it's okay to ostentatiously have premarital sex in front of your children? . . . [Diana was] an ordinary and pathetic and confessional—I've never had bulimia! I've never had an affair! I've never had a divorce! So I don't think she's better than I am.

And this hate-mongering death wisher is on TV, in the newspaper, online, and number one on the bestseller list. What does it say about us that we allow it?

* * *

There are a few stories you always hear about Ann.

Eric Alterman describes how he "first met Ann Coulter in 1996 when we were both hired to be pundits on the new cable news station, MSNBC. Still just a right wing congressional aide, she had been hired without even a hint of journalistic experience but with a mouth so vicious she made her fellow leggy blonde pundit Laura Ingraham look and sound like Mary Tyler Moore by comparison."

Ann was ultimately fired from MSNBC for looking over at a Vietnam veteran—a disabled Vietnam veteran, no less—and saying "People like you caused us to lose that war."

Coulter's column in the *National Review Online,* where she famously wrote, after seeing 9/11 celebrations in Arab countries, that we should "invade their countries, kill their leaders and convert them to Christianity," was dropped when she followed up with a piece in which she wrote, "Congress could pass a law tomorrow requiring that all aliens from Arabic countries leave. . . . We should require passports to fly domestically. Passports can be forged, but they can also be checked with the home country in case of any suspicious looking swarthy males." Commenting on why they fired Coulter, the online magazine said, "We ended the relationship because she behaved with a total lack of professionalism, friendship and loyalty," accusations that might have included her calling the editors "girly boys."

She earned the ire of many veterans and Democrats I know by ridiculing former senator Max Cleland because during the Vietnam War, he dropped the grenade that cost him the use of his legs and arm. As if the way you lose the use of three limbs in a war is the critical factor, not the fact that you were serving your country at the time—much less the fact that you find in yourself the will not to be destroyed by it; that you come home from your service abroad horribly injured, and instead of ending up on a street corner, end up on the floor of the U.S. Senate, only to be taken down by a rich, privileged girl from Connecticut who has no clue what you've been through. Ann's ridicule certainly played a part in Max's losing his Senate seat to Saxby Chambliss in 2002.

Asked in a July 2003 interview with RightWingNews.com about two of her most famous quotes, she had this interchange with interviewer John Hawkins:

> **HAWKINS:** You've caught a lot of heat for a couple of quotes you made. In your column three days after 9/11, you said, "We know who the homicidal maniacs are. They are the ones cheering and dancing right now. We should invade their countries, kill their leaders and convert them to Christianity." You also said in an interview with the *New York Observer*, "My only regret with Timothy McVeigh is he did not go to the *New York Times* building." Do you stand by those quotes or do you think that perhaps you should have phrased them differently?
>
> **COULTER:** Ozzy Osbourne has his bats, and I have that darn "convert them to Christianity" quote. Thank you for giving the full quote. I have the touch, don't I? Some may not like what I said, but I'm still waiting to hear a better suggestion. Re: McVeigh quote. Of course I regret it. I should have added, "after everyone had left the building except the editors and reporters."

What most people do who hear things like this is, they get so mad at Ann that they start wondering, How can I destroy her? And the first thing they think is: Her personal life.

The personal life of someone who looks like her must totally contradict what she has to say to all her God-fearing followers.

You figure, she has all these religious-right followers. Do they really relate to her and her lifestyle? You think, I wonder if her personal life conflicts with what she pontificates.

You know she wants you to go there, just so she can accuse you of getting personal. You know she used to go out with Bob Guccione Jr., because that's in all the interviews; she mentions it all the time. She also writes about having had a Muslim boyfriend, even as she reminds people not to get personal, and about living on chardonnay and cigarettes, which she actually confirmed in the *Time* interview.

"Let's say I go out every night, I meet a guy and have sex with him. Good for me. I'm not married."

Go right ahead. It's okay with me.

There are many who have gone looking. None have returned with anything very shocking that meets the test of credibility. It's not my game.

There are entire websites devoted to the size of Ann's Adam's apple. Yes. By otherwise seemingly intelligent people. Do not be seduced. She is just a regular woman from Connecticut. For my part, I really don't care who she sleeps with. Those who do haven't come up with much. I just wonder what all her God-fearing fans on the religious right think of it all?

Using personal attacks or otherwise, there's no easy destroying of Ann. No obvious skeleton in the closet of a liberal conversion, a secret law review article calling for legalized abortion, that sort of thing. It takes more work than that.

But then, it would be worthless if it was that easy. She'd just get replaced with a clone.

Ann is difficult to bring down because she has always been a believer. She came to her conservative views in college, has been writing about them since, and however deeply held they are they have always been hers. She herself has no patience for latecomers like the other blondies, and she is what she is. She may leaven it for public consumption, but it is what she really believes that she plumps up for publication.

Former conservative David Brock, author of *Blinded by the Right*, claims that Ann's conservatism was superficial—not the product of serious study, serious thought, serious academic work, all of which may be true; certainly there is no great theory in any of her books—but it was always strident and always absolutely hard core. Indeed, as he describes her in his book, in her lawyering days Ann was more excited by his stories about the Clinton sex scandal than he was himself—and he was reporting them. Her hatred of all things Clinton knows no limits.

She is not a moderate. She is not an old-fashioned conservative. She is out there on the right tail of the right tail of the bell curve of the electorate, and it is her genius that she can ever appear to be more mainstream than that. She is for real.

She is also the smartest of the group.

She knows exactly what she is doing. And she is scary as hell because of it.

3.

THE COULTER CULTURE

Even Islamic terrorists don't hate America like liberals do. They don't have the energy. If they had that much energy, they'd have indoor plumbing by now.

—Ann Coulter

Do you laugh or cry at Ann's glib jokes? Her latest one was to call Al Gore gay. She had already said Bill Clinton was a latent homosexual. She was serious about that. The Gore comment was a joke.

I do not allow my children to make gay jokes. I have explained to them why they are not funny. Will someone explain this to Ann?

Speaking at a National Conservative Political Action Conference, Ann famously said: "When contemplating college liberals, you really regret once again that John Walker is not getting the death penalty. We need to execute people like John Walker in order to physically intimidate liberals, by making them realize they can be killed too. Otherwise they will turn out to be outright traitors."

What kind of a society turns a purveyor of hate into a television personality?

Why is this woman being given air time?

Why do we call this news?

What does this say about us?

Those are the questions I keep coming back to as I read and listen to Ann. And, believe it or not, the puzzle is trickier than you think.

The immediate answer is, of course, that she gets ratings. She rates because we watch. Why do we watch? What is that about? The obvious answer would be to say that Ann is entertaining—she is beautiful and funny and as she puts it, amusing.

"Most of what I say," she e-mailed her *Time* interviewer, "I say to amuse myself and amuse my friends. I don't spend a lot of time thinking about anything beyond that."

What amuses her serves others. That's what my friend Neil, one-time (pre-Bush) Republican and gun-toting sometime conservative, keeps insisting. And he doesn't just mean the networks' ratings and her publishers' book sales.

Neil's a history buff, and his point is that demagogues generally serve the corporate interests of those who afford them a forum. When you think about it, there are certainly many examples of this. If I mention any of them, Ann will accuse me of comparing her to Hitler. Now why would I even think of that?

A different Neal, Neal Gabler, writes in *Life: The Movie,* "If the primary effect of the media in the late twentieth century was to turn nearly everything that passed across the screens into entertainment, the secondary and ultimately more significant effect was to force nearly everything to turn itself into entertainment in order to attract media attention."

If Ann Coulter were a product, you'd say she was perfectly packaged to sell. In a crowded climate, her image is clear and distinct.

It is very noisy out there in the world of public discourse, over on those screens. Compared to the number of movie channels and sports channels, the places where you can even do some discoursing is relatively small, and there's a whole lot of shouting and shooting going on. Every day, there are a thousand ideas, ten thousand press releases, hundreds of loudmouths, members of Congress, governators, cabinet members, talkers, trying to get in a word edgewise, while the whole world competes for attention on the screens.

This is what it is actually like. The fax machines whir constantly with press releases coming in competing for attention. Books pile up on the desks of every junior producer for every radio and television show. People are hired whose only job is to get would-be "legal experts" on television to comment on big cases. It never ceases to amaze me what people will do to get on television. On the other hand, no one will ever get in trouble for booking Ann Coulter.

When I ask people how I did on television, no one ever says, "You sounded great." They all say, "You looked great." It is a visual medium, not radio with pictures.

What makes Ann so easy to sell is that it is all of a piece: The image, the message, the vision, it's all about her, as much as "Arianna" is about Ms. Huffington, only more so.

As outrageous as Ann is, few in my informal survey think she would get the attention she does if she were a man—or an overweight, gray-haired woman.

Ann Coulter is all sharp-edged angles, diamond hard. In a room full of noise, her image is clear enough, sharp enough to break through. She shatters the glass, and you look up.

Banker and liberal George Soros can compare Bush to Hitler, as he has, but how many times do you want to see that? Ann Coulter on the attack is much more fun to watch. She is a demagogue for the twenty-first century, one who proves that you can never be too thin or too mean, too blonde or too bitchy.

She brings the vulgarity of the blogger's world, where she is a favorite target, to television in an acceptable form.

But she is more, as they say, than a pretty face.

She brings entertainment values to the pursuit of politics. The entertainment values provide an out to those who want to avoid their real responsibility for providing her a forum. Just entertainment, they can say. Not so fast.

For she is not simply an entertainer. She calls herself a public intellectual. I call her a politician. The classic definition of politics is who gets what, when, where, and how. Ann is a force in that process.

The first thing that Ann accomplishes—and that belies all those who complain that Ann does not help conservatives—is that she moves the entire ideological curve to the right. She creates a new point on the scale. By staking out her positions where she does, she makes others on the right appear moderate by comparison. Or at least more moderate.

She makes the *National Review* crowd look reasonable by comparison. She makes Bill O'Reilly look responsible by comparison. If she didn't exist, they would have to invent her. Otherwise, people might start thinking they were as conservative as they really are.

But what Ann is all about, her impact on politics, isn't simply to shift the curve to the right. Ann doesn't simply appeal to people to be more conservative than they might otherwise be. What she appeals to is baser than that.

She moves the line to the right, but it's a downward drift as well, a trip to the dark side of our soul. She puts a pretty face on an ugly trip. Both pieces are essential. This is not empty entertainment. It is worse than empty.

Los Angeles Times columnist Tim Rutten was right when he pointed out on *Larry King Live* that meanness is an essential element of Ann's success, as essential as good looks.

Like many effective media demagogues, Ann plays to the lowest common denominator of derision, labeling the hero a coward, her opponent a traitor, the wife or widow a whore. She says what we wouldn't and shouldn't say, and by saying it in acceptable forums, makes it seem acceptable and appropriate.

What characterizes a Coulter attack? Its purpose is to offend and provoke. It is delivered with a glib style. That is the whole point of the exercise.

In today's fragmented media culture it's not enough to say "the *New York Times* is too liberal," because all the conservatives are saying that. You have to say you wish someone would blow up the *New York Times* building, and then you've got their attention.

As she herself wrote on June 21, 2006: "A word to those of you out there who have yet to be offended by something I have written or said: Please be patient. *I am working as fast as I can*" (emphasis added).

It pushes the level of discourse downward. It divides people. It is invariably mean, and mean-spirited.

In seeking to offend, she plays to the worst of us, and laughs smugly when she finds it. Then she calls herself a Christian. Am I the only one who finds this both strange and strangely familiar?

That the attacks are executed by a beautiful blonde (oh, she's beautiful enough, Neil!) in a short skirt with a vicious wit makes it suit the needs of our times. You wanted a woman; you have one. *Our kind, not yours.* A bad joke on feminists.

Ann does not appeal to the better angels of our nature. She does not call out the part of politics that is about bringing people together. She is not an American dream girl. She is about suspicion and exclusion: I got mine, don't think I'm going to make it any easier for you to get yours.

Let her loose and politics ends up soulless. But good-looking and definitely entertaining.

The fulfillment of the high-speed crash between news and entertainment is ultimately a fatal accident.

Television does have rules about what can be said, but they relate to the words you can use, not the things you can say. Ann damns people as whores, dismisses entire races (Muslims) as terrorists (well, maybe only

10 percent of them), but so long as she doesn't use the "s-word" or the "f-word" to do it, it is "fun" and a "pleasure" to have her on. Or so the hosts say when she is done.

The claim that the broadcaster merely provides the forum underestimates the importance of his contribution. The forum is the scarce resource; it is the key, the essential element that turns Ann from a crack with a cult following into a national figure with four bestsellers to her name. Television puts Ann in a place where she can spread her message to those who would never read her book, which is essential to her political impact.

What is lost in the process is more than broadcast standards. She appeals to the worst in us, and you don't have to like her to be affected by her. You can swear all you want, you can switch channels halfway through, but her presence still serves the interests of her cohorts on the right. They still look good. The dialogue still goes down the tubes. Does she care? She's the one who claims she's just trying to amuse herself and her friends. Who cares what damage she does to everyone else in the process. . . .

* * *

Her *Godless* book tour provides a classic example of this phenomenon at work.

Consider the example of the Jersey Girls. Perhaps the most famous quote from *Godless* is the attack on the four 9/11 widows—the Jersey Girls—who spearheaded the effort to create the independent commission to investigate the 9/11 disaster: "These broads are millionaires, lionized on TV and in articles about them, reveling in their status as celebrities and stalked by grief-arazzis. These self-obsessed women seemed genuinely unaware that 9/11 was an attack on our nation and acted as if the terrorist attacks happened only to them. . . . I've never seen people enjoying their husbands' deaths so much . . . the Democrat ratpack gals endorsed John Kerry for president . . . cutting campaign commercials . . . how do we know their husbands weren't planning to divorce these *harpies*? Now that their shelf life is dwindling, they'd better hurry up and appear in *Playboy*."

Beginning with an interview with Matt Lauer on *Today* to publicize *Godless,* and continuing in the days and weeks that followed, Ann did major harm to the cause of victims' rights, of giving a voice to victims. She managed, in a stroke, to challenge the credibility not only of the Jersey Girls, but of victims everywhere, as well as taking a major shot at the 9/11 Commission. And she managed to—dare I say it—seduce most of her liberal critics into half agreeing with her along the way.

Three quarters of the respondents to Bill O'Reilly's website agreed with Ann about the widows. O'Reilly pronounced himself surprised.

These are the women whose mission had been to force the government to deal with the security issues that caused 9/11 and that still leave the United States vulnerable. These are the women who brought us the 9/11 Commission. Buying into Ann's critique is delegitimizing them.

This is not a small thing. Nor is it limited to these victims.

What is striking in all the interviews of Ann is how many of her critics, especially her liberal critics, bought into her so-called "good point"—that victims have no business, or less business, in public discourse about the subject involving their victimization because they are too immunized from criticism.

I can't think of one person who said that her fundamental point was wrong. I can't think of one time she was paired with a victims' rights advocate to take her on, on that fundamental newsworthy point.

This happens a lot with Ann—especially, may I say, with liberal men. They are blinded by the blonde. They want to agree with her, even when they know they shouldn't, so they find something on which they can.

But if you ask me, she is wrong. Or let me put it politely, there are two problems with Ann's argument—and, dare I add, I do speak as a

victim, and a victims' rights advocate who spent years fighting to give a
voice to victims.

The first is the assumption that being a victim immunizes you
from criticism. On what planet? I've been speaking out as a rape victim
for decades, and my life's been threatened, I've received contraband deliveries to my hotel room in advance of speeches, buckets of hate mail,
been told that I enjoyed the experience, been mocked for it. . . . The
list goes on.

No one gave the Jersey Girls a free pass on anything because their
husbands died. All that being a victim gives you is a chance at the mi-
crophone—the same thing money, power, connections, a vulgar
tongue, a short skirt, long blonde hair, and other forms of experience
give to others.

The other problem with Ann's argument is that it assumes that
being a victim is all the victim has to add to the conversation, and
therefore that victims bring nothing and excluding them costs us nothing. This is rarely the case.

The reason victims speak out, and participate, is that the experience of victimization teaches you something, pushes you to become involved, to educate yourself, and then you may actually have vital
information to share.

As a matter of fact, and speaking as objectively as I can, I would
argue that that is what happened with the Jersey Girls, who ended up
becoming, by virtue of losing their husbands, experts in the security
failures that produced 9/11 and that leave us vulnerable still. Along the
way they've been criticized plenty and opposed plenty, by those like
Ann who didn't believe it was necessary to have an independent commission investigate 9/11. I think most people would agree that the Jersey Girls were right on that point and Ann was wrong.

But notice the brilliance of her tactics. For a substantial number of
people, she turned these women into whores, and they will never re-
cover from that. Ann didn't just encourage you to think differently of

these women; she encouraged you to think less of them. The instincts that she appealed to were baser ones.

And it wasn't just these women; it was all victims—across the board. Now, whose interest does that serve? I'm listening, Neil; ridiculing victims as a bunch of whiners, getting them off the stage, does not exactly hurt corporate America by getting rid of its critics. But I don't subscribe to the same kind of wild conspiracy theories about loud-mouthed pawns of corporate masters that my friend Neil does, I just think she's attacking to confuse and divide.

What Ann sells is not subtle; it is often hateful and sometimes scary.

Consider some of the words she has used in her assault on Muslims and the religion of Islam—not just her one shot about invading and converting them, but all these others: "Bumper sticker idea for liberals: News magazines don't kill people, Muslims do."

"The rioting Muslims claim they are upset because Islam prohibits any depictions of Muhammad—though the text is ambiguous on be-headings, suicide bombings and flying planes into skyscrapers."

"Muslims ought to start claiming the Quran also prohibits indoor plumbing, to explain their lack of it."

"Making the rash assumption for purposes of discussion that Islam is a religion and not a car-burning cult."

"If you don't want to get shot by the police, Mahmoud Ahmadine-jad, then don't point a toy gun at them. Or, as I believe our motto should be after 9/11: Jihad monkey talks tough; jihad monkey takes the consequences. Sorry, I realize that's offensive. How about 'camel jockey'? What? Now what'd I say? Boy, you tent merchants sure are touchy. Grow up, would you?"

"Baby formula doesn't kill people, Islamic fascists kill people."

Entertainers who say such things drunk are generally banned from the industry for life (or at least people like me would so argue). Those who say them about Catholics or Jews become political pariahs. She says them about Muslims in witty lines and gets invited on the *Today* and *Tonight* shows.

If you were a dark, swarthy man, I can't imagine you'd find it funny that she thinks discriminating against you makes things safer. If you're a Muslim, I can't imagine you like being characterized as dirty and smelly.

What is wrong with being mean to get attention is that it plays to the worst in people, and in doing so it tears at our social fabric. What is worse is when it crosses the line and becomes hateful, or is capable of being understood that way. What is worse still is when you single out a group that is already suspected, hated, and viewed with suspicion. Note that she doesn't go on the attack against WASPs.

It's easy to turn people against Muslims right now. It's easy to inflame people by writing lines about how we should "invade their countries, kill their leaders and convert them to Christianity." It's not that Ann is the only one who thinks those thoughts. Far from it. That's the reason you don't say them.

"It's probably only 10 percent of them," Ann told the *Guardian,* "but that's still millions of people. This is something we have to be honest about."

Hence her enthusiasm for what American liberals condemn as "racial profiling" in airport security. She thinks it's "retarded" that guards can't just frisk "people who look like the last two dozen terrorists" who hijacked planes on September 11, but instead "have to shake down white paraplegics in wheelchairs."

Ann claims to have done research on which airlines discriminate, so she can prefer those. "I think airlines ought to start advertising: 'We have the most civil rights lawsuits brought against us by Arabs,'" she tells the *Guardian.* "Not so fast, Mohammed," is her laugh line. Ha ha.

If you've ever stood in line while an old white woman in a wheelchair was being searched, or been searched yourself, as I have, much less by people who recognized me, it's easy to wonder what's wrong with this system. Middle-aged white women are rarely terrorists.

What's wrong with racial profiling?

First, how long will it take for terrorists to figure it out and give the contraband, ammunition, whatever to women, South Asians—that is, to whoever isn't being profiled? Indeed, there were initial suggestions in the recent British case, where terrorists were allegedly plotting to use liquid explosives to blow up planes over the Atlantic, that there may have been plans to use women as part of the plot. How dumb do you think they are?

Second, what about Timothy McVeigh? Terrorists, we should remember, come in all colors and nationalities, including native-born U.S. citizens.

Third, how do you win the cooperation of a community if you single them out for disparate treatment? The recent arrests in Britain of homegrown terrorists reportedly depended on the cooperation of the local Muslim community. Without that cooperation, who knows what might have happened? Cooperation requires trust. Discrimination does not create trust. Hatred and contempt of the sort that Ann spews does not build trust that leads a community to literally turn in its own sons and daughters to police.

Fourth, the only check on the severity of the intrusion on privacy is exposing ourselves to it. This is the classic we-they problem: The danger of abuse is always greatest when "we" make rules applicable to "them," and less when the rules apply to all of us.

What was that joke again about Mohammed?

The conventional wisdom is that Ann Coulter is a product of a polarized country and a polarized culture, in which we have become used to screaming at each other across the cultural divide; that she is simply the most extreme example of the divisions, suspicions, and hatred that characterize America.

There is little doubt, certainly, that Coulter is part of the new world of twenty-four-hour news cycles, and news networks; of the merger of news and entertainment.

Other than her brief stint on the Paula Jones case, she catapulted from a junior job on the Senate Judiciary Committee to a position as a pundit on national television, hardly the place most people start. She got the job by making a tape of herself saying outrageous things and sending it to Fox News and MSNBC at the time they were both starting out. Fox passed; one of my friends who saw the tape back then said "outrageous" didn't begin to describe it. MSNBC made her one of their first hires, and even though they occasionally fired her (two or three times, anyway), they kept rehiring her, and putting her on their air. And still do.

Moreover, 9/11 itself undoubtedly raised the temperature of political debate in America. As my friend essayist Anne Taylor Fleming points out, the heat Coulter gives off has become more acceptable since 9/11. Being hated makes it seem easier and more acceptable to hate right back. Ann's name-calling seems tamer given what we've been called, and what's been done to us. Verbal vengeance feels good. Fame and infamy have become one.

But the electorate is not nearly so polarized as she is polarizing. The critical point is to recognize her as a dynamic force in our politics, not a reflection of it. That is the difference between someone who is entertaining and someone who is powerful.

In the second edition of his extremely smart book *Culture War?*, Morris Fiorina, with his colleagues Samuel Abrams and Jeremy Pope, proves to anyone who will listen exactly what the electorate looks like in general, and as regards some of the hot button issues in particular.

The choices generally presented to people in political discourse are polarized: *Yes* or *no* are generally the only two possible answers. The people who appear on television are polarizing: Ann and her matched opposite, which is not who I really aspire to be.

But Americans? Fiorina's point is that most of them are in the middle. Questions about ethics for them have more than just a yes or no answer. There are a lot of gray areas. And this is as true in red states as in blue states. They look almost the same. If you understand this, then you can understand how Coulter works.

Consider the issue of abortion. (Briefly, for now.) Most Americans would like to agree. Reach common ground. So what Ann and her clan of pretenders do is go find sub-issues to fight about. Instead of being willing to join in the consensus, instead of allowing a consensus to evolve, they will *create* an issue, the more gruesome the better, to divide people up. And so was born, literally, the issue of "partial birth abortion." A non-medical procedure, created as an issue for purposes of keeping the abortion fight alive. Just what we need. Actually, most of us don't.

The numbers Fiorina uses to back up his arguments are undeniable. Looking at all the national studies from 2000 and 2004, Professor Fiorina concluded that: "Avowed liberals continue to be scarce in both blue and red states, but avowed conservatives are by no means a majority in red states—pluralities in both red and blue states classify themselves as centrists."

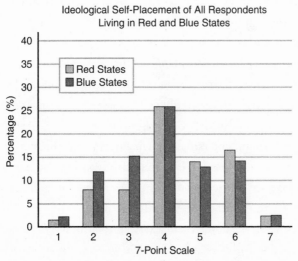

Both Red and Blue State Residents Are Basically Centrists

What you have here, Fiorina points out, is a bell curve. On the 1–7 scale, there are more 7s than 1s, but there aren't many of either; the 4s predominate; and if there are more conservative 6s than liberal 2s, you still need those 4s to win.

The 4s are the moderates. The people in the middle. What it takes to make a majority.

And what do the 4s care most about? Economic issues and security. Not moral values.

And here's the other key point: When it comes to moral values—or what Ann would have you believe are the only moral values, abortion and gay rights—most Americans tend to be tolerant, moderate. They're still in the middle.

The one person they don't agree with is Ann, who says:

"The swing voters—I like to refer to them as idiot voters because they don't have set philosophical principles. You're either a liberal or you're a conservative if you have an IQ above a toaster."

Now, what you do every day if you are a talk show producer or a cable programmer or even the speaker of the House is look for stories or issues that let you frame the questions as *Yes* or *No*, with more people on your side (if you have one) than the other side. That is what you do to people; not who they are.

The reason Ann attacks liberals is that the only way for her to win is to polarize. Like the schoolyard bully, she goes looking for the one group smaller than hers, simultaneously playing victim (of the press) and attacker.

The entertainment value of such fights—and the fact that gerrymandering has produced a Congress largely composed of safe liberal and conservative districts—adds to the false sense of politics as a clash of absolutes, with all the negatives that entails.

And the most unfortunate part is that it doesn't describe the country, which is not polarized in that way, but in which Ann Coulter, and those of us who are used to do battle with her, become polarizing forces.

The only way a right-tailer like Ann can ever win an argument is by going on the offensive against hard-core liberals. That's why she calls names, focuses on Cindy Sheehan and Michael Moore, tries to marginalize and whip up the religious fervor.

If the electorate is a bell curve, she's at eight plus, hurling grenades at number one, hoping to make it a liberal against conservative debate focused on the furthest extreme of the left she can find. She has chosen to attack the only group smaller than hers.

It used to be that there was a difference between an appearance on a talk show and a floor speech, a difference in terms of the tone and tenor of the comments, as well as their substance. That difference has not only disappeared, but the television studio has totally replaced the floor as the arena for jousting and the stage for political combat. That there are indeed studios inside the chambers of Congress only underscores the point.

Politics and television become one and the same. And in the process, place and tone change. The only way Ann Coulter wins is by controlling the terms of the dialogue.

If the middle ever gets a chance, the middle wins. If pragmatic progressives get to talk, they win. If the left does its imitation of her, yes, they can lose too. But she's better at that game: If she can scream extremities, define the debate, and marginalize the left, she wins.

* * *

"No liberal has to have security. Though I'd like to change that," says Ann.

What do you think that means?

Would Ann like to see liberals physically attacked?

Is she encouraging her supporters to go out and attack us?

It certainly sounds that way, doesn't it?

Ha ha. My kids don't think it's funny. Neither do I, actually.

I disagree with Ann fundamentally. But I would never want to see her hurt in any way. I can't even believe I would have cause to write this sentence. But this is how low she brings us.

Sometimes I wonder if she understands the power of her words to change a moderate America into a culture of polarized hatred and intolerance.

How could she not? Isn't that just what she was trying to do last summer?

4.

THE INTERVIEW

It was the interview everyone would talk about for the rest of the summer, the one that would define *Godless,* catapult it to the top of the bestseller list, and make Ann Coulter even more famous than the *Time* cover girl already was.

In retrospect, you could have predicted it. That is, after all, why they booked her.

There is simply no better place to launch a new book than on *Today.* Publishers fight to get their authors on. *Good Morning America* is good, but *Today* is better. Higher ratings mean more potential book buyers. It is no exaggeration to say that the woman who books authors for *Today* is one of the most powerful people in publishing, second only perhaps to Oprah herself.

But you don't just want to be on *Today* any old time. No, you want to be on when the most people are watching. That means the first hour, the seven o'clock hour. And if you're really, really lucky, say a former president or first lady, or a candidate for president, or you've just been pulled out of a mine, maybe you can hope for the top of the seven o'clock hour.

Or if you're Ann Coulter.

Why book Ann Coulter on Today, *at the top of the show, to launch her new book?*

Why? What makes it important? On a day when bombs are exploding in Iraq, when the president's poll ratings are reaching historic lows, when the administration is (by my lights) playing right-wing politics with the gay marriage issue, why does the highest-ranked morning news show in America choose, as its most important guest, a right-wing religious zealot selling the idea that God is on her side and her opponents are Godless?

Or is "important" not the goal? Is it "entertaining"? What is the standard? Why pretend to be a news show?

This is not, you can be sure, what Ann Coulter was thinking. Not at all.

It was 7:05 A.M. on June 6, 2006.

She had the perfect time slot.

She was in her trademark outfit: black cocktail dress, no sleeves, short skirt. Just like on the cover of the book.

Someone said she tottered onto the stage in her high heels. Manolos?

She sat opposite Matt Lauer, as ready as you can be on the first day of a book tour.

Clearly, he was onto something. He leaned over.

LAUER: Ann Coulter, good morning. Welcome back.
COULTER: Good morning.

They never start with the book, she must have thought.

Why should he start with the book? Start with what's important. Let her try to defend this administration. . . .

LAUER: David Gregory [NBC News Chief White House Correspondent] just mentioned, if you ask people in this country what they care about today they say Iraq, they care about gas prices. Things like gay marriages and flag burning are way, way down on the list, yet that's what the president's talking about this week. That's what the Senate's taking up. Why?

COULTER: I don't know what people are talking about or how David Gregory knows that. But I do know that gay marriages amendments have been put on the ballots in about twenty states now and have passed by far larger numbers than Bush won the election by.

But Ann Coulter loves gays, of course. . . .

LAUER: But the president—but the president talked about it in 2004 and then basically never talked about it again until now. Obviously we're in an election cycle, gearing up for the midterm elections. Isn't this just an overt way to say to this social conservative base, "Look, I'll talk about it again, come out and vote for me," even though that base knows he's not going to talk about it again for the next two years?

Classic Liberal Media Question, Ann must be thinking. . . . That might be because it's a smart question. In fact, that's precisely what George Bush is doing.

COULTER: I think they also know he's not running again. So why does he care?

Why does he care? Come on, Ann—he's a politician, the head of the party. If Republicans lose the midterm, he loses the midterm. Give us a break here. Don't treat us like we're stupid. . . .

LAUER: Here's how [columnist] E.J. Dionne puts it in the *Washington Post* this morning: "The Republican Party thinks its base of social conservatives is a nest of dummies who have no memories and respond like bulls whenever red flags are waved in their faces." Do you agree with that?

Now he quotes from the Liberal Media—and asks you to agree that the party thinks its base are a bunch of dummies. This is what she must be thinking: It just keeps getting better. . . . *Of course E.J.'s right, but that's beside the point. . . . The right does get its pound of flesh.*

COULTER: That the base are dummies . . .
LAUER: Yeah.
COULTER: . . . or that Bush thinks that?
LAUER: That they—that basically they think he can wave a red flag and they're going to run to the polls and respond to him.
COULTER: They don't need—I'm saying, they don't need to respond to him. Why would he be pandering to anyone? He's not running again.
LAUER: Well, but—well, he's not running again, but they want the voters to turn out in the midterm elections. They don't want to lose control of the Congress.

That's right. This "he's not running again," line doesn't hunt at all. Sometimes you wonder with Ann. Does she know these answers she gives don't work? Does she care? Is she really interested in electoral politics at all?

COULTER: Well, maybe they want to do what the voters want, and it's—I mean, whatever you can say about whether or not Bush has a mandate, the mandate against gay marriage is pretty strong. I mean, it passed by, like, 85 percent in Mississippi. Even in Oregon—and that was the state that the group supporting gay marriage fixated on—spent—they outspent their opponents by like 40 to 1.

It was not 40 to 1. It was not even close to 40 to 1. Three to one, if that. This is a Coulterism. Some call it a mistake. Others call it a lie.

LAUER: Let me try it this way.

You know what she's thinking now: "This is not about the book!"

COULTER: It passed even there.
LAUER: Do you think George Bush . . .
COULTER: There is a mandate against gay marriage.
LAUER: . . . do you think George Bush in his heart really cares strongly about that issue?

Good for Matt. He's not giving up. Ann Coulter claims she likes gays. Okay. So say something. . . . What's the president doing? Is he pandering? Playing politics? Does he believe in this? Do you?

COULTER: I don't know what anybody cares in his heart.

How about yourself? Is this what you believe in your heart of hearts?

LAUER: Would you take a guess? I mean, you know, people around the president, the vice pres. . . .
COULTER: I know what Americans think, because they keep voting over and over and over again. Overwhelmingly they reject gay marriage.
LAUER: The president's approval ra—
COULTER: So why is that a bad thing, for politicians to respond to what is overwhelmingly a mandate?
LAUER: Because they seem to selectively respond to it at times where we're in an election cycle.

Yes. Which is known, of course, as playing politics.

> COULTER: I don't know. I mean, on the one hand, you say, isn't that important? On the other hand, you say, well, it took them a while to get to it.
>
> Maybe they—he didn't—it took a while to get to because it's not that important.

Come again? It's important or it's not important. Do you think she cares? You know what she's really thinking: Are we ever going to get to the book . . . ?

> LAUER: The president's approval ratings right now in the low thirties. What's the main reason for that in your opinion?
> COULTER: He hasn't read my book yet.

You don't think I know what's going on inside this girl's mind??

> LAUER: No, really.
> COULTER: There's an important book that comes out today, Matt.

How cute do you think she's trying to sound when she says that? And you know it isn't working with Matt Lauer, God bless him . . .

> LAUER: What's the main reason for it in your opinion?
> COULTER: I don't know. I mean, I think his stand on immigration probably isn't helpful.

Miss Forthcoming, she'd call herself . . .

> LAUER: Okay, let me tell you what you said—I asked you that very same question October of 2005 [when] you were here. At the

time the president's approval ratings were about 40 percent. Here's what you said at that time.

He is going to discuss the news if it kills him . . .

COULTER: (Clip from previous *Today* show) I think all he has to do is—he's made one mistake: Harriet Miers. He just has to eliminate that mistake and everything will be fine.

LAUER: "He just has to eliminate that mistake, and everything will be fine." She eliminated herself.

Do you think she's thinking to herself: Does he play gotcha with liberal authors? Miss Victim, perhaps??

COULTER: I didn't realize he was going to make additional mistakes.

"Additional mistakes." Actually, if she had something to say about something, this would be the world's perfect opportunity to say it.

LAUER: Okay, so is immigration the only mistake? What about Iraq? I mean, don't we tend to find a scapegoat issue when the real reason is Iraq and that's a hard problem to fix?

COULTER: I don't think so. I mean, and that's the one thing he's doing right and that the Democrats are incapable of doing, and that is fighting the war on terrorism.

LAUER: But now I'm talking about the war with Iraq, not the war on terrorism?

Oh! Good one for Matt. She will never let him get away with that.

COULTER: Right. Right. I consider them the same thing, thus . . .

Actually, we are finally, finally at the point where a majority of Americans have come to see that the two are distinct. This is the key to—everything.

LAUER: All right, let me give you some . . .
COULTER: I mean, we didn't invade Guatemala.

What?

LAUER: . . . let me give you some quotes from your book, all right? These are random.
COULTER: Yes! Now we're getting to the subject *I wanted.*

Really. What a surprise.

LAUER: "Environmentalists' energy plan is a repudiation of American Christian destiny, which is Jet Skis, steak on the electric grill, hot showers and night skiing. Liberalism is a religion, a comprehensive belief system denying that Christian belief in man's immortal soul." And you go on to say, "Liberalism is the opposition party to God." How do you think Democrats who believe in God are going to feel about that statement?

First of all, who makes steaks on an electric grill? Also, how often do you go night skiing? Hot showers I do like, but so do most environmentalists. I think you can still be an environmentalist and take a hot shower. . . .

COULTER: They probably won't like it. They don't like a lot of things I say.

Duh!

LAUER: Is it a fair statement, you think?

COULTER: Yes.

LAUER: How about this one?

COULTER: Yes, that's why I wrote a book about it.

LAUER: Referring to liberals again. "To a liberal, 2200 military deaths in the entire course of the war in Iraq is unconscionable, but 1.3 million aborted babies in America every year is something to celebrate."

COULTER: Yes.

LAUER: Do you think people celebrate?

COULTER: They manifestly do. There are huge rallies for it.

Rallies for abortion, Ann? Or in defense of abortion rights? Here we go with the game. . . . Here comes the riff. . . .

LAUER: But do . . .

COULTER: That is the one issue that's more important to the Democratic Party than any other.

LAUER: Do you think they celebrate the right to choose . . .

COULTER: I mean, Bill Clinton, the last—the last candidate . . .

LAUER: . . . or the actual abortion?

Thank you, Matt.

COULTER: . . . the Democrats got into the White House was Bill Clinton. I take that as a fair assessment of whom the Democrats will choose as their representative. Bill Clinton sold out every single special interest group: the criminal rights group, the welfare bureaucrats. The one group he would not stand up to were the abortion ladies. Vetoing bans on partial birth abortion—a gruesome procedure—passed by overwhelming majorities in the House and Senate. Twice Clinton vetoed that.

So now Bill Clinton's problem is that he remained loyal to the pro-choice position. . . .

Shame on him. Imagine that. Having the courage to veto bans on a gruesome procedure, just because the people who passed it didn't bother to include an exception where there might be a serious genetic defect or a health risk to the mother. . . .

LAUER: Do . . .

COULTER: That tells you what the Democratic Party thinks about abortion.

Yes, it doesn't play politics with women's lives.

LAUER: Do you believe everything in this book—do you believe everything in the book, or do you put some things in there just to cater to your base?

She really does believe them. This is the amazing but true part. Scary, but true.

COULTER: No, of course I believe everything.

Here it comes. . . .

LAUER: All right. On the 9/11 widow—widows, and in particular a group that have been outspoken and critical of the administration: "These self-obsessed women seem genuinely unaware that 9/11 was an attack on our nation, and acted as if the terrorist attack only happened to them. They believe the entire country was required to marinate in their exquisite personal agony. Apparently denouncing Bush was an important part of their closure process." And this part is the part I really need to talk to you about. "*These broads are millionaires lionized on TV and in articles about them, reveling in their status as celebrities and stalked by grief-arazzis. I've never seen people enjoying their husband's deaths so much*" (emphasis added).

Coulter: *Yes.*

Lauer: Because they dare to speak out?

Coulter: To speak out, using the fact that they're widows. This is the left's doctrine of infallibility. If they have a point to make about the 9/11 Commission, about how to fight the war on terrorism, how about sending in somebody we're allowed to respond to? No, no, no. We always have to respond to someone who just had a family member die . . .

Lauer: Did I say the people in the middle of the story?

Coulter: . . . because then if we respond, "Oh, you're questioning their authenticity." No, the story is . . .

Lauer: So grieve, but grieve quietly?

Coulter: No, the story is an attack on the nation.

Lauer: And by the way . . .

Coulter: That requires a foreign policy response.

Lauer: And by the way . . .

Go Matt. . . .

Coulter: That does not entail the expertise . . .

Lauer: . . . they also criticized the Clinton administration for their failures leading up to 9/11.

That is of course correct.

Coulter: . . . that does not—no, not—not the ones I'm talking about. No, no, no, no.

Lauer: No, they have.

Coulter: Oh, no, no, no, no, no, no.

Oh, yes, yes, yes, yes, yes. . . . But they did make ads for Kerry, that is so.

LAUER: They have. But is your message to them . . .

COULTER: No, no, no. They were cutting commercials for Kerry. They were using their grief in order to make a political point. . . .

LAUER: So . . .

COULTER: . . . while preventing anyone from responding.

LAUER: . . . if you lose a husband, you no longer have the right to have a political point of view?

COULTER: No, but don't use the fact that you lost a husband as the basis for your being able to talk about it while preventing people from responding. Let Matt Lauer make the point, let Bill Clinton make the point. Don't put up someone I'm not allowed to respond to without questioning the authenticity of their grief.

LAUER: But apparently you are allowed to respond to them?

So it seems, doesn't it. . . .

COULTER: Well, yeah, I did.

LAUER: Right, so in other words—and they—and they . . .

COULTER: But that is the point of liberal infallibility. Of putting up Cindy Sheehan, and putting out these widows or putting out Joe Wilson. No, no, no, you can't respond. It's their doctrine of infallibility.

Note how they always attack Cindy Sheehan.

LAUER: But what I'm saying is . . .

COULTER: Have somebody else make the argument, then.

LAUER: I'm saying is I don't think they've ever told you, you can't respond, so why can't they make the point.

COULTER: Look, you're getting testy with me.

It seems like she's getting testy with him.

LAUER: No, I'm just . . .

COULTER: Oh.

At this point the audience moans. They're on Matt's side. Duh!

LAUER: I think it's your dramatic statement. "These broads," you know, "are millionaires" . . .

COULTER: Yeah, you think I shouldn't be able to respond to them.

LAUER: . . . "stalked by grief-arazzis. I've never seen people enjoying their husbands' deaths so much."

COULTER: Mm-hmm. They're—yes, they're all over the news.

LAUER: The book is called *Godless: The Church of Liberalism.* Ann Coulter, always fun to have you here.

Always fun to have you here? If this is fun . . .

COULTER: Hey, where's Katie? Did she leave or something?

Where did this girl go to charm school? Where does she get her lines?

LAUER: She did.

The man of class . . .

It was over by 7:17 A.M. She couldn't have been more pleased. The Jersey Girls—she could have done the attack in her sleep.

The interview was posted on YouTube before she got to her next one. People passed around the link to it all day long. You can watch it yourself. It's even better after you've read it.

"That was great," Ann told George Gurley of the *New York Observer* in an interview a month later. "I could've kissed Matt Lauer after that interview . . . we can keep this party going all summer."

She did.

5.

THE AFTERMATH: THE MAKING OF A MOMENT

The interview became something more in the hours that followed. It moved as she did. Her schedule had been set. She went from *Today* to a studio to record the Michael Graham radio show for the Boston market. "I'm a huge Ann Coulter fan," Graham said that morning. "She gives great radio. She's got strong opinions, she's funny and she's articulate. And let's face it, she's smoking hot." Then she went to Fox's *Hannity & Colmes* and to MSNBC's *The Situation with Tucker Carlson.* In the meantime, word of the interview started to move online.

Did you hear what Ann said?

11:08 A.M.—Salon.com, War Room, by Tim Grieve: "The core of Coulter's point isn't necessarily wrong: It's a little unseemly to argue facts and consequences with somebody who can claim the high moral ground that comes from personal devastation. But a Republican like Coulter is hardly in any place to make such an argument, and there's no call for making it in the nasty way that she does."

The pattern was set: Basic point "isn't necessarily wrong," but so nasty. . . .

The only official reaction on June 6 came from Representative Anthony Weiner, who issued the following statement: "Like an insecure child, it's always been clear that Ann Coulter is prepared to do anything to get attention. Even for someone like her who crawls along the sordid bottom of the media world, this is a new low."

So was the larger phenomenon: Everyone was talking about Ann.

On Fox, Alan Colmes tried to argue that the Jersey Girls weren't liberals; Sean Hannity was with her all the way. On MSNBC, Tucker Carlson was generally very supportive. But in one memorable exchange, Ann added more fuel to the morning fire:

CARLSON: I want to focus in on this reoccurring problem that I think you have. I read a lot of your book, three hundred pages long. I think a lot of it's reasonable. It's very smart. I agree with the vast majority of it. The headline tomorrow, however, will be confined to your exchange with Matt Lauer and that single sentence about the widows enjoying their husbands' death so much. And people who know people who perished on 9/11 or average Americans are going to think Ann Coulter is a whack job and a bad person, and I'm not buying her book. And I'm not listening to her ideas. Isn't that self-defeating to say things like that?

COULTER: I guess we'll see by my book sales. I don't think they will say that. If people are going to use personal tragedy in their lives to inject themselves into a national debate, I'm sorry. You can't just say, "We're off limits. Oh, now, we're going to invoke the fact that our husbands died and you can't criticize us." They were specifically using their husbands' deaths and there were hundreds in fact thousands of widows.

You see how she spells success? Book sales. Ann looks out for Number One.

CARLSON: It doesn't mean they were enjoying it. Their husband's gone, and their kids are there and jeez, it's depressing.

COULTER: And so are the thousands of widows who are not cutting campaign commercials for Clinton [*It was Kerry, not Clinton, but does Ann care? No.*] These women got paid. They ought to take their money and shut up about it.

That last line. "These women got paid. They ought to take their money and shut up about it." A new clip to circulate.

It was all over the net that night. . . . *The widows should shut up.*

Tucker Carlson was right. He just didn't know how right he was.

The next morning, June 7, Ann Coulter woke up to find herself on the front page of the New York *Daily News:* COULTER THE CRUEL.

It was a good picture; Ann was reportedly thrilled. Later in the day she posed with copies of the front page, and signed autographs of it for fans.

She would eventually also make the cover of the *New York Post* and the *National Enquirer.*

Was it even noticed that the Jersey Girls themselves responded, poignantly? Lorie Van Auken was quoted in the *Daily News:* "Having my husband burn alive in a building brought me no joy. Watching it unfold on national TV and seeing it repeated endlessly was beyond what I could describe. Telling my children they would never see their father again was not fun. And we had no plans to divorce."

Ann would later claim to be misquoted; she didn't say they enjoyed seeing their husbands die, just their being dead. Obviously a major difference, yes? Another instance of the mainstream press treating conservatives unfairly. Clearly, you had to be there. . . .

Howard Stern played the clip of Ann and Matt at 6:35 A.M. and called her "seriously deranged" and said her comments were "despicable." Coming from Howard Stern, that got her much more attention.

At 10:37 A.M. the Associated Press did a release: "Ann Coulter lambastes some 9/11 widows in new book."

ABC and NBC started putting together stories for the evening newscasts.

The person whose response counted most spoke out at 1:50 P.M. Senator Hillary Rodham Clinton criticized Coulter for her "vicious, mean-spirited attack" on the 9/11 widows, suggesting that the book should have been called *Heartless* instead. If you are Ann's PR person, this is something you can only dream of. Wish for. Imagine.

The full text:

I know a lot of the widows and family members who lost loved ones on 9/11. They never wanted to be a member of a group that is defined by the tragedy of what happened.

I find it unimaginable that anyone in the public eye could launch a vicious and mean-spirited attack on people whom I've known for the last 4½ years to be concerned deeply about the safety and security of our country.

Perhaps her book should have been called *Heartless*.

Ann went to town. She responded to Hillary on the radio from a book signing in Huntington, Long Island, that afternoon, which she was doing with Sean Hannity, three hundred fans, a protesting city councilman whose letter of protest she tore in half, and only a few other dissenters. She also sent e-mail to reporters.

This is what Ann said about Hillary Clinton's comments:

If she's worried about people being mean to women, she should talk to her own husband.

If Mrs. Clinton is going to start being concerned about angry women, perhaps she should go talk to her husband who was accused of rape by Juanita Broaddrick and was groping Kathleen Willey at the moment Kathleen Willey's husband was committing suicide.

Ann had lots of people jumping that day.

In New Jersey, two members of the state assembly called for a boycott of the book on the grounds that Coulter is "a leech trying to turn a profit off perverting the suffering of others."

Governor Pataki issued a statement criticizing Coulter: "I was really stunned and I don't think it's at all fair or accurate."

Mayor Bloomberg avoided a question.

Republican Representative Peter King, who had had his own clashes with the Jersey Girls, and had said that they should not be considered representative of all 9/11 widows, said her comments "went beyond all limits of decency. . . . Ann Coulter has become a legend in her own mind."

She was all over the evening news. Both *NBC Nightly News* and ABC's *World News Tonight* did reports. In the ABC report, network correspondent Jake Tapper focused on the tradition of meanness in politics and interviewed David Hogberg of the *American Spectator*. "It crosses the line into incivility . . . and stuff that's nasty when she refers to them as self-obsessed or enjoying their husbands' deaths," Hogberg said.

The NBC report featured former White House adviser David Gergen talking about the controversy. "It's the ugliness of the charge that she's making, the ugliness of the words that she's using that are drawing attention to her," Gergen said. "But it's almost as if she's a figure in a circus. And you're saying, 'Oh, my God. Can you believe that?'"

That day, Ann also began what would be her multiweek domination of the cable talk-show circuit.

Senior *Newsweek* analyst Howard Fineman, talking on *Hardball with Chris Matthews,* said: "I think Ann Coulter is getting exactly what she wants, which is attention. She got the gift of all time when Hillary Clinton responded. So now she has the whole world arguing over her, especially in New York. I think Ann Coulter often has interesting and provocative things to say about the clash between liberalism and conservatism. I think some of the stuff she said here is over the line, and I have a pretty high tolerance for this kind of stuff because I believe that the more we argue, the better we are as a country, but I think some of the personal comments were just over the line."

The big news in the talk show world was Bill O'Reilly. People who would never care what Bill O'Reilly said were now invoking him as the sane arbiter of the respectable conservatives' line. That's because he said this: "Stop Ann Coulter before she bombs again. Most Americans reject that kind of vitriol because it is mean and counterproductive. . . . So if Ann Coulter is trying to persuade people to her view, the personal attack is foolish."

And this: "I think this kind of stuff does conservatives more harm than good, because it basically reinforces what the left is trying to sell, that the right is mean, out of control, whatever other adjectives you want to put in there."

Neo-conservative blogger Andrew Sullivan ran eight items on Coulter on his page in an opening spurt, getting into the spirit of things by calling her "a drag-queen-fascist-impersonator."

On June 8, the *New York Times,* Coulter's favorite whipping boy, which she would later accuse of ignoring her book, did its first story on the controversy—which meant that anyone who hadn't covered it yet, would.

"Clinton Calls Comments on Widows Mean-Spirited."

The *Times* story, by Raymond Hernandez, reported on the initial *Today* interview, as well as the subsequent back-and-forth with Mrs. Clinton. There would be three more *New York Times* stories in the next week, including one of the toughest, by media columnist Alessandra Stanley. Four stories amounts to nothing, apparently, for Ann. After all it was Clinton in the headline, not Coulter.

That same morning, radio host Don Imus got into it with Republican campaign strategist Mary Matalin, another Coulter defender, on his show *Imus in the Morning:*

Imus: What did you make of the Ann Coulter deal?

Matalin: I take her larger point that in the absence of being able to make persuasive arguments, you roll out messengers that can't be—you know, it's politically incorrect to argue with. But I—I, you know, the verbiage is a little—little stressful.

Imus: So you thought her comments about these women was—were inappropriate?

Matalin: I take her larger point, which is—

Imus: Well, why can't you comment on what she—calling these women harpies?

Matalin: Because that's not her point.

Imus: Harpies and—

Matalin: That's completely not her point.

Imus: Well, no, but I mean, saying that they were happy their husbands got killed?

Bernard McGuirk [producer]: Their husbands were going to divorce them.

Imus: And—yes, that they're getting long in the tooth, and maybe ought to think about appearing in *Playboy,* which is an option—

Matalin: What do you think about her point? Her point that you can't—you know, Cindy Sheehan—you can't—if you throw yourself in the political arena, that you should be able to, you know, to address political issues, and people should be able to speak back to you?

I like Mary a lot, but note that she does it too: We were discussing Ann Coulter, so how did the discussion manage to be about Cindy Sheehan in the next breath? Favorite whipping girl?

IMUS: I agree with her point.

See, she does get smart people to agree with her underlying point, which is more than they should do.

MATALIN: Well then that's what I agree with.

Two for the underlying point. What is the underlying point? That Cindy Sheehan isn't immune from criticism? Did I miss the period in time when Cindy Sheehan was immune from criticism?

IMUS: I agree with her point. But I think it's repugnant and repulsive and gutless to—and cheap and cheesy to call these women all these names. I mean, it's just—whether it's right or not, I mean, you just—that's just something—you know, you just don't go there.
MATALIN: Well that's her stock in trade.

And that justifies it, Mary?

IMUS: But I'm surprised that you won't condemn her for these repugnant remarks.
MATALIN: I don't know her. I haven't read the book.

Mary and her husband James Carville must not socialize with Ann and Drudge. Different cities, different circles.

IMUS: Well, you don't have to know her. You know what Hitler did. Did you know him? And you can condemn what he did.

Oh no! Watch out for Hitler. . . .

MATALIN: Are you comparing her to Hitler? See, this is the point.

IMUS: No. No, I'm not. I'm just—of course not. I'm just saying—

MATALIN: This is completely the point she's making.

IMUS: All right. You know me. You condemn me all the time.

MATALIN: You lefty crazy people run around, calling us "extra chromosome" and "Hitlers" and "Nazis" and everything, and nobody says anything. She calls somebody a "harpy" and you'd think that, you know, the whole world was on fire.

At noon that day, Ann appeared on *The Radio Factor* with Bill O'Reilly.

COULTER: (Defending her attack on the Jersey Girls) I'm attacking the whole technique, the whole system, and the fact that people, even like you, will say, "Well yes, you can attack them, but you have to use these certain words." Well, why?

O'REILLY: Well, attack the argument and not the person.

COULTER: No, but that is—no, don't give me rules on this particular area—

O'REILLY: I can give you rules. It's my program.

At 6 P.M., Ann appeared on *Lou Dobbs Tonight*. Lou Dobbs said to Ann: "You are basically . . . the opposite of Michael Moore." Ann replied: "I reject that. . . . I am the right-wing Mark Twain."

What do you think Mark Twain would say to that?

Later, at 8:56 P.M., David Horowitz on *The O'Reilly Factor* said: "Well, Ann Coulter is a national treasure, and her point is right on the mark."

A national treasure . . .

On *Hannity & Colmes,* Ann went so far as to say that she wasn't at all sure that the Jersey Girls wouldn't, at this point, rather keep their fame than have their husbands back. Democratic strategist Laura Schwartz, a guest on the show, was appalled.

> COLMES: Do you think for one second these women would not give up every piece of celebrity and notoriety they have to have their husbands back?
>
> COULTER: Oh, I don't know, to give up $2 million and . . .
>
> COLMES: To have their husbands back.
>
> SCHWARTZ: Oh, my God, what are you saying, Ann?
>
> COLMES: To have their husbands back.
>
> COULTER: Appearing in *Vanity Fair.*
>
> COLMES: They would not give up. I want to be clear on this. They would not give this up to get their husbands back?
>
> COULTER: I don't know. I can't read into their hearts. But it isn't as obvious to me as it apparently is to you.

How can you say this, Ann? How can anyone say it? Even if it's just for effect, how can you say it?

> COLMES: Really? You don't think so?
>
> SCHWARTZ: Ann, you know . . .
>
> COLMES: You've got to be kidding me.
>
> COLMES: Laura, you can respond because I can't deal with her.
>
> COULTER: Why can't I respond?
>
> COLMES: You just did. You just did.

There were plenty of negative stories, but they all spelled her name right, and kept her in the news.

The *Boston Herald:* LIBERAL DOSE OF OUTRAGE FROM "MERRY" 9/11 WIDOWS; THEY RIP CONTROVERSIAL CONSERVATIVE COULTER.

The *Daily News:* BLATHER SELLS, SO BIG MOUTH KEEPS SHOVELING.
Was Ann upset?

Not according to the reports. The *Daily News* story, by Jonathan
Lemire and Adam Lisberg, read: "Oh, Please, Tell Me How Bad I Am:
Ann Coulter Thrives on Criticism."

A number of conservatives weighed in with their own concerns:
Hugh Hewitt, talk show host, Townhall.com editor: "Ann Coulter owes
an apology to the widows of 9/11, and she should issue it immediately.
This is beyond callous, beyond any notion of decency."

Cliff Kincaid, editor of *Accuracy in Media:* "If she really believes
this [the widows enjoyed their husbands' death], she is completely out
of touch with real-life human beings and the reality of what terrorism
does to people. If she doesn't believe it and made the charge only to create controversy and sell books, then she is devoid of a conscience."

Joe Scarborough, MSNBC's *Scarborough Country:* "It seems to me
there are so many targets out there, why go after the 9/11 widows? I
mean, it almost suggests to me that the *New York Times* and the *Washington Post* were dead on today when they said that Ann Coulter knew
exactly what she was doing, she was trying to whip up a firestorm so she
could sell some books."

And Mickey Kaus, blogger extraordinaire, famous for his *kausfiles,*
chronicled the whole thing, with a pro-Ann spin.

Of course, Ann had other defenders as well, some famous, some
simply writing letters to newspapers.

Karen Hanretty, a Republican strategist, on *The O'Reilly Factor,* defended Coulter: "If you read some of what Ann Coulter is saying and
you put it into context, I don't think it's mean spirited. I think a lot of
it is sort of tongue in cheek. . . . It was satire."

In the *Los Angeles Times,* columnist Meghan Daum applauded her
"subtly arch commentary" and wrote: "The woman isn't a pariah, she's
a comic genius, an anthropologist with an edge, the adopted love child
of Oscar Wilde and Gore Vidal."

Indeed, satire became the main line of defense. But as Georgette Mosbacher, herself something of a defender, would argue, satire implies that you don't believe what you say. And Ann clearly believed what she said. . . .

From the *Washington Times* Letters section: "She's my heroine, a true patriot and the saint of the conservative movement. She does not bow at the altar of political correctness. We can always depend on Miss Coulter to tell it like it is and to give voice to what so many of us are thinking," wrote L. Ryan, Berwyn Heights.

The Hill asked a sample of members what they thought of Ann Coulter. Rep. Zach Wamp (R-Tenn.) said: "Ann Coulter is tough as nails and strong-minded. She probably falls in the category of a person with a lot of credibility that needs to be careful what she means. She's very smart and does her research, but words matter. Words are powerful; they rise nations up and bring nations down."

Rep. Kenny Marchant (R-Texas) said: "Ann is an intelligent, thoughtful journalist who communicates the message of conservatives very effectively with a flair for entertainment."

Rep. Charles Gonzalez (D-Texas) said: "Simply put, it is about decency or, in Ann Coulter's case, lack thereof."

Rep. Jim Costa (D-Calif.) said: "I don't spend much time thinking of Ann Coulter. I do believe she is part of a class of pundits that are the equivalent of political wrestling: The outcome is fixed."

Rep. Vernon Ehlers (R-Mich.) said: "I've never met her, never listened to her; that's all I could tell you. You'll have to find someone younger or more Ann-oriented. I do, however, know Laura Schlesinger. She seems to have gone downhill these days."

Ann didn't waste time responding to the criticism: "I wrote the book to get a reaction and to get people to read it," she told Neil Cavuto of Fox News on June 9.

"Harpies and witches is what I think they are, which is why I used those words. And I must say I certainly have spotlighted the issue with my alleged name calling," she told *Time* the same day.

Larry King devoted his entire CNN show to discussing her with other guests the next Monday night. On the program, Tim Rutten, the *Los Angeles Times'* respected media columnist, took on David Horowitz, one of Ann's most prominent defenders, he of "national treasure" fame.

Asked by King why Coulter's form of marketing gets results, Rutten said: "Well, because, unfortunately, this is a very mean society these days, and it's one in which the differences between people have been personalized, people—no one's just mistaken anymore. No one's wrong. They're dishonest. They're treasonous. They're conspiratorial. No one's ever incorrect. They're a liar. So we've lost the habit of being civil to each other. Ann Coulter is an enabler, a facilitator of all this. And commentators like her. They are. I'm sorry, David, but they are. . . . Let me say the unsayable in this sophisticated company. You know, we've talked about marketing and so forth. You don't come to a serious issue like this and you don't come to people who've experienced this thing with a shtick. You come with honesty. You come with your heart in your hand. And you're sincere. And you're serious. And you know what? This isn't serious. And that's the worst thing about it."

Horowitz responded: "I disagree. I think this is serious. I think that Ann has done [us] a service. And I don't think people understand it, obviously, at all. There's a great human—there's a great human tragedy. There's also a political argument. It wasn't Ann who crossed the line. It was these widows who crossed the line. They have called Bush a liar. They have accused him of being responsible for 9/11. . . . Look, they have a right to go into the political arena. But then they've got to, you know, take the heat."

Rutten had the last word: "Why is being called a name—why is being called a witch or a harpie part of being in the political process?"

Rutten's right, by my lights.

But what's fascinating about all this is that, no matter what he thinks, she has him talking about her. It was already a week later. That means everybody has been talking about her for a week. She has made it through a weekly news cycle, which means she is on her way to making it through the summer, which means, more important, that she will sell a lot of books, which means she will get her larger message, her religious or political message, depending on how you define it, into the hands of a lot of people.

Who has rewarded her meanness and divisiveness? Every media company in America has competed for the honor. Why was she on *Today* in the first place? Because she sells; she rates. People hate her or love her, but they don't actually turn off the television.

She is everywhere. Until and unless (it has yet to happen on cable news) the public, or the relevant segment that watches television reacts against her, she will continue to be the first guest everyone wants when there is a "conservative" issue. As Howard Kurtz, the *Washington Post's* media columnist, explains: "When the staff of *Today*, or any other program, book Coulter, they know exactly what they're getting: A woman whose vituperation they can decry even as they milk it for market share." Is it a coincidence that it was Brian Williams of NBC who asked "Have you no shame?" of Coulter's much-repeated NBC interview? Believe me, when bookers talk, her name comes up sooner than Senator Chuck Hagel.

Not only is she selling books, putting her revolutionary tome, such as it is, in the hands of the readers she wants, at a time when no election is taking place the next day (and a presence like hers on the tube might be harmful to her side), but consider this as well: She is both controlling and driving our national dialogue.

It is a week when the war is going badly, there are more dead in Iraq, the president's numbers are sinking, gas prices are climbing—and yet who is dictating the agenda for that extra three minutes in the national news, who is everywhere on television, what is the topic we're discussing, not how many kids died, or what the president did, but Ann—whether she went too far, and then more about her, whether she's right about the widows, whether they went too far as icons in supporting Kerry, what they got paid, that they should shut up and take their money . . . and not go bother us with that pesky 9/11 Commission, which is what they did.

And for those who would ignore her, this time anyway, consider this question, too: Do you think NBC was pleased with the *Today* interview? Which means, will we see more of her? Did she expand her power, or lose power?

"This is of course exactly what she wants," columnist Joe Klein told the *Guardian* the following weekend about the tumult that Coulter had created. "She's a really cancerous example of the American political disease. You know, there's a whole generation of people in this country who think a serious political discussion is Ann Coulter and Michael Moore yelling at each other. It's driven serious, nuanced conversation out of the market."

The book debuted in first place on the *New York Times* bestseller list.

Part of what made it a Coulter Moment was certainly that she stepped over the line, and in doing so she took control of the discourse. Could she have made the same point without calling the widows names, insulting them? Yes, but then would she have been on the front page of the *Daily News,* on Leno, on the evening news? She could choose targets who weren't national icons; she could have short hair and wear black pantsuits and drop all the applause lines. But would anyone pay attention?

Both the left and the right use victims—even 9/11 victims—to make points. No one who attended the Republican Convention in New York City in 2004 could miss the symbolism of 9/11 there. The Republican ads in 2004 featured 9/11 body bags. Democrats do it, Republicans do it, even the president of the United States does it. For weeks after Ann made her point about the Jersey Girls using their status as victims to make their point, she was shown various pictures of the president calling the vice president on 9/11, which were sold as memorabilia to capitalize on 9/11, along with the body bag ads and the rest, and asked to explain what the differences were. After a while, she just refused to answer. There was no answer.

So why make a major media moment about *this*?

Ann's response, no doubt, would be that she didn't pick it, the liberal media did. It was all Matt Lauer's fault. When he finally got to the book, this was the sentence of the chapter that he picked. But that's only half true. She wrote the sentence. And while there are a great many controversial sentences in *Godless,* she had to know that when you attack American icons as harpies who have enjoyed their husbands' deaths, someone is bound to notice, particularly when you do it in a black cocktail dress.

When Matt launched the attack, and in the days that followed, Ann could have changed the subject. Instead she rode the horse. She knew she had one. She stuck with it. She built on it. She built on the case against the widows: That they took the money, that they wouldn't trade it back. Then she complained that the liberal media had repeated it, playing, yes, victim herself.

On June 15, Ann pointed out, critically, that liberals didn't care that she'd written a whole book attacking them for being godless, only about the lines attacking the widows. Appearing on CNBC's *Kudlow and Company,* she said, "I do want to pause to enjoy the fact that you pointed out I call them [liberals] godless. And liberals are cool with that. Just don't attack those four liberal women in New Jersey. But godless, yeah, okay. No one seems to really mind that."

But when Ann did get attacked for the theme of her book, she refused to address it. On one occasion, Democrat Mary Ann Marsh tried mightily to engage Ann on the theme of her book on *Hannity & Colmes* and Coulter did no more than mock her—first for not reading the book, and then for reading more of it than she'd initially let on. What she never did, however, was answer Marsh's substantive objections.

The conversation is revealing. Marsh had done her homework but Coulter trapped her, and then she simply ridiculed her. Meanness shows up here in more ways than one:

MARSH: The fact that Ann's book is number one is just further proof that the only person making money off a book that exploits 9/11 and religion for political purposes is Ann Coulter, and I think that leaves some people . . .

HANNITY: Have you read the book?

MARSH: You know, I've read all the parts that are available free online. . . .

HANNITY: You read all the parts in the paper.

MARSH: So I want to thank Town Online, no, not the paper, straight out of online, I haven't bought the book. . . . I think the more important fact is that Ann has written this book in a way that really—it uses religion to sort of start a new holy war, by trying to divide political parties along the lines of religion, and that really is using religion to divide political people.

Watch how she gets diverted by admitting she didn't really read the book, because she wanted to make the point that she didn't pay for it. You can only accomplish one thing. . . . (Crosstalk)

HANNITY: . . . intelligent discussion, because you didn't read the book, but you attack the book. And I always find that difficult to debate with. But, Ann, one of the things you wanted to have happen here is you felt that the more controversial nature of the book was ignored by the media, and the fact is you are saying liberalism is a godless religion. You're glad to now move onto this decision.

COULTER: Right, but apparently liberals are cool with being called godless. That doesn't disturb them at all.

MARSH: I'm raising religion right now.

Keep at it . . .

COULTER: I'm a little tired of liberals exploiting my book to get on TV and sell newspapers.

COLMES: That's why I get on TV, I know that. Hey, Ann, I have a follow-up to Jay Leno's question.

Oh, Alan! No . . .

COULTER: Yes?

COLMES: Have you ever had sex with a conservative? (laughter)

HANNITY: Oh, personal.

COLMES: All right. I'll give you a pass on that.

COULTER: Everybody's avoiding the *Godless* title.

COLMES: I see. All right.

MARSH: No actually, I'm the one who's actually raised religion in this conversation and it really—the book really strikes as blood money, Ann. The fact that you're getting these . . . (Crosstalk)

COULTER: You don't know what you're talking about. You haven't read it.

Ouch.

MARSH: I've read plenty of chapters online, okay?

COULTER: Starting a holy war? (Crosstalk)

MARSH: Why don't you answer the questions, Ann, about how you're using religion to start a new holy war to help Republicans to win elections?

COULTER: If you read the book, you'd realize that's a completely irrelevant question. Okay, Alan? (Crosstalk)

Ann's answer, complete with the "Okay, Alan," is about as rude and dismissive as you can get; there's an unwritten convention on television that if you're at all a decent person, you say it's a good question, not an "irrelevant" one, and what Ann is really saying here is, "I'm done with this woman forever." No sisterhood here. . . .

So what about "holy war"? Of course Ann never uses the term. But she puts God on one side in a political battle, sets up the schools and education, in the last third of the book, as the potential bounty of political activity, and provides the ideological fervor for political involvement. She plays the religion card in support of political ends. Holy war? Pick your terms. But don't change the subject, or crack jokes.

> **Marsh:** Well, the title is *Godless: The Church of Liberalism.* How could that be irrelevant?
>
> **Hannity:** Let her answer.

Let her answer?? Hold on a minute. She hasn't been willing to answer.

> **Coulter:** It's not exploiting religion. How is it exploiting religion? It's describing a religion.
>
> **Colmes:** You talk, Ann, about—
>
> **Marsh:** You called Episcopalians barely a religion in that book.
>
> **Coulter:** Oh, I guess, Miss "I Haven't Read the Book" has paged through it a bit.
>
> **Marsh:** I said that upfront I did.

And that's it. At that point, Colmes changes the subject to the picture of the president the Republican Senate Campaign Committee had used as a fundraiser, the one that showed him calling Vice President Dick Cheney, in the hours shortly after the planes went into the twin towers on 9/11. Alan is challenging Ann on a blatant use of a victim in a political event. Ann of course refuses to answer. Hypocritically, she claims it wasn't the same, since the Senate Campaign Committee had sent out the picture rather than the

White House. So, in this case, it was okay to exploit 9/11. And Marsh never did get an answer to her questions about religion, and the Episcopal Church remained "barely a religion" with no follow-up questions to Coulter on the point.

So much for Ann wanting to talk about the subject of her book.

Mostly in interviews, even friendly ones, it never even got that far. What happened was that questioners could barely manage a comeback, or a relevant one, when Ann began a summary of the actual substance of the book. It lacked the bite of calling the widows harpies. Her description of her book, perhaps intentionally so, lacked the bite of the book itself.

It hardly could be an accident that so masterful a manipulator of the media, so clever a mistress of the one-liner, would summarize her own book as follows, in this revealing exchange with Lou Dobbs on CNN, who asked where the "Jersey Girls" fit in the book:

> **COULTER:** It is part of the chapter. I mean, the theme of the book is that liberalism is a religion. It's a godless religion. I describe their tenets, their doctrines, their beliefs in miracles, in the supernatural, their temples, their clergy. This is a chapter on the liberal doctrine of infallibility, and that is they used to have complete, 100 percent domination of the news and prevent us from responding.
>
> **DOBBS:** Ann, I had the same reaction as I read your book, talking about the catechism, if you will, I mean, I had the same reaction to right-wing free traders. They have a faith-based view of economics . . . (goes on to discuss economics . . .)

But of course . . .

Or consider her much-touted interview with Jay Leno, in which the substance of her book came up in the last fifteen seconds:

> **LENO:** All right. The book's title—
>
> **COULTER:** Godless. Which liberals don't mind.

LENO: Explain what you mean by that. Explain what you
mean. . . .

COULTER: I mean, no one's complained. I think if somebody
called me godless, I'd take notice of it. No, they're obsessed
with this one section of one chapter. But the point of the book
is that liberalism has become like a religion. All the bad things
associated with religions, which I don't think you see that
much from God-based religions, by the way.

At this point Ann turns to fellow guest, comedian George Carlin. . . .

Though I think you do.

. . . and turns back to Leno.

But the self-righteousness, the intolerance, the refusal to
countenance differing beliefs. (*Wait—is she talking about herself?*) And by denying that it's a religion, I mean, they have
their own cosmology, their own worldview, their own belief in
miracles. They promote themselves through the schools,
through the government, the children are baptized in the religion of global warming, of recycling, of safe sex, but you can't
have a moment of silence. I mean, that is preferring one religion over another, and they advance themselves by denying
their religion. And this is the religion of liberalism.

LENO: Well, the book is called *The Church of Liberalism, Godlessness.* Ann, thank you. Always fascinating to have you.

Imagine if she'd ever figured out how to publicly market the rest of the book.
"Always fascinating to have you," says Jay Leno of NBC.
"Always fun to have you," says Matt Lauer of NBC.
"Have you no shame?" says Brian Williams of NBC.
What about his own network? Have *they* no shame?
How hateful and mean do you have to be before you stop being
"fascinating" or "fun"?

The *Washington Post*'s Howard Kurtz quotes *Today* executive producer Jim Bell, who says: "She made news. I think our audience is smart enough to figure it out and reach their own opinions. It's not our job to censor people. Besides, she's good television."

News? Exactly what news was that? That someone could be even more vulgar and tasteless than we heretofore thought possible on national television, and it would be considered an accepted part of public discourse?

That *Today* was willing to provide a forum for that display? So long as she's good looking, mind you.

By that standard, it was NBC who made news, not Ann Coulter.

And it was hoping to make news when it had her there.

Why else book her?

She is the shock jock of public debate, after all: You have the book, you know what's in it, you know what you're getting when you book her, you're asking the questions, asking for the lines.

And she delivered. Everybody replayed the interview over and over. It was an advertisement for *Today*. You think that makes them happy? It was a "successful" interview by the standard that counts. Its reach, its explosive impact, was enormous. Will she be on for her next book? Yes. She has proven herself, once again. She did what she had to do.

There are many people in our society who express hateful opinions with which I fundamentally disagree. The first amendment guarantees that government will not censor their right to speak. As a civil libertarian, I'm used to fighting for the rights of unpopular speakers to engage even in speech I hate.

But on television's top rated programs? There is no first amendment right to appear on *Today* or *Tonight*.

That's not a first amendment issue. It's not a free speech question.

The government isn't trying to censor Ann Coulter. I'm not trying to censor Ann.

I'm just asking the people who are giving her the megaphone why it is that they think she deserves that kind of voice in order to amuse herself and her friends with her after-lunch pajama chat, as she puts it, at the expense not simply of civility, but the whole idea that politics is about the give and take of compromise and not the absolutes of belief.

And I'm directing that question not at the networks, because I know better. They respond to only one thing, which is people. That's all.

So I'm directing it to you.

6.

THE WILLIE HORTON STORY AND RACE POLITICS

Ann's *Godless: The Church of Liberalism* attack begins with Willie Horton and the death penalty.

This is an old chestnut. For those of you old enough to remember, Willie Horton was the man whom the late Lee Atwater, famed campaign manager for the first George Bush, vowed to make into Michael Dukakis's running mate in 1988—meaning he would tag Dukakis with Horton's crimes to his detriment.

Horton is a symbol of a brilliant campaign to some, and of the power of racism to others; the force of the crime issue, or the foolishness of liberals.

Horton was the convicted first-degree murderer who committed rape while out on a weekend furlough from a Massachusetts jail. As governor, Dukakis had refused to meet with the victim and her family, and stood by the program under which Horton was furloughed, rejecting criticism of the program that allowed furloughs for first-degree murderers. When Dukakis became the Democratic nominee for president,

Willie Horton became one of the most visible issues in the campaign—short for crime or race or toughness or values or all of the above, depending on who you talked to.

Horton's name was first mentioned by Al Gore during the New York primary as a criticism of Dukakis's furlough program, then quickly dropped. But, beginning in the summer of 1988, Horton became a staple of the Bush stump speech, and he was the subject of two of the most memorable ads of the 1988 campaign. One was widely criticized for combining the images of Horton and Dukakis and sending the not-so-subtle message that associated the Democratic nominee with the worst black criminals in our society. In retrospect, it was that ad that was viewed as the epitome of use of racism in the negative campaign against Dukakis. The press did not wake up to the significance of any of it until it was over.

For most of us who lived through it, it is not a period we are eager to revisit.

Why bring it up here? Why tell the story again?

Is Ann teaching history, as she suggests in a later interview with *Time*? Or could it be she understands that whatever she might think, the Willie Horton story must be retold because it remains an obstacle between older blacks and the Republican Party, who remember it as a time when some Republicans were willing to play the race card to win.

I think the Anns have a CR fantasy. So of course does DM. For those falling behind in initials, I'm referring to Condi Rice, and to Dick Morris, who would like Rice to run in the 2008 presidential election.

The fantasy is that they can make inroads with older conservative black women who agree with them on abortion, and who would be drawn to a ticket with Condi in the number two slot. All they need to do is get past the Willie Horton racist campaigning business.

The "backbone of the Democratic Party" is a "typical fat, implacable welfare recipient," according to one of Ann's columns.

That won't help.

The way Ann tells it in *Godless,* the story of Willie Horton is not a story about racism—in fact, it has nothing whatsoever to do with the fact that Willie Horton was black.

Her purpose in telling the story is to make the point that he was just Willie Horton, that the Bush campaign really wished he was white.

The idea, for Ann, is that he was just a guy. That it had nothing to do with the fact that he was black. Nothing at all. That's what makes it significant. That's her reason to begin here.

Problem is, she's got it all wrong.

I was there.

* * *

While Ann says everything begins with Willie Horton, she actually begins with the death penalty.

Here is what she wants to have happen.

She wants you to fall into the trap. The trap is: You say you're against the death penalty, and she says, "Oh, you're in favor of saving murderers, and killing babies." Ha ha. That shows who liberals really care about—unlike conservatives whose interest in life, as Representative Barney Frank pointed out some years ago, begins at conception and ends at birth. Both sides can play this game. But why?

There is only one set of questions worth debating about the death penalty.

What kind of system does it take to administer it fairly? How good is good enough? What process is due when the penalty is death?

If you are against the death penalty, those are the questions you want to ask, because it is the only way to frame the debate if you want to win.

If instead you let Ann frame the question as whether you are "for" or "against" the death penalty, she will win. Upward of 80 percent of

Americans are for the death penalty, if you ask about a child moles-ter/murderer who we're sure did it—with everyone except the people you don't need to be debating ready to trip the switch, approve the in-jection, and so forth.

I do a road trip routine on the death penalty with Professor Barry Scheck, who is best known for being one of the DNA experts on the O. J. Simpson "dream team." In the meantime he has spent decades doing DNA work for indigent defendants on death row as a cofounder of the Innocence Project. We've done it for ten years—and this is what it comes down to: We don't debate religious issues.

Whether you're for or against the death penalty is essentially a mat-ter of belief. You would think people like Ann would embrace that. You can't prove deterrence, any more than you can prove the opposite. Ret-ribution is a question of belief.

Whether someone deserves the death penalty depends on whether you think it is just for the state to apply it.

Unless you enjoy losing a debate in which no one's minds are ever changed, why debate it? Me, I get paid to do that sort of thing, but I still like to stake out a winning position.

The question that fair-minded people, in middle of the bell curve, will stop to think about, the question that has lead numerous states to consider whether to impose a moratorium on the death penalty, is whether our current, sometimes sloppy, sometimes worse than sloppy criminal justice system is fair enough, accurate enough, and reliable enough to administer a penalty where mistakes are simply unacceptable (to almost all of us, anyway).

Ann says there has never been a case where we have been demon-strably wrong in our application of the death penalty.

That's just silly. *Demonstrably* is obviously the key word. We correct the mistakes we know about. Mistakes we don't know about, we don't know about. Once someone is dead, the incentive to uncover the mis-take is largely gone. But one thing anyone who has spent any time at all in the criminal justice system knows is that the system is far from perfect, and that mistakes do get made.

I was a Supreme Court law clerk when the death penalty was reinstituted in this county in 1979. The first man to be executed against his will was a man named Spinkelink, in April 1979. His petition to stay alive came to my boss at nine o'clock at night on the day he was supposed to be killed. He had until midnight to live, unless we acted. My co-clerk, Jim Liebman, who has gone on to a celebrated career both practicing and teaching as an opponent of the death penalty, and I were sitting in chambers waiting for it. We treated the papers as if a man's life depended on it. The light in my old Maverick was broken, so Jim brought his flashlight, and we read aloud as I drove to Justice Stevens apartment in Arlington. We looked for mistakes. Both of us felt like throwing up. You have a man's life in your hands, literally, and you're trying to make sure there are no mistakes. What if we were the ones who made one?

The case had already been reviewed by a number of courts before it got to us. The petition itself had, as I recall, already been turned down by another Justice. It didn't matter. We studied it as if ours were the first sets of eyes to see it. We examined each claim of error. Our best bet was, I think, a Fourth or Fifth Amendment claim. We got to the Justice's apartment, and he read it too.

Then he called Justice Potter Stewart, whose vote would be needed if there were to be four votes (the two regular dissenters from the grant of death—Justices William J. Brennan and Thurgood Marshall—plus the two more required to grant review and stay the penalty automatically) to see if Justice Stewart thought there were any cert-worthy issues here. He didn't. We sat for a few moments. There were no mistakes, none we could find, none he could find, none that Justice Stewart thought were worthy of the Court's review. He handed us the unsigned petition to drive back to the Court.

Justice Marshall was there when we got back. He delayed the execution until morning, when the Court met in full session to dissolve the stay. Spinkelink was killed that day. An American Airlines flight from Chicago to Los Angeles crashed that same day. "Death and destruction," I remember saying to Justice Stevens, overwhelmed by the grimness of it all.

In those days, every petition in a capital case got read. In those days, my boss was in favor of the death penalty. These days, death cases at the Court are handled routinely. There are no midnight drives. People don't stay up all night looking for mistakes the way we did. Mostly, just one clerk reads death petitions, except for my old boss, Justice Stevens, who has yet to join the "pool" in which one clerk does the review for all the Justices.

These days, Justice Stevens has changed his mind about the death penalty. Why? Not because he has changed his fundamental "beliefs," as far as I can tell, but because of the way we administer the ultimate punishment. Because we do it too routinely. Because there is too much room for error, and too little care to ensure that those errors will be caught.

Justice Stevens was the junior Justice when I clerked for him, back in 1978. He had been on the Court a year then, the worst seat, the smallest chambers. He did not consider himself a liberal, and frankly, neither did I.

Today, Justice Stevens is the Senior Justice. The networks now celebrate his birthday. He says he really hasn't changed his views very much and, with the exception of the death penalty, I think that is true. He is now considered the Court's leading liberal.

* * *

As for Ann's claim of no demonstrable mistakes, the fact is that there are a number of websites devoted to just that issue. The Innocence Project, co-directed by my friend Barry Scheck, exists to make sure such mistakes aren't made. No thanks to Ann, of course, but thanks to people like Barry, volunteer investigators and lawyers, and others, we are probably doing better than we have any right to expect in preventing mistakes in capital cases. But even so.

My favorite mistake story is the story of Earl Washington, who gave five confessions, four of which were thrown out, and the fifth of which landed him on death row, even though he knew none of the details about the crime or the victim, such as what she looked like or how many times she was stabbed, and had an IQ of 69, and a desire to please, and was lead to the crime scene twice. I tell stories like this and people don't want to believe it. But none of these points got raised by his defense lawyer at trial, and then finally, when it was held that he had received inadequate assistance of counsel because exculpatory biological evidence hadn't been introduced, the error was held to be harmless because after all, he confessed. And it took nine years for DNA testing to exclude the possibility that Washington could have raped the woman. He "confessed" in 1983, and was finally released from prison in 2001.

And Washington was lucky. He wasn't executed in the interim. He could've been, and no one would have categorized it as a mistake. They would have said, "Of course he was guilty. He confessed."

You can read the story for yourself at http://www.innocenceproject .org/case/search_profiles.php and http://www.pbs.org/wgbh/pages /frontline/shows/case/cases.

* * *

Ann's only other answer to crime in *Godless* is a very long love letter to Mayor Rudy Giuliani. Need I add that he also favors sticking forks in the heads of babies, to quote the description of someone I know . . . and gay rights. He is an average moderate, tolerant American, in those respects.

As for the crime rate, my friend Bill Bratton was the chief of police in New York for much of Rudy's tenure, and he is the chief here in Los Angeles now, and the crime rate has declined steadily in both places, so maybe *he's* the hero. I've worked with some of the very smartest people in this field for more than two decades, and the efforts and factors that go into a change in the crime rate go so far beyond who the mayor is that it really isn't worth debating.

* * *

Ann writes: "The only reason the Democrats cried racism over the Willie Horton ads was that it was one of the greatest campaign issues of all time."

She claims that the Democrats exploited racism the way they always do.

Not so. Ann is right that it was vice presidential nominee Lloyd Bentsen who finally brought up the racism issue in 1988. But she has the rest of the story wrong.

So wrong.

It was a terrible issue. That's why it took so long to raise it. People, especially white male people, questioned Dukakis's strength and toughness. Crying racism, as Ann puts it, doesn't make you look strong, which was one of Dukakis's big problems.

More important, it doesn't help you appeal to white voters in a racially polarized electorate, which was Dukakis's other big problem at the time, especially because the more polarized the electorate was, the worse we did. We already had the black vote. We were losing because we were doing so badly among whites. That was the real reason the campaign rule was to *not* attack the Willie Horton campaign as racist. I didn't make that rule, but I was under orders to follow it. The only one who wasn't was Lloyd Bentsen. That's why he was the one to raise it, and that's why it took so long to bring it up.

What Ann's chapter on Willie Horton also ignores is the question of timing. By the time Lloyd Bentsen went on *This Week* and first mentioned the "racial elements" in the Republican Willie Horton campaign, the damage had all been done. By the time of all the quotes that

Ann counts, in her Lexis search, finding all the mentions of Willie Horton and racism, the contest for the presidency had already shifted decisively in Bush's favor. Miss Lexis-Nexis can count, but either she doesn't know enough or chooses not to pay attention to the critical factor of timing. Yes, there were lots of stories about Willie Horton and racism, but they were all triggered by Bentsen's comments, which in effect removed the gag rule.

This is how the *Financial Times* of London reported on the final days of the campaign: "Class and race have emerged as the dominant themes which Governor Michael Dukakis, the Massachusetts Democratic candidate, will try to exploit in the final two weeks of the 1988 presidential campaign in his effort to close the gap with Vice President George Bush, the front-running Republican. They are a far cry from the message he delivered to the Democratic convention in Atlanta in July. . . . Mr. Dukakis, who early in his campaign apparently decided that a top priority was to win back white, working-class 'Reagan Democrats,' seems to have realized that Mr. Bush has trumped this card."

It was October 23 when Bentsen raised the race issue. Seventeen days before the election. Eight days after the second debate, with its memorable question from Bernard Shaw about what Michael would do if a man raped and killed his wife Kitty (what Bill Clinton and I used to call, in debate prep, the Willie Horton question). We were all set with the answer. The problem was recognizing the question. That was what Dukakis missed.

By the time Bentsen asked about race, the election was all but over. The reason the press finally chronicled the issues of race and Horton was because they discovered, after the fact, that Lee Atwater had pulled off his campaign, that it had worked, and that the media had functioned as his silent, sometimes hapless partners in crime. Yes, you can find a story here or there earlier on saying there were furlough programs in other states, and Ann cites them; but for months, day after day, Bush mentioned Willie Horton in every speech and the press repeated the charge; Willie Horton ads and propaganda were distributed uncritically, and the damage was done.

I'm not saying it was all their fault. We knew it was coming. We could have done something about it. We didn't. Fair point. But to pretend that, from day one, the press was attacking Bush for attacking Dukakis on Horton is just flat wrong. It didn't happen that way. They wouldn't have felt so guilty if it had.

Ann argues that Willie Horton wasn't a "metaphor" for anything, as I described him, "but a real murderer and rapist who had already killed a person before being released from a life sentence by Dukakis, whereupon Horton savagely beat a man and raped a woman." She says it wasn't the age-old "image" of the black man raping the white woman as her husband watched, as African American Democratic strategist Donna Brazile described it, that was so powerful, but "the real case, and I'm not sure how that image would be improved if it had been a white man raping a woman while her husband watched."

Ann argues that race simply didn't matter, either in terms of crime policy or presidential politics: "The whole mythology of the racist Willie Horton ad is a joke. Even the victims' ad that showed Horton's face would not be deemed racist by anyone who had ever been to our planet. Was this Vermont circa 1780? No! It was Massachusetts in the 1980s. Some criminals in twentieth century America are black. Meanwhile, the Bush campaign bent over backwards to avoid any acknowledgment of the fact that Horton was black, going to the ridiculous extreme of showing all white people in prison. . . . The Bush campaign surely wished that Horton had been Chinese, Indian, German, Malaysian—an Aleut!—anything but black. But the issue was simply too important to drop just because liberals would call Republicans racist."

There were, as Ann notes, two Willie Horton ads. I had no problem with the second ad, the official Bush ad, which showed a revolving door with a disproportionate number of white criminals circling

through it. You can watch the ad at http://livingroomcandidate
.movingimage.us/index.

The first ad is another story. Virtually everybody who has seen it,
with the exception of Ann, was troubled by the classic technique of
having the candidate's face revolving with the other face on a block,
when the other face was the worst and scariest shot you could ever possibly find of Willie Horton. There was a reason the Bush campaign
consistently distanced itself from this ad—the Swift Boat ad of its time,
the one everybody but Ann Coulter refused to admit any connection
to—and that was that collapsing the face of the Democratic nominee
with a black murderer and rapist was not just one of those coincidences
where you know the Bush campaign just wished he was white.

In fact, in all my conversations, including Atwater's famous apology for the campaign, I never once heard one suggestion that the Bush
campaign wished Willie Horton were white.

Nor was it just a coincidence, speaking in terms of either crime
policy or presidential politics, that he wasn't.

Pretending race isn't an issue doesn't make it go away—it just undermines our effectiveness in dealing with the real issue that is there.

* * *

On the day I am writing this, a gunman has opened fire on a sidewalk
in Los Angeles. Three people have been killed, including two children.

Now guess where.

White neighborhood or Black/Hispanic neighborhood?

Guess what color the shooters were? (Black)

Guess what color the victims were? (Hispanic)

Does it matter?

Four days later, police are trying to keep interest alive.

You know that wouldn't be the case with white victims in a white
neighborhood.

Would the reaction be different if the answers were different?

Are you kidding? So why pretend?

* * *

Ann writes that "some criminals happen to be black."

Can she really be so stupid? I don't think so. If she is, she has no business writing about crime. Or race. Or Willie Horton.

Violent criminals don't just happen to be black. The correlation between race and crime is significant, although it is not because of any causal connection—being black doesn't cause crime, but if you're walking down the street and wondering which of two men, one white and one black, is more likely to be a violent criminal, I think Ann would be the first to point out that it is rational to suppose that, all other things being equal, it is the black man.

Luckily, Jesse Jackson said the same thing some years ago, so it's safe to say it aloud without being accused of racism: "There is nothing more painful to me at this stage in my life than to walk down the street and hear footsteps and start thinking about robbery—then look around and see someone white and feel relieved."

A few years ago, I wrote a column for the *Washington Post* that said that in most American cities, 40 percent of all black men between the ages of eighteen and thirty-five are in prison, on probation, or on parole. The young intern fact checker called me, appalled. I suggested she get the number for the District of Columbia. It was 60 percent. As of 2001, I found reports as high as a one in three chance of a young black going to prison, much less probation or parole. One in three. Adjust by age and urban location, and you get closer to 40 percent. These numbers should be terrifying if you apply them to your own community.

"Some criminals happen to be black . . ." Who is Ann kidding?

It all correlates to education. If you look at who drops out of high school, you can find who commits crimes. If you look at who drops out of high school, you find a group that is disproportionately black and

Hispanic. If you look at the prison population, you find a group that disproportionately dropped out of high school and is black and Hispanic. This is all nothing new. This is sadly old. So is our failure to do anything about it. Go laugh at midnight basketball. It worked. So did some of the faith-based programs Princeton professor and George W. Bush adviser John DiIulio supported, which, curiously enough, in a book about Godlessness, Ann never even trumpets. I would gladly have joined her there. Common ground and all.

But of course Ann isn't really interested in crime. Or race and crime. Or faith, race, and crime. Or God and faith and race and crime. Just attacking liberals.

* * *

In 1988, the four-letter word in Democratic presidential politics was still race. No one said it out loud. But the explanation was simple.

How had the Democrats lost the South? Race.

What did "law and order" mean when Nixon ran on it in 1968? Race.

Why did the South vote Republican in national elections and Democrat in local elections? Race.

Why did you have to create districts that looked like porcupines to elect blacks to Congress? Because whites in states with large black voting blocks wouldn't vote for blacks. Without majority minority districts, there would be no minority representation.

The higher the percentage of blacks in a Southern state, the worse you were likely to do among white voters, the more likely you were to lose the state. That's why there was a list of states where Jesse Jackson wasn't supposed to go.

The more polarized the vote became along racial lines, the worse you were likely to do among white voters.

The Democrats spent every fall in fear, trying to figure out how to win white votes. Except Bill Clinton with his "Sister Souljah moment," where the nominee, having won the nomination with the support of black votes, renounced the extremist rhetoric of the musician Sister Souljah. "If black people kill black people every day, why not have a week and kill white people?" is what she was quoted as saying, to which Clinton said, "If you took the words 'white' and 'black' and you reversed them, you might think *David Duke* was giving that speech." Clinton was roundly criticized by black leaders, including Jesse Jackson, for what they viewed as a transparent effort to appeal to moderate voters and move the party to the middle.

But Willie Horton, of course, just happened to be black, according to Ann. Nothing to do with race. Nothing to do with history. Nothing to do with law and order. Nothing at all. Imagine saying this with a straight face. Imagine writing it today. Ann does. And by saying it and writing it, over and over, they ensure that nothing changes. It is not merely a sin of omission.

It is worse than that.

Because it's not just about a campaign ad, or even just about one candidate and one campaign.

Imagine that an epidemic like this one had affected any other community for as long as this one has, and what we might have done.

Imagine, dare I ask, that the Jewish community faced an epidemic in which 40 or 60 percent of our young men were denied a chance to have a productive youth—and we knew that would be the case, generation after generation?

Imagine that were happening to generation after generation of Italian Americans, or Irish Americans? Imagine six out of ten being locked up, put on probation or parole?

Would we start a prison expansion project, or would we set about to do something to solve the problem?

I don't believe in rehabilitating Willie Horton, but I'll be damned if I understand why a society would choose to build prisons for his kids and grandkids instead of schools. Why looking to the future, our focus would be on how to punish the next generation of criminals instead of how to prevent today's children from growing up into a life in prison. Ask any first grade teacher whether we're headed for trouble and she'll tell you. Ask the public if we should focus on prevention and they consistently say yes. So how is it that we don't ask, don't try?

I know the answer to that. The reason we don't try, or try very hard, the reason we live in a society that puts a priority on punishment over prevention is because our politicians became terrified of their shadows in the wake of Willie Horton. His legacy was that you could never be too tough on crime. The prison building boom was the racist legacy of Willie Horton.

Ann says, "Whether it is building prisons, mandatory sentencing, three strikes laws, or the death penalty, if it has to do with punishing criminals, Democrats are against it."

Ann is wrong about the Democrats, dead wrong, and I'm afraid she knows that and is just pushing the game onward, calling them weaklings who adore criminals so that she can continue the paranoia that feeds policy by slogan. If she doesn't know she's wrong, she's blinding herself to what's happened in crime policy.

Whatever the goal of the Bush campaign, the effect of the Willie Horton ad campaign was to teach a generation of politicians that no matter what the idea, what the proposal, what the slogan, there was only one answer if it was about being tough on crime. Yes. For it. No more Willie Hortons.

In 1988, after a long rehearsal for the first presidential debate, during which Bill Clinton tried over and over to come up with an answer for Michael Dukakis to use about Willie Horton, I sat with the Arkansas governor at a restaurant and he pulled out a napkin, took out a pen, and drew a line down the middle. On one side of the line were the Democratic governors who opposed the death penalty, on the other, the ones who supported it. The older generation—Dukakis and Cuomo—were on one side. The younger generation—starting with him—on the other. He shook his head, and made a simple point. You need to be on this side to win. Four years later, during the New Hampshire primary, Bill Clinton interrupted campaigning to go back to Arkansas to preside over the execution of a man who was sufficiently mentally handicapped that he asked them to save his dessert from the final dinner so he could have it later.

I'd like to believe that things are changing with respect to the death penalty—not because people have necessarily changed their underlying beliefs, but because DNA evidence has made it "easier" (in theory, in truth, if you're poor and don't have a good lawyer, it's really not easy at all) to prove that the system makes mistakes. But the underlying point about "toughness," and the crime issue as a test of toughness, instead of good policy, remains as true today as it was that night in the Chinese restaurant.

I wish I had a nickel for every time in the years since that a politician would explain to me why he had to vote for a bad bill, or couldn't support a good judge, or wouldn't nominate an able candidate, because of a "Willie Horton" problem. Poorly written "three strikes" laws that equalized non-violent and violent crimes as potential life-sentence third strikes, that allowed prosecutors to send old men to prison for life for stealing a pizza, would be passed by legislators who knew better, who could see the problems on the face of the statute, because they wanted to avoid "Willie Horton problems." Mandatory sentencing statutes had the effect of taking discretion away from judges, grown-ups, and people who operate in public, who are visible, and must explain their judgments. Instead, they transferred that discretionary power to kids, prosecutors, my former students, to be exercised invisibly in the charging decisions. Don't you understand, I would ask, and of course, everyone understood. Discretion is like toothpaste in the criminal justice system: if you squeeze at one end it comes out at the other. Everyone understands this, but you can't vote no.

Jerry Brown, who appointed Rose Bird—the liberal judge whose opposition to the death penalty led to a voter revolt against her and her fellow justices—is running for attorney general of California as the law-and-order Mayor of Oakland, with support from the police and a record of cutting crime. No one is liberal on crime.

Everything Ann says Democrats are against, I have seen them enslaved to, supporting in the name of one Willie Horton, determined never to lose another election, winking at me meaningfully, as if I were the last person to question a judgment like this.

After all, don't I know? Wasn't I there?

And now she repeats the old charges, lest common sense intervene along with the results of an aging, growing prison population whose incarceration no longer produces any crime-cutting effects.

For years, federal law unjustly discriminated between the sentences for crack and powder cocaine, punishing the former, used primarily by blacks, far more harshly than the latter. In an earlier book, I wrote about this discrepancy, and the corrosive effect it had on black juries, encouraging disrespect for the criminal justice system and even the sort of jury nullification that allowed O. J. Simpson to get away with murder. I sent the book to Bill Clinton, by then the president. He agreed with me. We should get rid of that, he told me, but we can't unless the Republicans are willing to do it on a bipartisan basis. Otherwise, we'll have a Willie Horton problem.

Always Willie Horton.

Afraid of their shadows.

And it's not just crime.

Shh.

* * *

After the Dukakis campaign I moved to Los Angeles. I got involved in local politics, started appearing on television, making some trouble. It was eleven years ago that my friend Lynne and I went to see the chancellor of UCLA about the fact that, for the first time she could remember, there were fewer than one hundred blacks in the entering freshman class.

Fewer than one hundred. How could that be? In 1995, no less.

Her family gives a lot of money to UCLA. I have a big mouth. Together, we were the Committee Against Discrimination. CAD. Something like that. Or MAD. I'm an expert in making up new organizations for the purpose of meeting with important people and demanding change. We were definitely mad.

The short answer to what the problem was, of course, was Proposition 209, the California ballot proposition barring affirmative action.

The regents were watching everything we did because of it.

So what, Lynne said. So what, I said.

Do better. Certainly you can take into account the obstacle these kids endured to make their numbers.

Eastern European immigrants, they said. That's who we get if we take into account the obstacles. . . .

What about all these kids who grow up here in Los Angeles and don't even know where UCLA is, I asked, pointing out that most of them think of my school, USC, as their hometown school. Certainly UCLA could do a better job of affirmative action, in the best sense of the word. What about starting with the kids in public school in Los Angeles? What about an outreach program—bringing them to UCLA every Saturday, getting the gifted kids early, literally the opposite of building prisons for Willie Horton's kids? A friend of ours, at the time, was president of the Los Angeles Unified School Board. She was eager to be part of the team. What team?

And what about a statement from the top about the value of diversity as an essential element of educational excellence?

How are you supposed to teach a class about civil rights, a class about the Los Angeles riots, a class about American history or slavery if you don't have enough blacks to go around for classes in your basic core curriculum? That's what excellence in education is about. I was on a roll. . . . I could have written the speech for him.

The chancellor looked at me as if I had lost my mind. Perhaps I wasn't familiar with Prop 209. You couldn't talk about race like that, he said.

We have to talk about race like that, I said. Most people would agree. That's not what they meant to prohibit.

He didn't give the speech.

* * *

"We're looking for two people to discuss affirmative action," the CNN producer tells me.

"Are you free at three?" What time you're free is the most important question in the game of booking. I'm free at three. Good news.

Just one question: Am I for or against affirmative action?

I explain. I'm a law professor, after all. I've been teaching in the area for years. The Supreme Court has yet to decide the University of Michigan admissions case, but I know which way the wind is blowing.

Here's what I think, I explain to the booker. I don't believe in automatically awarding points to people, in a bid or application, because of their race. But you should be able to take into account what those people went through to get those numbers, the obstacles they've overcome, that sort of thing. And where there's a past history of discrimination, or a very good reason to want diversity—for instance in the police department, or the university, for that matter—you should be able to take that into account as well. In the law, we call that a compelling state interest.

The booker pauses. Makes sense to me, she says. As a matter of fact, you make the most sense of anyone I've talked to today.

Good thing, say I pleasantly, the pleased professor, having explained a rather complicated bit of Supreme Court law in a few easy sentences. Because not only is that my opinion (and most people's in the bell curve, dare I add), but it's also the law of the land.

So, she says, would you say you are *for* or *against* affirmative action?

I see it coming.

I'd say I'm against affirmative action except in those limited cases where I'm for it. Or, if you'd prefer, I'm for it except where I'm against it.

She laughs, but this is not funny. You can have either, she says. For or against.

I laugh, but it is not funny. I am neither for nor against.

She asks again. I answer again. We are going nowhere. They are not having three guests that day.

She does not book me.

The whack-job on the left debates the whack-job on the right.

One says it has nothing to do with race. The other says it's only about race.

Nothing changes.

Eleven years pass.

Next fall, the entering class at UCLA will have fewer than one hundred blacks. There is a big story in the newspaper. No one can remember numbers this low. The same chancellor, now in his final year, says we will have to work harder.

* * *

Two Black Shooters. Three Hispanic Victims.

Seventy-five percent of the violent offenders in Los Angeles are young men of color. So are most of their victims.

Willie Horton just happened to be black.

Ignore race, and who loses? Not whites. Not Ann and her crowd.

Ann still wants to scream that race is not an issue, that crime is just about some individuals who do it and need to be executed, that the only question about the death penalty is whether you're for it or against it.

We are already sending pizza thieves to prison for life, executing at record clip, and still she is parroting the old charges. She attacks to drown out the possibility that without her voice, there would be no disagreement about both the need for enforcement and the need for prevention, about the reality of race or the necessity of addressing it.

7.

THE MORAL MAJORITY IS US

For the Right, morality is not about social justice or equality.

And when the pollsters talk about the dominance of moral values, they do not mean values in the broad sense; they do not mean what you and I mean.

When Ann calls us immoral, there are only two issues she is addressing. We know what they are. They come from the political playbooks, not from Scriptures.

Abortion and gay rights. Women and homosexuals.

Wedge issues. Intended to divide.

But here is the key point. We need not be defensive. We need not be afraid. The moral majority is us. We have not yet won gay marriage. But someday we will. And basically, we can win everything else if we frame it our way. Or rather, she loses every time if we frame it right.

So why does it never feel that way?

According to Ann: "No liberal cause is defended with more dishonesty than abortion. No matter what else they pretend to care about from time to time—undermining national security, aiding terrorist, oppressing the middle class, freeing violent criminals—the single most important item on the Democrats' agenda is abortion. . . . No Republican is so crazily obsessed with any issue as the Democrats are with abortion."

Here's what would happen if *Roe v. Wade* were overruled.

Abortion would not necessarily be legal or illegal. It would depend on state law. Every state legislature would be free to do something it has not been free to do since *Roe:* to criminalize abortions prior to viability or to impose whatever burdens they choose on the "right" to abortion.

Abortion would be on the agenda in every state legislature, which would mean it would be the hot issue in state legislative and gubernatorial contests across America.

A new generation of voters and would-be voters would have concrete reason to understand that their access to abortion—and potentially other reproductive services—would turn directly on the outcome of forthcoming elections. For the first and perhaps only time in their lives, they would see a reason to vote.

Explain to me why Ann Coulter would want this to happen.

Explain to me why this would be good, positive, and helpful to the Republican Party.

And I'll explain to you why she really only wants to focus on "partial birth abortion," the made-up term for a second-trimester abortion procedure rarely used but chosen for its gruesome characteristics to give conservatives something to be against. It's the only issue she can win. Maybe. At least if you don't explain to people why it is that a woman might need a "partial birth abortion."

People rarely change their minds about abortion in a debate. I'm not likely to come up with a new argument in the next few paragraphs that will always work to change the minds of those who disagree with you about abortion.

That's not how it works. How it works is that the questions change and that changes the answers. Whether there have been any other

changes in attitudes toward abortion in recent decades is much de-
bated. What is clear is that the country is fundamentally pro-choice.
The evidence is undeniable.

That's why you can win every argument.

* * *

This is how attitudes toward abortion are measured. Or at least it is one
of the basic methods, one that has been used for a long time. It's the
method that gives you the long view.

Every two years, a statistically relevant sample of the whole population is asked a series of questions about when, if ever, they think it
should be possible for a woman to obtain a legal abortion. The questions are phrased in the most neutral, unemotional way possible, in an
effort to measure beliefs, not fondness for political rhetoric and red
meat.

What's stunning, to me, is how many people say yes to at least
some of the questions.

Take the test yourself, for starters, and measure your own attitudes.

For thirty years, the question has been asked in this way: *Please tell
me whether or not you think it should be possible for a pregnant woman to
obtain a legal abortion if:*

1. The woman's own health is seriously endangered.
2. She became pregnant as a result of rape.
3. There is a strong chance of serious defect in the baby.
4. The family has very low income and cannot afford any more
   children.
5. She is not married and does not want to marry the man.
6. She is married and does not want any more children.

Two things are quite stunning about the charts that document
Americans' answers to these questions.

The first is just how stable they are. You can drive yourself completely crazy detecting slight dips in attitude toward abortion from
2002 to 2004, but they are slight. What is striking, overall, according to
Morris Fiorina in his book *Culture War?*, from which the chart below is
taken, is the flatness of the lines from 1972 to 2004. Fiorina constructed his charts from the General Social Survey and other studies of
public opinion and the Stanford professor and Hoover Institution senior fellow's point is that attitudes toward abortion vary far less than you
would think.

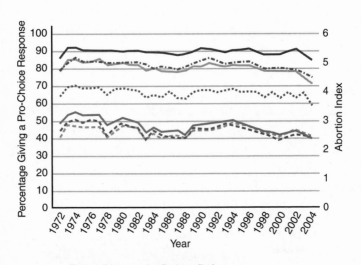

— Strong Chance of a Serious Defect
— Woman's Health Seriously Endangered
--- Pregnant As a Result of Rape
--- Married–Wants No More Children
— Low Income–Can't Afford More Children
--- Not Married
···· Abortion Index (Average Number of Circumstances Legal)

Popular Attitudes Toward Abortion Since *Roe v. Wade*
Source: Calculated from the General Social Surveys.

But Professor Fiorina's second point is even more telling. Virtually everybody in the country supports legal abortion in the first three instances cited in the survey questions. By huge, overwhelming majorities, in both red and blue states, Americans favor abortion in those first three categories. According to Fiorina's breakdown, "residents of the red states supported legal abortion in about 3.5 of the 6 circumstances, a bit lower than the national average, while residents of the blue states supported abortion in about 4 circumstances, a little higher than the national average."

Overall, the majorities on questions 1, 2, and 3 are just enormous, in the 80–90 percent ranges.

It is certainly true with abortion, more so than with most issues, that she who controls the questions determines the answer.

If you want to prove that the country (as of 2003) is equally divided (46 percent to 46 percent) between those who think abortion is murder and those who don't feel this way, and that the division is closer than it was in 1995 (40 percent murder, 51 percent not), you can. That's all true. But it is also the case that almost two-thirds of all Americans support the United States Supreme Court's decision in *Roe v. Wade* protecting a woman's right to choose, prior to viability, whether to continue a pregnancy, and that Republicans and Democrats, Catholics and Protestants, even churchgoers and non-churchgoers all tend to agree that there are at least those three circumstances—a risk to the health of the mother, rape, or a strong chance of a serious defect—when a pregnant woman should be able to secure an abortion.

Fiorina writes: "The fact that the differences among Americans are as small as they are is widely understood by social scientists and widely obscured by political debate."

Consider what that means. There really is a consensus in this country about abortion. It's just that most people don't know about it.

And Ann takes advantage of that fact to turn people against each other.

Knowing that there is a consensus, however, can at least help you win the argument—not by convincing anyone, but by asking the right questions instead of falling into her traps.

If you're in an argument, and you ask someone (Ann Coulter, for instance), should a woman be able to get an abortion if her health is endangered, Ann will say no—but 90 percent of the people listening will disagree with her.

If you ask, should a woman be able to get an abortion if she became pregnant through rape or incest, Ann will say no—but 80 percent of those listening will disagree with her.

If Ann starts going on about partial birth abortion, and you say, but what if there is a strong chance of serious defects in the baby—you win the argument.

And if she says, but most of the cases don't involve serious defects, look at Ann, or whomever you're talking to, and ask: Will you make an exception for those that do? They won't. But if they will, ask if they will also make an exception for the health of the mother, when it is endangered.

Ask them how much danger the mother must face before they will recognize an exception.

Ask them how much additional risk they think a mother should bear.

Reasonable danger? Serious health risk? What pound of flesh do they want from women?

On the issue of abortion, there is indeed a gap between the extreme and the middle, but the gap is between the extreme that Ann represents, and the rest of America, which supports a woman's right to secure an abortion in at least some circumstances (my definition of pro-choice) and has done so since 1972—even at a time when the country didn't support *Roe,* which they do now.

There is a gap between the overwhelming majority that wants to find common ground, and the only group that doesn't. And what group do you think that is? Surprise: it is the small minority, the right tail of the right tail, that supports a total ban on abortion. They are the only ones who don't want compromise, don't want common ground, don't want peace.

How can it be that we've won and it feels like we've lost?

This is what happens when the losing side makes all the noise, when that noise is mean and sometimes vulgar, and when they are dominating the discourse and insisting on continuing the conflict.

* * *

Here's something even more "fun" to note, if anything can be fun in a debate about abortion.

It is also, potentially, very significant.

The only cases where a majority doesn't support abortion are the truly elective middle-class situations: where a married couple chooses not to have more children, or where a woman is not married, and doesn't wish to marry the man.

These are what I call the "doctor's office abortions." These are the abortions that white middle-class women get in doctors' offices, that college girls get in clinics, and that suburban women get from their own OB/GYNs.

Imagine what would happen, speaking purely politically, if *these* abortions were to be outlawed.

Talk about all hell breaking loose.

Talk about bad news, electorally speaking, for the party considered responsible.

Remember those numbers—about the one group that, had it voted for Kerry in the same numbers as it voted for Gore, would have elected him. Those were women. Plain old-fashioned married suburban and rural women. The kind of women who can occasionally get pregnant when they don't mean to, or can't afford to, or aren't married, or know women this can happen to. They are women who may one day find themselves happy they have a right to choose.

Abortion is not a voting issue because the overwhelming majority of voters in this country are pro-choice and they don't need to
vote the issue.

Want to make them?

Want to force them to?

Prohibit the abortions they say they're against.

Of course we would never hope for that, we're too decent, but just
imagine it happened. Who would vote in that election? Who would win?

You know that is the game Ann would play if she had our hand.

* * *

The Supreme Court describes the abortion question as a "clash of absolutes," as if both positions have equal weight and the task is somehow
to figure out how to navigate between them. Not so. In fact, there is a
small minority of absolutists on one side, and everyone else is in the
pro-choice middle.

It's hard to imagine anyone who would be "for" abortion in *every*
circumstance; no state has ever allowed that, and no one I know has
ever advocated it. The Constitution, certainly, has never mandated it.

Moreover, the fact that you believe in sorting things through
doesn't mean you necessarily believe in the government sorting them
through for you. One of the most interesting groups is the significant
percentage of voters who see abortion as murder, but support *Roe v.
Wade* anyway. It is not necessarily inconsistent. The essence of a right to
privacy is the right to keep the government out of a decision, even one
you might make differently from the one you're granting the right to.
The reason we allow abortion in all circumstances prior to viability is
not that anyone approves of it in all cases, but that it is not the government's business to be setting forth what the acceptable reasons are, and
sit in judgment of the individual's exercise of her "right to privacy."
After all, what could possibly be more anathema to a right to privacy?

The abortion case deserves study because the losers have done more than score points for noise. It isn't just that they have made us "feel" bad, robbing us of the "pleasures" (no, Ann, I'm not calling abortion a pleasure, no way) of victory. The Coulter Culture has not only distorted the debate, it has turned settled questions into debatable points.

How many times do we have to defend *Roe v. Wade* before it will finally be considered settled law?

How many times do we have to win the same parental consent cases, over and over, against state legislatures that refuse to take into account the health of pregnant teenage girls, and would instead use them as pawns in their own ideological battles?

How many times do we have to fight the partial birth abortion fight—an ultimately worthless, stupid, made-up fight, one that will be replaced with some new fight the minute it is decisively concluded by the Supreme Court, having interfered with the way doctors practiced medicine and hopefully with the lives and health of not too many women?

The problem with the abortion fight is that cultural tyranny has effectively restricted choice. The move to the right has been not simply ideological, but practical and real.

They've done this by cleverly restricting the issues that ever come up for voters to ones that either don't affect the majority of voters, or that they don't understand, or that they think they understand but they don't. And they've done this through pure intimidation.

Consider then, Ann's favorite issue, "partial birth abortion." Most people have no idea what it is. With reason. When they hear about it—about an intact baby's brain being sucked out, for starters—it sounds so awful that of course, they're against it. What's to be for, in that rendition?

Ann goes on a bender of an attack on the fact that liberals say there is no such thing, medically speaking, as partial birth abortion. But liberals are right, it is a legal term, made up by Senate staffers and anti-abortion

activists, literally sitting around at night looking for something to prohibit that sounded so grisly and awful, that even the majority that was
pro-choice might be on their side.

She quotes a dated, but perfectly accurate, 1995 interview on *60
Minutes* of a Colorado doctor (she calls him an abortionist), Warren
Hern, who, when asked to define the term, responded sensibly enough:

> **BRADLEY:** What is a partial birth abortion?
>
> **HERN:** Well, I'm not really sure I know. The—there's no such
> thing in the medical literature.
>
> **BRADLEY:** Would most doctors in this country know what a
> partial . . .
>
> **HERN:** No, there's no such thing.
>
> **BRADLEY:** It doesn't exist?
>
> **HERN:** No.
>
> **BRADLEY:** So where does this term come from?
>
> **HERN:** Propaganda term. It's a political term; has no medical
> meaning.

Ann doesn't deny that it's a made-up term, that it has no medical
meaning, that it is a propaganda term. Her answer is: So what? So are a
lot of terms we use. To quote: "This is as opposed to precise medical
terms, like choice and back alley abortions." A silly point: choice and
back alley abortions are not the subject of criminal laws that penalize
doctors and patients if they misunderstand them.

She goes on: "This is pure sophistry, along the lines of liberals pretending not to know what liberal means. [*I wouldn't want to have to define it at the risk of going to prison if somebody disagreed.*] Battery and
sexual assault aren't medical terms, either. They're legal terms, descrip-
tions of what the law prohibits. The fact that the medical community
has not dignified this particular form of infanticide with a name doesn't
mean legislatures can't ban it."

Ann's analogy doesn't hold water. The problem is that "partial birth abortion" isn't "a *particular form* of infanticide"—that's the point.

It would be bad enough, really very bad, for a legislature to tell doctors how to practice medicine by dictating which of a number of recognized medical procedures they could use to perform a legal abortion. That gets into the whole question of why the legislature is practicing medicine in the first instance; of its interfering with the doctor-patient relationship and not letting the doctor do his job of protecting his patient's health.

But partial birth abortion laws go well beyond that, or at least they may, precisely because it's not clear what medical procedures the legal term "partial birth abortion" is intended to encompass.

The advocates of the laws tend to argue for the narrow interpretation, saying they were only intended to reach abortions performed through intact deliveries, ID&X, which accounts for as few as 15 percent of 1.4 percent of all late-term abortions, depending on whose numbers you take. Opponents argue that the broad wording of such bans could potentially also reach the more common D&E procedure, which is used throughout pregnancy. The vagueness of the language, and the absence of fair warning that results, is the first reason these laws, with few exceptions, have been tossed out by the courts.

The other reason is that the drafters of these laws have chosen not to include any exceptions to their bans for the health of the mothers. They have shown themselves firmly determined to lose rather than admit that the health of the patient—the one who is to survive the procedure—must come first.

They have done this even though the Supreme Court has made it perfectly clear how you write a constitutional "partial birth abortion" statute, to wit: narrowly and with an exception for the health of the mother. They have refused either because they fear that the exception will account, as it could, for all of the cases, or because they would rather lose than win.

Consider what would happen if they did win. The late-term abortions at issue here include many performed for precisely the reasons people approve of abortion by the very largest margins: Because a potential birth defect has been detected through genetic testing, or because a problem has developed which threatens the woman's health.

Explain that to people and their attitudes will shift immediately. Succeed in actually banning these abortions, and you'll have a political revolution.

But we can't even get to that point in the discourse. What happens instead in these debates is that people like Ann start talking about brains being suctioned out, and toes and toenails, and most people just don't want to listen, which is how she wins.

What is striking is that if the anti-abortion crowd wanted to write a "partial abortion law" that could pass constitutional muster, they probably could have. But the amazing thing is that they haven't, not yet anyway. (There is a case coming before the Court as I write this.)

They are curiously similar in this regard to the parental consent crowd. It has been clear, and I mean crystal clear, since 1979, how you write a constitutional parental consent law, just as it was quite clear, even before the Court's opinion in *Stenberg v. Carhart* (2000), throwing out the Nebraska partial birth abortion law, what you needed to do if you were going to stand a chance in that area.

It's not my job to lay the whole thing out, but suffice it to say, if you want to require parental consent, there has to be some "out" for the kid who is pregnant by Dad, or who will get beaten up by Dad or Mom if she tells them. And it's remarkable how many states keep failing to provide this out. There also always has to be an out for the health of the mother, and the anti-abortion crowd is just allergic to that one. They'd rather lose than put it in, so they do, more often than you'd imagine.

Which raises the question, if you're just a little bit cynical, whether that isn't the point of the whole exercise.

If you wanted to stretch out this process of fighting about *Roe v. Wade* for a lifetime or two, not get rid of it mind you, just keep it as an issue and stretch out the fighting about it—if *that* was your goal—exhausting the other side just plain *fighting* about it, using it as an organizing tool, while in the meantime making it harder and harder to gain *access* to abortion, particularly if you live in a rural area, or are later in your pregnancy, isn't this the strategy you would follow?

Coulter herself speculates at one point that if you really wanted to test *Roe,* you would test *Roe.*

Maybe they're afraid of achieving their goal.

Will society thank them for forcing a teenager to be a mother? What happens the first time a woman becomes infertile because she couldn't use the preferred abortion method? What happens the first time a woman carrying a baby with a birth defect claims she is being denied access to an abortion?

Whose side will the public be on then?

The cynic would say: Let them win. It's the only way they'll finally lose. The only way American women will stand up and fight for the right to abortion is if they lose it. But we don't play that way. It wouldn't be right. It would cost too much.

In the meantime, in more than 60 percent of the counties in this country, you cannot find a doctor or a clinic willing to provide a safe, legal abortion. That number is up 43 percent from ten years ago.

Who knew that you would have to be a hero to be a gynecologist?

Who knew that the children of gynecologists would be writing memoirs of growing up in fear?

* * *

Excerpt from testimony delivered to the Texas State Legislature:

My name is Julia _____ . I am here today to tell you my story, and the story of my son, Thomas. I hope and pray that you will choose to open your ears and truly listen.

I was born and raised here in _____ . I was raised in the church and I was raised a Republican because my family believed in small government, that had no place in our private lives. I was raised to be pro-choice for the same reason. I was a straight-A student and athlete throughout school, and I graduated from _____University. I have a gold medal from the State Track Championships and I even attended Girl's State. In short, I am the girl next door. I am your daughter, or your granddaughter. I am as all-American as apple pie. And *I* am the face of late-term abortion.

In June 2002, on the first anniversary of our marriage, my husband and I conceived our first child. We spent the next five months attending uneventful doctor's appointments, debating names, and decorating the nursery as we watched my belly grow.

In November, when I was 22 weeks pregnant, we received news that would forever change our lives. A sonogram at the perinatologist's office revealed that our son, Thomas, had a condition known as arthrogryposis. The doctor's face spoke volumes when he returned from fetching a medical book to confirm the rare diagnosis. He explained that arthrogryposis was a condition that causes permanent flexation of the muscle tissue. The condition could be caused by over 200 different diseases and syndromes, with a wide array of severity.

He asked for permission to do an immediate amniocentesis, and for the first time he used the word "termination." It was then that I first realized the gravity of our situation.

My husband and I were shocked and struggled to comprehend what we were being told. It would take two weeks to receive the results of the amniocentesis, which might reveal the cause of the arthrogryposis, but we already knew that the prognosis was not good.

The ultrasound showed that Thomas had clubbed hands and feet. His legs were fixed in a bent position and his arms were permanently flexed straight. He had a cleft palate and swelling on his skull—a condition that would likely kill him in and of itself. Due to his inability to move, Thomas's muscles had deteriorated to 25% or their usual size, and his bones to 25% of their usual density.

My husband and I were sent home to grapple with the news and face an unwelcome decision: Whether or not to continue with the pregnancy.

We talked a lot. We met with a genetic counselor, we met with our pastor, we called our parents, and we read the stories of other couples who'd faced this decision in a book called *Precious Lives Painful Choices: A Prenatal Decision-Making Guide.*

By the time the amnio results came back, we had two days left to make a decision before hitting the 24 week mark—after which, no doctor in Texas would terminate a pregnancy. The results were devastating. Our son had no chromosomal disorder. There was no explanation at all for his condition, and as such, no way to predict the scope of his suffering. We would have to make our decision based strictly on what the ultrasound had revealed.

My husband and I decided that we would have to use the golden rule. We would do for Thomas what we would want done for us in the same situation.

We tried to look at the evidence as honestly as we could. Even the best case scenario was abominable. Thomas would lead a very short life of only a few years at the very most. During those years he would be in constant pain from the ceaseless, charley-horse-type cramps that would rack his body. He would undergo numerous, largely ineffective surgeries, just to stay alive. He would never be able to walk or stand; never grasp anything, never be able to hold himself upright. He wouldn't even be able to suck his own thumb for comfort. And this was only if we were lucky. The more likely scenarios tended toward fetal death and serious health complications for me.

We made our decision with one day to go and left for Houston where we would end Thomas's suffering in one quick and painless moment. Though we wanted to stay at home, _____ was no longer an option, as all of the hospitals were religiously backed and there was no time to convene an ethics committee hearing.

In Houston, God graced us with some of the most compassionate people we'd ever met. The first was our maternal-fetal medicine specialist, who confirmed that the prognosis was even direr than originally thought. In a procedure very similar to an amniocentesis, Thomas's heart was stopped with a simple injection. In that moment, as I held my husband's hand, I met God and handed him my precious boy to care for, for all eternity.

Over the next 17 hours I labored to deliver Thomas's body. It was a painful experience, but the only option given to a woman at 24 weeks gestation. Thomas Stephen _____ was born into this world just after 6:00 A.M. on November 27, 2002—the day before Thanksgiving.

The loving nurse who'd helped us through labor cleaned his fragile body and brought him to us. We held our boy for the next hour as we said goodbye. Our own eyes confirmed what our hearts had already come to know: That Thomas was not meant for this world. The hospital's pastor joined us and we christened Thomas in the baptism bonnet I'd worn as an infant.

Thomas's life and death have changed our lives in ways we will never fully comprehend. I know he made me a better mother, a better friend, and a less judgmental, more compassionate human being. I know he is the reason I have the courage to stand in front of you today.

Through him, I've grown closer to God, who understands what it is to sacrifice your only begotten son in the name of mercy.

During the summer and fall that followed Thomas's death, my husband and I lost two more children during first trimester miscarriages. We lost three children within the space of one year. On January 17th of this year, our prayers were finally answered with the birth of our daughter, Hannah. If anyone knows about the value and sanctity of life, I assure you, it is us.

I am here today in my son's honor to tell you that life doesn't always follow an easy path. And that life is almost never a black and white issue to be governed by others. I am here to put a face on the issue of abortion for all the families that cannot be here today. And I am here to beg you to remember me and Thomas each and every time you contemplate legislation that would deteriorate our God-given parental rights to do what is moral and just for our children.

Thank you.

Additional Information:

Since we lost Thomas, I have been blessed with the opportunity to meet many other parents like us through various support groups, internet message boards, and a blog (Web log, or online diary) that I write about our difficulties growing a family. I received the following, unsolicited letter from someone who had read about Thomas online:

Please believe me that I do not usually write to total strangers but I felt compelled to tell you that your blog has changed me in a profound way.

I have been ardently pro choice for most of my life and fervently pro life for the last 4 of those years. The big reason for the switch? I terminated my first pregnancy 4 years ago, at 11 weeks. And lived to regret it with a force I could never have imagined. I have since acquired a psychiatrist, a therapist, a truckload of anti anxiety and anti depressant medication and ugly red scars on my wrists and ankles that are impossible to hide. I have been hospitalized many times on the wards where you aren't allowed to keep your shoelaces. I have never forgiven myself for signing papers requesting that my first baby be scraped away from me like so much plaque off a tooth.

And I decided that we do our sisters a great injustice, offering termination as a choice, when it causes so much pain. The hardest choice so often masquerading as the easy one. Termination, I screamed, should not be presented as a choice. It isn't fair to anyone.

Reading your blog, I realized that the right to terminate should never be taken away. As much as I have suffered greatly because I was given the choice to end my baby's life, your son would have suffered greatly if you had not been afforded that same right. Everything I believed in changed dramatically 4 years ago. It changed again today reading your blog. My staunchly pro-life stance has been blind and ignorant.

I apologize to you for every time I spoke against the right to abort. I am truly sorry for every pro-life candidate I ever voted for. I am, above all, so very very sorry for your loss.

Every February 8th I sit and cry for the little life that ended so fast, so wrongly. No one ever knew of him but me and so his name goes unspoken, his life goes unnoticed by the world. I often wish someone other than me knew of him, would love him and would miss him. Would think of him. I know how powerful that wish can be, that wish that your unborn baby not be forgotten or overlooked.

Your unborn baby has changed everything for me. Thomas Stephan was never born. But he made a difference. And so have you.

I cry for my son, my Jack. I cry for your son, your Thomas. And I thank God you chose to share your story.

Barbara

* * *

How much choice you have depends on who you are. For teenage girls, the situation is particularly dire. Not rich, college girls, mind you. Mostly poor rural girls.

It's one of those girls. The poorer, the younger, the further from the big cities she lives, the more vulnerable she is, the worse off she is. The ideal person to force to be a mother!

In 1979, in *Bellotti v. Baird,* the United States Supreme Court held that it was unconstitutional to give parents an absolute veto over their daughters' abortions. The thinking, at least, was that whatever you think of parental rights (and a majority of the Court thought quite a bit of them), you could not expect a girl who was the victim of incest, or a girl who was being beaten by a parent, to tell that parent that she was pregnant and get permission for an abortion. The Court also said there needed to be an exception for "mature minors." So the Court wrote a road map: All you needed to do if you wanted to pass a constitutional parental consent law was create a "judicial bypass" procedure whereby a girl who was in danger of being abused, or was a "mature minor" could *simply* bring a lawsuit and convince a judge either to let her have an abortion, or at least let her decide on her own.

Every once in a while, you hear a story about a judge ordering a delay in one of these cases. But in all the years since 1979, I don't think I've ever heard of a single case where a teenager has gone to court and actually been denied a right to an abortion.

No, the problem isn't the girls who go to court, but all the ones who never get there.

Quick: How many of you reading this would know how to go to court by yourself with the clock ticking and get a court order?

No? You would if you went to a fancy college and went to the health clinic to get an abortion. Then they'd refer you to the appropriate women's counseling/referral/legal services group, which would hold your hand through the procedure—the legal procedure, I mean—and you'd be fine.

But say you're not a fancy girl who goes to a fancy school. Say you don't know how to find a women's legal services group. Say you think about going to a state, one of the twelve, someplace like New York or

Connecticut or Washington or Oregon, say, that doesn't have a parental consent law.

Say you do something really radical—excuse me, criminal—like asking a grandparent for help. Excuse me, not just help, but to give you a ride.

CRIME.

That's right. The Senate voted to make that ride a crime last summer. That's the politics of abortion in action.

If a grandmother gives her granddaughter a ride to a state without a parental consent law to get an abortion, she could commit a crime.

Does the Senate have nothing to do at all?

It was all part of another pre-midterm effort to play politics and secure the right wing base of the Republican Party.

Senator Dianne Feinstein actually introduced an amendment to the bill that would have exempted grandparents, clergy, aunts, and uncles from the criminal prohibitions against interstate transportation . . . and the amendment failed.

Now, you might ask: How can this be? If this is truly a moderate, decent, compassionate country, why would we punish a grandmother for driving her granddaughter to have an abortion?

The answer, of course, is that we wouldn't. Did you even know about this bill? Of course not. You weren't paying attention. It doesn't affect you. It won't. Nobody is actually going to enforce this law against anyone's grandmother.

They're just going to use this law to win votes and scare girls.

Who does that sound like?

Obviously I'm no expert, but it doesn't sound very Christian to me.

* * *

Will the Supreme Court overrule *Roe v. Wade*?

No.

It will not.

Why do I say that so firmly?

Four reasons.

First of all, my ability to count. Justice Kennedy joined the O'Connor opinion in *Casey v. Planned Parenthood,* the last time *Roe* was challenged. Casey was a 6–3 decision. If all of the new justices, all two of them, go with the dissenters, who included Rehnquist, that will bring them up to four: Roberts, Scalia, Thomas, and Alito. There will still be five votes for the "Kennedy" position in *Casey*—Stevens, Kennedy, Souter, Ginsburg, and Breyer.

Second, something comes over justices when they join the Court, and my guess is that it will come over Chief Justice Roberts, at least. Call it *precedentia.* The disease of being afflicted with respect for precedent. Not wanting to be known as the modern *Dred Scott* Court, the Court that upheld slavery. Not wanting to cause unrest and discord. Feeling the heavy weight of the robe; it makes you want to vote to uphold precedent. *Roe* looks like very old precedent.

Third, note that overruling *Roe* takes the Court completely out of the action on abortion cases. All of a sudden, one of the most important areas for the Court to decide cases simply disappears. What brand of human nature is it for the new guy in charge to want to do that? Give up all your power? When you just got it?

Fourth, as it turns out, it wouldn't even be good for Republicans. It's not all that hard to figure that out. Not that those kinds of considerations would ever have anything whatsoever to do with how decisions are made at the United States Supreme Court.

Never? Just ask President Gore.

What that means, in practice, is that we keep fighting about what restrictions can be placed on the right to abortion, while waiting, hoping, for a future in which non-surgical abortion, early genetic testing, and most important, improvements in prevention, hopefully make at least some of these questions irrelevant.

* * *

Prevention. This is what we should be fighting for.

It is a much better issue. No forks in babies' heads. No pictures of fully formed fetuses.

How do you make abortion safe, legal, and rare, as Bill Clinton used to say?

Prevent unwanted pregnancies.

How do you divide the crazies on the right from everybody else?

Talk about prevention.

Talk about Plan B, the morning-after pill, which until very recently Wal-Mart was refusing to stock in any of their pharmacies because they had made a "business decision" not to carry it.

What kind of "business decision?" The kind that said that they feared the anti-abortion people, the right tail of the right tail, more than the vast majority of Americans, including the majority of their own shoppers, who are women.

So even though they stocked birth control pills, not to mention Viagra, and even though Plan B is nothing more than a concentrated version of the same chemicals as those in birth control pills, Wal-Mart refused to stock Plan B.

Planned Parenthood announced a boycott. Not much happened. There were some negotiations. Things were quiet for a while.

And then just last spring, I noticed a small item in the paper. Wal-Mart to stock Plan B. A new "business decision." No more explanation than that.

Wal-Mart got the message.

Who could be against prevention?

You know who.

And don't forget about embryonic stem cell research. She's against that too.

* * *

The vote on embryonic stem cell research came in the Senate last summer, just in time to throw meat to Ann's friends on the religious right.

The issue could not have been framed more perfectly. The bill was drafted by a Republican member of the House, Michael Castle of Delaware. It didn't apply to any of the controversial issues regarding creation of new embryo lines or anything like that. It only dealt with frozen embryos in fertility clinics that were going to be destroyed. How could it possibly be better to destroy the embryos altogether than to use them for potentially life-saving researching?

All the bill said was that instead of throwing these embryos away, the federal government would support research on them.

Research over destruction.

What possible pro-life position could favor destruction over life-saving research?

Polls taken before the vote, admittedly by organizations that supported expanded federal support for stem cell research, found 72 percent of the public in favor of broader rules allowing federal dollars to support research on stem cell lines in these circumstances.

A majority of both Houses of Congress, requiring substantial defections from the president's own party, voted to support the legislation.

And what happened?

The president, surrounded by his choice of victims—in this case, children and their families born through donated eggs—vetoed the bill. Democrats, not to be outdone, paraded their own victims, those suffering from diseases and injuries, notably spinal cord injuries, that might be addressed through embryonic stem cell research.

Victims, victims, as far as the eye could see.

Meanwhile Ann had her own list, which she had actually "copied," of how all the same results could be achieved through research on adult stem cell lines, rather than the embryonic lines at issue here. No one else agreed. What other argument was there? Choose destruction. Choose your victim.

This time Ann did not object to the use of victims.

* * *

What's your take on the Supreme Court's ruling that anti-sodomy laws are unconstitutional? Ann was asked.

"Gay sex may well be a mystery of life, but I'll be damned if I can find it in the Constitution," she answered.

Someday, our children or grandchildren will look back on us and wonder why we had such a difficult time with gay rights. There will come a time when gay rights are fully accepted, the way that nondiscrimination against women and minorities is accepted today. But that day has surely not come yet.

The consensus in the country today is against gay marriage. Ann was right about that, in her interview with Matt Lauer. It is also the case, however, that a substantial majority of Americans don't think the issue is important enough to merit amending the Constitution.

On every other basic issue relating to discrimination against gays, though, including the issues of gay school teachers—where even a few years ago, most Americans favored discrimination—there is today a growing consensus in favor of gay rights.

The law is changing, and so is public opinion, and the right is very angry and threatened by that.

In 1986, the United States Supreme Court ruled in *Bowers v. Hardwick* that the right to privacy did not extend to the right of adults to engage in private, consensual homosexual activity, and that the state of Georgia could constitutionally continue to criminalize such activity. From the day the decision was handed down, gay activists and their straight supporters vowed to work to overturn it. It took seven years. Finally, in June 2003, in *Lawrence v. Texas,* the Supreme Court did so, striking down a Texas law that criminalized sodomy.

The Christian Right declared it to be the end of the world. As the Reverend Lou Sheldon, chairman of the Traditional Values Coalition, put it: "This is a major wake-up call. . . . This is a 9/11 . . . the enemy is at our doorsteps."

Or as my friend, conservative Moral Majority veteran Cal Thomas, put it: "Has the end of the world arrived because the Supreme Court ruled no state may prohibit private, consensual homosexual conduct? No, the end of the world is being handled by the Supreme Judge. But the end of the Constitution has arrived, and that is something about which everyone in this temporal world should be concerned."

In fact, everyone wasn't all that concerned. One poll found that a third of all voters thought the decision was a disaster, while the rest either supported it, didn't care, or didn't think it was important enough to care about.

Most Americans, according to the most recent polls—60 percent, down from 75 percent—do believe that sexual relations between two adults of the same sex is wrong. But that doesn't translate into a majority for criminalization. In fact, solid and growing majorities support equal employment opportunities for gays and lesbians, even if they disapprove of their sexual conduct. Indeed, a majority of Americans support nondiscrimination—even with respect to the sensitive profession of public education that is teaching.

Moreover, the differences among demographic groups on these measures are smaller than you might guess. According to the latest Gallup Poll data, there are very small differences between men and women, between whites and nonwhites, when it comes to support for gays and lesbians. Moreover, the regional differences are not as great as one might expect on legalization of gay relationships: The difference between the South and the West runs approximately 20 points. Indeed, even 40 percent of weekly churchgoers believe that homosexual relations should not be criminalized, thus supporting the Supreme Court decision.

What all of this suggests is that, so long as you stay away from gay marriage, it is difficult to lose an argument about gay rights. This country is far more tolerant than one would think, listening to the shouting.

If you fight about gay marriage right now, you're liable to lose.

So fight about whether it's important enough to be in the Constitution.

Fight about the basics, and you're likely to win.

Ask: Should people be punished for being gay? For engaging in homosexual relationships?

See what Ann says. My guess is, she'll crack a fag joke. I look for serious commentary and that's what I find.

When they start talking about special privileges, say: No one wants special privileges. Gays and lesbians want the same rights every citizen has to be treated fairly, based on individual ability, rather than being judged based on their identity as a member of the group of gay people.

Should gays be protected from discrimination based on sexual orientation?

Do they have the same right as everyone else to be judged on the basis of ability, and not discriminated against based on sexual orientation?

Should the law protect them from discrimination?

Ask Ann. And then ask everyone else. Everyone else, or almost everyone else, will say yes.

See if she ducks.

Ask her if gays have a right to teach school.

A right to equality and fairness in health care and housing.

A right to enter into civil unions to secure the advantages of a domestic relationship such as insurance, survivorship, and so forth.

Ann doesn't answer any of these fundamental questions in her book, or in any of the columns I've found, even though she does address gay rights, or as she calls it, "Queer Theory."

What she chooses to address, however, and maybe this is the answer to all of the above, is not any of the issues facing gays and lesbians today, but how absurd it was of heterosexuals, and particularly of the former surgeon general, C. Everett Koop, to spread the false fear of heterosexual AIDS in order to avoid "stigmatizing" gays.

What could be more ridiculous?

She's changing the subject and changing the question. And this is her constant tactic.

Now, all of this is, first of all, ancient history. The campaign against heterosexual AIDS to which Ann is referring dates back to the 1980s. It was thoroughly exposed by the writer Michael Fumento in his much-talked-about book, *The Myth of Heterosexual AIDS,* which Ann cites and relies on.

The question, then, is: Why go through it all again here? Maybe she was just looking for an example of liberals (or well-intentioned Reagan appointees, in the case of Koop) playing fast and loose with science—although Ann hardly gives him credit for his good intentions, suggesting he should have been "distributing condoms in gay bars and at Madonna concerts where they might have done some good" instead of in kindergarten classes. Of course, Ann offers no proof that he or anyone else ever did the latter (this is one of Ann's major bloopers), and it's not clear to me that Ann and her friends would actually support the former.

More important, she has nothing to say about the stigma of homosexuality, and particularly how it attached to AIDS in the mid-1980s; how to deal with it; who was responsible for it; much less what she thinks of it.

Indeed, her whole point seems to be to remind everyone that AIDS does discriminate, and that gay men have multiple sexual partners.

This is a theme she returned to later in her *Godless* summer, in her memorable attack on Bill Clinton's sexuality.

During her sixth or seventh appearance on the NBC network to promote *Godless,* this time on CNBC's *The Big Idea with Donny Deutsch,* she called Bill Clinton gay:

COULTER: I think that sort of rampant promiscuity does show some level of latent homosexuality.

DEUTSCH: Okay, I think you need to say that again. That Bill Clinton, you think on some level, has—is a latent homosexual, is that what you're saying?

He really can't believe she said it. So he begs her to say it again.

COULTER: Yeah. I mean, not sort of just completely anonymous—I don't know if you read the Starr report; the rest of us were glued to it. I have many passages memorized. No, there was more plot and dialogue in a porno movie.

DEUTSCH: I'm not paying any attention. I'm still stuck on Bill Clinton. Don't—now, isn't that an example of mean-spirited? Isn't that just a mean-spirited low blow? No pun intended.

COULTER: No. Which part of what I said?

DEUTSCH: I think this . . .

COULTER: Well, you can read *High Crimes and Misdemeanors* if he wants some low blows.

DEUTSCH: Okay. No, no. Here's a—here's a president of the United States . . .

COULTER: There's merely a comment.

DEUTSCH: . . . a former president of the United States, and just saying, "You know what? I think he has latent homosexual tendencies."

COULTER: No. I think anyone with that level of promiscuity where, you know, you—I mean, he didn't know Monica's name until their sixth sexual encounter. There is something that is—that is of the bathhouse about that.

DEUTSCH: But what is the homosexual—that's—you could say somebody who maybe doesn't celebrate women the way he should or just is that he's a hound dog?

COULTER: No. It's just random, is this obsession with his . . .

Deutsch: But where's the—but where's the homosexual part of that? I'm—once again, I'm speechless here.

Coulter: It's reminiscent of a bathhouse. It's just this obsession with your own—with your own essence.

Ann Coulter, sex expert . . .

Deutsch: But why is that homosexual? You could say narcissistic.

Coulter: Right.

Deutsch: You could say nymphomaniac.

Coulter: Well, there is something narcissistic about homosexuality. Right? Because you're in love with someone who looks like you. I'm not breaking new territory here. Why are you looking at me like that?

Yes, why, Donny? Why . . . ?

Is it possible she doesn't know that other people don't talk this way, and that there is a reason they don't—that we don't equate being gay with being a narcissistic philanderer.

Was this, as it was described by one writer, an effort to revive sales of *Godless* with some gay-bashing after the novelty of attacking widows had worn off?

I don't know what goes on in Ann's head in moments like these, and my view is that it really doesn't matter. It's the rest of us who need to be considered. I teach my kids that "It's so gay" is not an acceptable joke. My gay friends agree.

Here is the follow-up to the Donny Deutsch interview: Ann's conversation on CNBC's *Kudlow and Co.* with Peter Beinart, a monthly columnist for the *Washington Post,* editor-at-large of *New Republic* and author of *The Good Fight: Why Liberals—and Only Liberals—Can Win the War on Terror and Make America Great Again.*

Slate.com's Mickey Kaus, a major Coulter fan, thinks Ann got the best of the conversation: "Am I wrong to think Beinart . . . comes off . . . as a posturing fool, who somehow successfully bullies Kudlow?" I think he is wrong. But judge for yourself. And remember, Coulter claims to like all gays. With friends like her . . .

COULTER: . . . It's sort of standard, feminist doctrine 101, and psychological doctrine that wildly promiscuous heterosexual men, you know, still believe in a place called Fire Island. I don't think it's that hard to believe, except that it happens to be, you know, being said about feminist great hero Bill Clinton, so they pretend they've never heard this before. I—I'm—I don't know why this should be a particularly startling statement. . . . [snip] . . .

I have taught gender discrimination for twenty-five years. This has never been "standard feminist doctrine 101."

KUDLOW: Peter Beinart, what is your response to Ann's remarks on Clinton?

BEINART: It's a statement of a bigot. Pure and simple. To suggest that gay people are somehow inherently more promiscuous than straight people and that straight people who are promiscuous are—therefore have latent homosexuality tendencies, and, look, Larry, I'll—let me throw it to you. It's not enough for people like me, for liberals, to say that when Ann says that, she's being a bigot. You need to say it. As a conservative who agrees with her on issues, it's up to you, because you don't believe in a conservative movement that is bigoted. You don't believe that's what the Republican Party stands for. It's up to you to say that it's bigoted and to distance yourself from it.

I think what Peter Beinart is doing is terrific. Mickey Kaus thinks the opposite.

KUDLOW: Well, I would . . .

COULTER: Do you have some problem with gays?

BEINART: No, in fact—in fact, I think you are—you are the one who's making . . .

COULTER: I like gays. I like all gays, and not just the ones who are Ann Coulter drag queens.

She likes all gays. And that of course is why she begins her book Godless *with the most famously anti-gay passage from the Bible. That's why she tells fag jokes. It's funny. I wonder if tortured gay teenagers, of whom there are tragically many, find it funny.*

BEINART: You . . .

COULTER: I like gay just fine. What's your problem?

BEINART: Well, it's a strange way to show . . .

COULTER: Why is that so insulting?

BEINART: To make—to make classically bigoted statements about them is a strange way to show your affection, Ann.

COULTER: Classically bigoted statements? You're denying that gays are . . .

BEINART: In fact, the idea that somehow gay men are inherently more promiscuous than straight men is an old chestnut of anti-gay bigotry. You surely know that. You said it anyway. I— Larry, I think it's really up to you to tell Ann that you find this bigotry unacceptable in the conservative movement.

COULTER: I love these—I love these constant demands that every other conservative on the planet denounce Ann Coulter. I refuse to allow . . .

KUDLOW: I'm a friend of Ann Coulter . . .

BEINART: Well, I don't—I don't—you know, I criticized—I criticized Michael Moore when I disagree with him.

COULTER: Wait. Where are all those heterosexual bathhouses? I must have missed that period of the '70s.

She won't give up. She still won't admit that she was wrong.

KUDLOW: I am a friend of Ann Coulter's. That's no secret. I have read her books. I basically admire her values. But, Ann, I guess when you go down that road, I don't know. You kind of lose me on that. You just kind of lose me. I just don't see it.

COULTER: Well, I don't—what am I losing you on?

BEINART: Good for you.

KUDLOW: I think it—I think it detracts from your overall . . .

COULTER: What am I losing you on? Forget, you know, the general I disagree, blah, blah, blah, blah, blah. What are you disagreeing with me on?

BEINART: It's called bigotry, Ann. What part of bigotry don't you understand?

COULTER: Are you claiming that gays are generally not more promiscuous? Is that what you're claiming? Are both of you maintaining that gays are not—some segment of gays are not more promiscuous than heterosexuals? Is that the big point here?

KUDLOW: I . . .

BEINART: I'm saying that I don't know that there's any empirical evidence whatsoever here.

COULTER: No. I'm asking Larry here.

BEINART: And it's a—it's a—it's a bigoted stereotype that you are fomenting.

COULTER: You don't know any evidence that gays are more promiscuous than heterosexuals?

BEINART: Where's your—where's your evidence, Ann?

COULTER: Where have you been?

BEINART: Where's your evidence?

COULTER: It's a fact.

This is Ann's idea of a fact. Something she believes to be true. Unsupported by those things people like me taught her about in law school like citations.

BEINART: Give me the evidence. Cite chapter and verse. You have no evidence whatsoever.

COULTER: I just cited the bathhouses. We don't have heterosexual bathhouses. It's well known.

BEINART: What—it's like saying—it's like saying Jews—Ann, it's like saying Jews love money more. Everyone knows that's true. Where is your evidence?

COULTER: It is well known that gays . . .

BEINART: It is well known.

COULTER: I—every time I try to give the evidence, you get after me.

BEINART: That's your evidence? It's well known? Okay. Give me the evidence.

COULTER: Okay. You got to stop talking now. . . .

In another follow-up, this one with Chris Matthews on *Hardball,* she reaffirmed her description of Clinton, and went on to make a "joke" of calling Al Gore a "fag."

When a young woman in the audience objected to the joke, she pulverized the young woman. It was a joke, she said, not answering the woman's question at all, "Thus the audience laughed except Little Miss Smarty Pants here."

"Little Miss Smarty Pants?" Pure Coulter.

Remember how she dismissed Mary Anne Marsh for having the gall to actually ask her about the religious aspect of the book? She ridiculed her too.

For having the decency to object to a fag joke, you get called a name.

What do you call a mean bigot who thinks she is funny? Ann.

And why keep giving her a forum? Hello, NBC?

No one is quite sure how many gays and lesbians vote Republican. No one is quite sure how many gays and lesbian voters there are, period, much less how many are in the GOP, but the Log Cabin Republicans, an organization of gay Republicans, has tried mightily, albeit with limited success, to convince the party to steer a more moderate course on gay rights issues.

Nonetheless, you know it's an election year when the party throws red meat on the burner. Red meat being an issue like the "Defense of Marriage Act," one of those totally useless pieces of legislation meant to defend at the federal level an institution that isn't even defined federally from attacks that aren't coming and require no defense.

But I don't know how the Log Cabin Republicans could read Ann's book, or watch their party in action, without feeling precisely the "stigma" that Ann ridicules Koop for caring about.

And for the life of me, I don't see why you stay in a party that treats you that way.

8.

SEX

If you don't hate Clinton and the people who labored to keep him in office, you don't love your country.

We're now at the point that it's beyond whether or not this guy is a horny hick. I really think it's a question of his mental stability. He really could be a lunatic. I think it is a rational question for Americans to ask whether their president is insane.

Clinton is in love with the erect penis.

He was a very good rapist.

—Ann Coulter

* * *

Bill Clinton was Ann's number one issue. She would not, and will not, let it drop.

It was how she made her name. The President the Rapist. The President the Sex Harasser.

The accusations the right brought against the president, the behavior that gave rise to it, our felt need to marshal a defense against the grave punishment being threatened—all of that *did* do harm to feminism. I think we should admit that. They did it to us; he did it to us; we did it to ourselves.

And now, it sometimes seems like she couldn't care less. She laughs.

She writes: "I have always been unabashedly anti-murder, anti-rape and anti-false accusation—and I don't care who knows about it!" Ha ha.

She's against rape and against false accusations of rape. Hooray for her. Who isn't? And she doesn't care who knows about it, because she's taking such courageous positions. I bet she also likes apple pie and would be willing to advertise that.

For her, this is one big joke. For feminists, it is anything but.

For us, reforming the laws governing sexual abuse was one of the great, unadulterated triumphs of the 1980s and 1990s. The fact that our triumph has been compromised, the fact that its fate is now in doubt, and that we are in some sense complicit in that, is not something to be dismissed lightly, or with humor, but a serious question, an unintended consequence, a painful product of a terrible period for which the Anns bear their share of responsibility.

Ultimately, I believe she knows that, which is why she and her cohorts will simply not let the old Clinton issues rest when it comes to the candidacy of the next Clinton, Hillary Rodham Clinton.

When I first began writing about rape law, there were two crimes—one that I termed "real rape," and the other, not-real or "simple rape." In real rape, a stranger with a gun or knife, or someone "inappropriate" like a black person, forces you to have sex and of course you don't resist—and that's a real rape. In a not-real rape, someone you know or someone appropriate—a date, or in those days, a boss even—acts in such a way that if the sound were off we might be in doubt as to whether it were rape or sex.

By definition, in a not-real rape, it doesn't matter what you say. *No* meant *yes,* or it meant nothing. That was the battle I fought. That and the one that defined consent solely as the presence or absence of force.

Those were big fights. And *are,* you want me to write. Yes, and *are.* But there was a moment when I would have left that out, a moment when I look back, even in my own writing, and find that I think it's won.

Every state reformed its laws. Every state enacted shield laws. Women were at the table to write the new laws. We got everything we asked for. New rape units were set up in police and prosecutors' offices. Crisis centers were expanded. The whole rhetoric changed. No one argued that *no* meant *yes* anymore.

On the civil side, sex at work was recognized to be coercive in certain circumstances: The question was power; the wrong was the abuse of power. In determining that, we convinced courts and legislatures, a man's past record of bad acts is relevant; a woman's sexual past is generally not. For a moment, we won. Or at least we won a lot. And we have.

A combination of factors ended the moment, made us wonder in retrospect if it ever existed after all. Circumstances conspired against us powerfully. A new generation of anti-feminist Anns came of age, and their ammunition could not have been better, or their target juicier— they had a blue dress with DNA and the president of the United States, a special prosecutor and a crazed Congress, a newborn cable industry and the punditry to go with it. And it hardly helped that we feminists were making pretzels of ourselves, to put it nicely, as they used everything we'd managed to accomplish and turned and wielded it like a weapon against our friend the president.

In this effort, of course, they had powerful allies, and the primary impact on Ann Coulter and company was to serve as a career stepping-stone. The subject matter of the attack hardly seemed to matter for them. It was incidental. It happened to be that rape and sexual harassment were convenient tools for women like them to wield against the president, so they became champions of the victimized and the harassed, allegedly so. And it happened that in this particular instance, opposing the president put them on the side of supporting the woman, which is not necessarily the expected conservative stance. But it didn't matter because, while it happened that Paula Jones was complaining that the president had harassed her—she claimed he exposed himself to her, which is such a far-fetched account of Bill Clinton's behavior that I've never credited it. The worst thing can be an innocent client, which may be why he refused to settle the case, to his detriment. Nevertheless, the Paula Jones case could have been a lawsuit over widgets and, if it had the potential to help bring down Bill Clinton, Ann Coulter was signing up and signing on.

The reason she expected different reactions from us feminists, the reason anyone might, was that for us it *did* matter.

There will be a price to be paid, I used to think, and of course there is. Every time we attack the trashing of a victim we are reminded of how Clinton lawyer Bob Bennett trashed Paula Jones. Every time we utter the word *power,* we are reminded of the most powerful man in the world.

Now that we've returned to our usual sides, I cannot write a line about a victim of sex abuse, express a thought about a rape or sexual harassment case, without being reminded by someone that I took a somewhat different position when it was Bill Clinton who stood accused. Ann loves to chastise me about that.

There is a credibility problem, and it is ours. Since the Clinton years, there is a perception of a conflict in our positions on sex abuse such that people laugh when we get tough. What about Bill? they ask.

This is what I tell my students: Imagine it was your brother or your husband who stood falsely accused, who'd been charged with rape by someone who really was a nut, a crazy girl. Imagine it was your kid, I tell my friends. Then tell me what the rules should be. How are you going to make sure your best friend is going to be able to get off, when he's falsely accused by a girl who appears on the surface to be perfectly normal?

The answer is that hard cases make bad law.

That is what happened to liberal feminism. We were forced to apply the rules we made to the man we helped to elect and vitally depended on (and, in my case, had counted on as a friend), and it was no mean trick. We twisted them the same way everybody else did.

The difference is we had made the rules, and now we have to re-make them.

* * *

I am standing in Boston in front of a group of academics and practi-tioners in the fields of sex abuse and victims' advocacy. There must be sixty, seventy people in the room, most of them law professors who are also activists, run clinical programs, a few of them my fellow board members of the Victims Rights Law Project, which has brought me to town to keynote this conference.

It is the middle of the Kobe Bryant mess. For those who have for-gotten, that was the time when charges were pending against the Lak-ers star arising out of what he claimed was a consensual encounter with a local college student at a Colorado inn where he was staying prior to knee surgery. I put the case to the roomful of experts: If it were your daughter, and she came home and told you she'd been raped by Kobe Bryant, and you believed she was telling the truth, how many of you would call the police and then follow through with a criminal complaint?

Not a single hand went up.

This from the people who were in the business of making it possi-ble to complain.

We who changed the law understood precisely why we wouldn't want to use it in these circumstances, to wit: We would not want to see our daughter get destroyed. And destroyed she would be. Nuts-and-sluts time. Her sexual past. Her mental health. The whole nine yards. Hello, Paula Jones. What's good for the goose is good for the gander.

And we would all be on opposite sides.

But you might be asking: How can that be? Isn't that precisely what we changed? Isn't that what we promised those other parents, around some other dining room table, wouldn't happen to their daughter if she complained?

Lamar S. Owens, the 5′9″ quarterback of the 2005 Navy team who, in a storybook tale of success, went from backup to beating Army, was charged with raping a fellow midshipman. He was also charged with conduct unbecoming an officer, and with violating a military restraining order to stay away from the woman.

The *Los Angeles Times* described the case this way: "The defense attacked the credibility of the alleged victim, saying she was prone to binge drinking and that she was so drunk that night she did not know if she had invited Owens to her room, much less what happened later. In contrast, Owens was portrayed by friends as an upstanding young man who would not have behaved as the woman said."

A court martial jury of five Naval Academy officers returned a verdict of not guilty on the rape charge, which carried a penalty of up to life in prison, and guilty on each of the two lesser offenses, which carry punishments of two years apiece. Owens's attorney immediately moved for dismissal of the conduct conviction and predicted it would be thrown out.

Now, say you're representing Owens, as Reid Weingarten, one of the finest lawyers I know, was. Your client is a twenty-two-year-old kid, headed for a career working in surface warfare in the navy after graduation, whose ex-girlfriend gets drunk and invites him to her room, and he's dumb enough to go, and now she's saying he raped her, and the navy isn't going to decline to prosecute, any more than a lot of local district attorneys would, especially because there's a restraining order keeping these two apart.

How do you deprive a defendant such as Lamar Owens of the right to show that his ex-girlfriend was a binge drinker whose behavior that night was fully consistent with her behavior in the past? His entire future is on the line. In any other circumstance, you are entitled to show that the way a person is acting, the car they're driving, the force they're using, is similar to what they've done in the past. How can you, in the interest of fairness, not to mention the constitution, deprive a defendant standing trial for rape of the right to introduce that same kind of proof to raise the reasonable doubt necessary to save his life?

It's also in these close, high-profile cases where the press has begun to change the rules of the game adopted a decade ago to protect victims. There has definitely been a shift in the winds, as closer cases are being prosecuted on lesser evidence. Where a decade ago it was accepted that a rape victim's name should remain confidential—a hard-won victory that we justified on the grounds both that complaining of rape still carried a stigma, and rape was among the most underreported of crimes—today that consensus is unraveling, as more and more news organizations are questioning what they see as the "imbalance" in protection between the accuser and the accused. This shift is coming at the same time as the number of "news organizations" is expanding exponentially with the Internet making it difficult even to define what counts as a news organization. And the reality is, all you have to do is type in "Kobe Bryant's victim," or "Duke rape case victim," and you have yourself a name.

The balance argument that comes up in this context is particularly troubling because it has broader applications beyond the naming issue. The idea that the accuser and the accused should stand in the same position, whether for purposes of disclosing their name, or admissibility of other evidence, confuses the fact that one has been found, on the basis of probable case, to be allegedly a criminal while the other is allegedly a victim. It also potentially equates the sexual pasts of the two, when that makes as little sense. The fact that the woman has engaged in consensual sex in the past doesn't really prove much about whether she's engaging in consensual sex on the night in question; after all, consensual sex in this day and age is for many people a relatively common event, so proving that you've engaged in it in the past means nothing. Now if you could prove a woman had complained of rape in the past that would be the equivalent of proving that the man had engaged in forced sex in the past, and both should be admissible.

* * *

Every year or two, there is a big case that will define how everyone thinks about rape or sex harassment—at least until the next big case comes along. I remember the days when the plane would pick Kobe up at the hearing in Colorado and race him back to the playoffs at Staples Center. The crowd would cheer as the "alleged rapist" would take to the court. What are they cheering for, I used to ask myself. You used to cheer for Bill, someone would always remind me. Such is the game. Many people noted that Kobe was always at his sharpest on court dates. Now, Kobe drives to work like everyone else, and the Lakers are no longer in the playoffs.

This year's big case is the Duke lacrosse case—what began as a party with an exotic dancer at the house rented by the three captains of the Duke lacrosse team, and ended up in a racially divided community demanding action of its embattled district attorney who, facing a challenge in his first bid for popular election and a strong minority challenger, sought the indictment of three white lacrosse players for the rape of a black college student and single mother. He did so in advance of appropriate procedures being followed in his own office and notwithstanding obvious problems with the photographic identifications.

None of which, of course, means that the woman is lying about what she claims happened in a bathroom in the house. But can the prosecutors prove it?

Conservatives are having a field day with this one. After a slow start, they have been pounding on the prosecutor.

I am on the radio with Sean Hannity and Ann. They are killing me. Just destroying me. We are discussing the details of the case. I am arguing that we should wait for the public trial. Ann is arguing for the prosecutor's head.

I remember the days when Ann was on the woman's side. I wonder if she does. I don't have time to remind her. It takes all my energy to play two against one.

And here is the worst part: We do not yet know the half of it.

Ann is claiming that the only reason the prosecutor brought charges in this case is that his political future was on the line, that he was pandering to blacks (ah, race matters). She is calling him names I can't repeat.

I am in the impossible, feminist position. Because I am a woman, a victim, a rape expert, I am expected to support the prosecutor's decision to indict. But did he have enough evidence to indict? Did he follow his own procedures in deciding whether to indict?

In the coming months we will learn, from the discovery materials the district attorney is required to turn over, that the prosecutor went to the grand jury for an indictment before he even performed DNA tests (it turns out there was no match). One of the investigators was still collecting prices for DNA tests while the DA was giving interviews. He announced to the press that he was certain that a rape had taken place before excluding the possibility that the woman's physical symptoms were the result of sex with another man (turns out she'd had sex with her boyfriend within the preceding twenty-four hours). They were still investigating the woman's whereabouts in the twenty-four hours leading up to the party when they had already been to the grand jury. The prosecutor relied on a photographic identification procedure that reportedly violated the standards of his own department. If the discovery is any indication, his case is sitting on quicksand.

None of this means the woman made up the whole story. But at the very least, standard procedure should have been to await the results of tests, and then, given the results, the inconsistencies in the woman's statements, the fact that at least one of the boys seems to have an airtight alibi, investigate further before indicting anyone.

Instead, the train had already left the station.

How could a grand jury indict on so little?

Because a grand jury will indict a ham sandwich. That's why prose-cutors have the power to ruin people's lives. That's why I tell my students, if you want to play God, go be a prosecutor. That's why, have you noticed, so many of the other Anns seem to be "former prosecutors."

If this had been a normal case in a normal time, you would slow it down. Wait for the DNA test to come back. Wait to see what the story is with her physical evidence.

And this is what you would have found out: No DNA on her. None of hers at the house. No match. Nada.

All you got is kids who live in the house. Active young men, if you know what I mean.

The only match is her boyfriend. She had sex with him the day before.

There are problems with all her IDs.

One of the kids has a watertight alibi.

Her statements have inconsistencies that can be explained away, but make her a very vulnerable witness.

In other words, you have an unbelievably weak case.

Again, that doesn't mean she's a liar. But it means it's not winnable. And prosecutors aren't supposed to prosecute unwinnable cases.

And you would've explained to the kids in the office: This is why we wait. Look at those lives we didn't ruin.

That's what you would've done.

Twenty-six years ago, I wrote guidelines for one of my prosecutor friends on how to handle such situations. To help avoid just such a situation.

Of course a district attorney still has to keep his job, and rape is that kind of crime. The community was screaming.

Fair enough. There are all kinds of things a district attorney can do to keep his job. Bring black leaders in to explain the evidence. Give interviews, even. Treat a grand jury like it's something real and have it reach the decision not to indict after actually investigating.

But there is one thing you actually can't do to keep your job, and that's to indict on inadequate evidence, which may be what happened here. It's certainly what it looks like.

I don't think it happened because the DA consciously said, *I need to get elected, I think I'll indict these kids.* It doesn't work that way.

What happens is that the community demands action. You try to respond. Instead of treating it like every other case, you start asking one question, the question you actually heard the district attorney answer in the early days of the investigation: *Do I believe her?* And when he said he believed that a rape occurred, you knew he was doing that . . . answering the wrong question, actually.

And the problem is, he really wanted to believe her. It made his life much easier if she was telling the truth. He had started a massive ship going, not just an investigation, but a media circus.

In the law, one of the hardest things to prove is bad-faith prosecution. Short of that, it doesn't matter anymore why the DA was so determined to indict. His critics will say it was just because he was thinking about his political career. His supporters will say he really believed her, and that a district attorney has every right to be responsive to the community that elects him. My guess is he really did believe her, but it certainly didn't hurt that he needed to. But one thing is clear: He's not going to change his mind now.

That means this case is going to trial, unless a judge steps in to stop it, which is something that rarely happens.

And of this you can be sure: No good will come of it. Trials do not tend to be healing experiences. Sides dig in. Things get more contentious, not less. Tempers are bound to flare. Reliving the evening in living color is not likely to be pretty. Hearing the racial epithets again, rereading the e-mails, all of that will not improve race relations, even if it has nothing to do with whether a rape happened or not.

Even before that, there will be the question of who serves on the jury, and what counts as a jury of their peers. Shall we start counting how many minorities there are, how many "Duke" people, how many of "us," and how many of "them"? Shall we watch how the two sides use those peremptory challenges, the challenges they can use for no reason at all.

You know what our friend Ann will say about that.

What would a fair jury look like?

If the woman takes the stand, she'll be slaughtered on cross.

If she doesn't, the prosecution doesn't have a chance.

No one will be convinced that the case was handled fairly.

If even one of the boys is convicted, there will be outrage in the Duke community.

If they're all acquitted, there will be outrage in the black community that three white boys got away with rape.

If the jury comes back and says they're convinced that a rape took place but they don't know who did it—the compromise approach—the black community will be even more outraged that the sister got used by the incompetent DA who rushed the case for his own purposes.

Conservatives will think they're crazy.

Conservatives will be outraged that three boys' lives were ruined because an ambitious prosecutor believed a lying "slut" (as in the nuts-and-sluts defense), which will be played to a fare-thee-well.

Victims' rights advocates like me will be depressed because we will worry, rightly, about all the messages being sent to legitimate victims.

Ann will write something cutting and mean.

* * *

Writing earlier about the Duke rape case and the disappearance and presumed death of Natalee Holloway, the young woman who disappeared while on her class trip to Aruba, Ann said (with her customary gentle touch):

However the Duke lacrosse rape case turns out, one lesson that absolutely will not be learned is this: You can severely reduce your chances of having a false accusation of rape leveled against you if you don't hire strange women to come to your house and take their clothes off for money. Also, you can severely reduce your chances of being raped if you do not go to strange men's houses and take your clothes off for money. (Does anyone else detect a common thread here?) And if you are a girl in Aruba or New York City, among the best ways to avoid being the victim of a horrible crime is to not get drunk in public or go off in a car with men you just met. Everyone makes mistakes, especially young people, but the outpouring of support for the victims and their families is obscuring what ought to be a flashing neon warning for potential future victims. Whenever a gun is used in a crime, there are never-ending news stories about how dangerous guns are. But these girls go out alone, late at night, drunk off their butts, and there's nary a peep about the dangers of drunk women on their own in public. It's their "right."

I don't know anyone who actually walks around talking about a "right" to drink your butt off alone late at night. Everyone I know is busy giving their kids lectures about what a bad idea it is to do that, and trying to figure out how to deal with the fact that the criminal law has yet to solve this set of problems.

It's fine to say girls should be more responsible too, but what does that mean? Or rather, what do you do when they aren't?

There was an important Pennsylvania case a few years ago in which the court held that force was still a requirement in rape. Sounds simple enough, until you consider the circumstances and what they reveal. The case took place in a college dorm. As the Pennsylvania Supreme Court describes the circumstances, the boy didn't use force and the girl didn't consent; she didn't leave the room, even though she could have; then again, she also didn't want to be having sex with him, she does say no, he ignores her, but he doesn't force her.

I've taught the case for a few years now, and from my middle-aged vantage point, I always ask the same questions: If she didn't want to have sex, why didn't she leave? How can there be non-consent if there wasn't force? The answers I get tend to focus on the passivity, the "going along," the silent intimidation (of an unarmed, half-asleep college boy, in this instance)—all the opposite, I should add, of what it must have taken the woman in this case to see the case through to its successful prosecution and then appeal. If she had the guts to go to the authorities and complain of rape, why not just leave? And how do we teach girls to leave without returning to the days where passive victims were routinely blamed, and those who didn't were considered fair game?

So when Kobe was charged, those of us who knew the most had every reason to be the most skeptical. It wasn't that we had any reason to disbelieve the victim; quite the contrary, our bias is to believe victims. It is also to protect them, and that's why every instinct I have in a close case is to protect the victim and use the civil system.

Which is not to say we would let Kobe get away with it. Not a chance. There would be a price to pay. The girl would need help, therapy, and he should pay for it.

The civil system is geared, far better than the criminal system, to serving the actual needs of the victim, as opposed to the needs of society. Professor Ellen Bublick of Arizona, a former student of mine, has done pioneering work in this area, exploring advantages that the civil system offers to rape victims. Obviously, it allows for a lower standard of proof, for starters, which means that all doubt does not have to be resolved in the defendant's favor.

But it is more than a question of determining just how convinced you are, itself an uncertain process. Do you love the red jacket, I sometimes ask my students, or do you just like it. . . . Does it matter how much it cost? Assume it's really expensive. That means you have to be really persuaded. If you're paying full retail, you have to love it a lot.

The civil law, the tort law, is all about the apportionment of loss, and the factors that go into this decision include responsibility as well as how you can best deter the loss in question. What's wrong with those involved knowing that if they sleep with someone without being very certain that she's agreeing to it, they're vulnerable to a civil suit; even if she bears some of the responsibility, if they bear more, they will pay; the party who bears the greater responsibility pays for the loss involved. If in doubt, don't. If you do, you pay. If that makes you stop, all the better.

When you take away the threat of prison and replace it with the question of apportioning loss, do you have much trouble finding Kobe responsible? What's wrong with requiring the deep pocket to pay for the injury he has inflicted? And to be more careful next time: Get her to sign the condom. Get her to sign a card. Get him to stop and think. Are these bad things?

But that's where Ann becomes problematic. She's right out there blaming the (probably) dead Natalee Holloway for claiming a "right" to party all night (which we don't know if she did). . . . Oh, but not really, just kidding.

The civil law depends on finding one party more responsible than the other. It depends, ultimately, on not equally blaming the victim. So, no, Natalee Holloway should not go drinking at night, if that's what she was doing. But she is not equally responsible for her rape or her death, if that's what happened.

There is a trap here that we can avoid. We teach our daughters to be careful. We teach them signs and signals that we never knew. My daughter does "no" circles that make me cry; the girls stand in a circle and get power from saying no together. But wait. Will our strength be used against the woman who does not play by our rules? Is it now against the rules to have a drink, go out at night, say yes? Does one yes mean three? That cannot be.

We need to define the rules, not let Ann do it in her half-serious, half-joking way.

The civil law is far more flexible to meet the needs of the individual case. My friend Susan Vickers, the founder of the Victims Rights Law Center, tells wonderful stories of how our organization (I'm on the board—you're about to meet my passions) has been able to come in and use the tool of the civil law to fashion an injunction to get a kid back in school, in the right classes, not with the boy who abused her; to fashion relief, in other words, which serves the victim and not the people.

A criminal case is *The people vs. so-and-so;* it's not the victim's right to vengeance, but the state depriving a defendant of his liberty; it's not a battle between two parties, but a contest between the government and the individual. That's why the state has to be put to its proof, why the individual is accorded certain rights. In a civil system, you're free to fashion relief that serves the needs of the injured party.

The purpose of a tort suit is to compensate a plaintiff for loss occasioned by wrongful (or sometimes just accidental) conduct. If you think of the Kobe Bryant case as a wrongful sex case, is there any doubt that had the woman had her lawyer call his lawyer the next morning, that lawyer would have been in a rather commanding position, and with every reason in the world to be so, to demand a healthy sum not to sue. . . .

Think about the simple tort of *wrongful sex.*

Like wrongful death.

Sex should be consensual.

It should not be coerced.

It should not be the product of force, or threats of force.

It should not be the product of threats or coercion.

Otherwise you should be liable in an action for wrongful sex.

Don't go looking it up.

I just made it up.

I wonder if Ann would go along with it. Ask her.

But then, the way she thinks about and uses sex, it's just a weapon in a fight against the Clintons. The challenge with the Anns is to remind them of the positions *they've* taken in the past, and force them to embrace them as meaning something more than tactical positions. To see them as a basis for common ground with *us* even, instead of just the foundation for a new generation of anti-Clinton assaults.

Not that I've given up on the criminal law in rape cases. Even if it should be used sparingly, for winning cases.

The criminal law was not a deterrent to what went on college campuses in the past because there was simply no chance that anything you did to a girl, short of beating her near to death, could get you prosecuted for rape. Ask anyone. *That* is not true anymore.

And even if successful prosecution remains unlikely, it doesn't take a quantifiably large risk to deter a would-be rapist, when the downside is your life being ruined. You remember those old equations, probability times loss. The probability can be quite small when the loss is high enough. Even being arrested is enough to ruin your life pretty effectively, sad to say. That's how deterrence works and in that sense, you could say it's succeeding.

All of which makes *rape* one of the most powerful words in the English language. To most young men, it's a four-letter word for hell.

Don't say no, I tell young women when I speak at colleges; say "rape." We have given enormous power to the word, and it should be used. If "no" is still ambiguous, "rape" is not. It has a better chance of penetrating the drunken haze. It reflects the exercise of a woman's power. Use it.

The point is: Use the deterrent power, not the deterrent. Use the threat of the criminal law, not the criminal law. Use the power you have as a woman to protect yourself.

But of course, none of these real issues are a concern to Ann. When she writes about rape, she prefers to be glib and distract.

She writes: "In addition to the consensus position that liberals are Godless, no one has made a peep about that swipe I took at Hillary, proposing that she have a chat with her husband before accusing others

of being 'mean' to women in light of Juanita Broaddrick's charge that
Bill Clinton raped her. Hillary beat a hasty retreat on her chubby little
legs and is now hiding behind Rahm 'Don't Touch My Tutu' Emanuel."

The book tour I went on to promote my book on Hillary Clinton
was like none I have ever been on. Wherever I went, I was followed by
people demanding that I meet with Juanita Broaddrick to hear out her
charge against the former president. Of course the statute of limitations
had long since expired.

I started noticing questions popping up. Did I support eliminating
the statute of limitations for rape? Could I see a trap coming? I told
President Clinton that I had been followed and harassed by irrelevant
questions. Even he was surprised. Still. He told me the whole story
about Juanita Broaddrick. It does not bear repeating.

I am sure they will try to harry Hillary the same way they did me.
There was Ann trying, when she took her "swipe" at Hillary.

But guess what? I don't think anyone is going to listen to her.

9.

PUBLIC SCHOOLS: THE NEXT BATTLEGROUND

For all the frenzy that's surrounded *Godless,* no one has ever pushed Ann at all on the real agenda of her book. And that's because, if anyone actually read past the first half of it, they didn't show it, and it isn't until the last five chapters that Ann shows her hand.

That the book has an agenda is beyond question: The entire second half of the book is nothing less than a scathing full-frontal attack on the public schools.

The attack has two parts. The first is extremely familiar: It is an attack on teachers unions. The second, far longer, is an attack on Darwin and the teaching of evolution.

I will happily leave the science to others to address, since neither Ann nor I are scientists. But schools, values, and education politics are another matter.

This is where Ann really locks down her agenda. She is trying to generate outrage and action. Most Americans do not believe in teaching pure evolution. So what does Ann do? Rub their noses in it.

Through her combination of attacking bad teachers and teaching bad science, Ann's goal must be to rile readers and parents to the point that they will want to take over their local school boards and take control of what is taught. Why else devote almost half the book to this?

There is, ultimately, only one answer to Ann and that is counteraction. She is right about taking control of local school boards and local schools. It *is* the right idea. What could be more important? Teaching the next generation is the right answer. But not her way. It isn't as revenge on the teachers, as an assault on science, as an act of political hari-kari. Or at least it should not be.

Everybody likes to complain about the public schools. Why not? It's easy to do, especially for those who don't have children in them, or children at all. You rail against the terrible test scores, point out how we suffer on the international comparisons, and then, at least if you're a Republican, you point a long finger at the teachers unions, and stop right there.

It works as a political attack because Democrats, particularly Democrats running for president, depend on teachers for support, particularly in caucus states, for the same reason that Republicans rely on church leaders.

Jimmy Carter discovered in Iowa in 1976 what Pat Robertson learned in 1988: It's all about who has access to buses.

For Democrats, they are school buses. For Republicans, church buses. Teachers and church groups. That's what does it in a caucus state, where getting people to turn out on a (cold) winter night is the key to victory.

There is no group that turns out for Democratic events like teachers. So there is no group more assiduously courted by candidates in the Democratic Party especially at the time of primaries and caucuses.

And this dependence has utterly paralyzed the Democratic Party on the issue of education. Instead of talking about the needs of kids, we spend most of our time talking about the needs of unions—about how to get teachers higher salaries and not about how to get kids higher test scores—and it never gets beyond that.

Ann's chapter on the union is entitled "The Liberal Priesthood: Spare the Rod, Spoil the Teacher." Her basic argument is that it's all the teachers—and the teachers unions'—fault.

What differentiates it from other attacks on teachers unions is that it's more vicious: "Most public schools are—at best—nothing but expensive babysitting arrangements, helpfully keeping hoodlums off the streets during daylight hours. At worst, they are criminal training labs, where teachers sexually abuse the children between drinking binges and acts of grand larceny."

This is another one of those sentences that could have sparked a media moment equal to what happened when she called the Jersey Girls whores. Notice that it has a great deal to do with Godlessness. . . .

It's worth pointing out that Ann provides no footnotes supporting these allegations. Ann has absolutely no proof the kind of criminal misconduct she alleges is the norm in our schools is anything other than extremely rare occurrences of criminality that tend to be punished severely.

The allegations are a vicious assault on thousands of teachers who do their best every day, making a fraction of what she does, in the hopes of making an actual difference in someone's life.

And it should go without saying that teachers unions have a job to do, which is to protect their members. There is a reason they're there: Teachers across this country can point to a very long history of arbitrary treatment at the hands of administrators and school boards, and their unions are what protect them. Many teachers fought the move to unionization because they considered it beneath their professional stature. They only acceded to join the "association," as they preferred to call the union, because the arbitrariness on the other side convinced them. They joined unions so they'd get paid as much as janitors and have protection against unfair administrators, which they needed. They joined unions because—for all the talk about the important work they do—their pay stank, and in many cases still does.

So it's not the unions that are the problem, but how the Democratic Party and some elected officials deal with the unions. You know what I mean. The people who are afraid of the teachers union. The ones who worry about what the teachers think before they allow themselves go to the bathroom. Profiles in gutlessness. And it's not the way to solve the problems we face in education.

But what's far more troubling is what Ann does, which is to bash the union and then offer nothing but bile as an alternative.

Ann attacks what she calls the "class size" shibboleth, claiming, again without any support from studies, that "reducing class size doesn't improve educational achievement; it reduces the workload for each teacher."

And her ultimate conclusion, other than what's to come in her chapters about the teaching of evolution, is that "there's nothing the matter with teachers that a little less unionization and more competition couldn't cure."

She follows this conclusion with the next four chapters on evolution in schools, in which Darwin is alleged to be both wrong and responsible for all the world's ills.

The man from Mars, reading Ann's book, might say: Why?

Why is this intensely political, mean, divisive, polarizing person devoting a third of her book to fossils?

Does anyone care?

The answer to that question is most assuredly *yes*. There's a substantial number of people who care deeply.

According to the scientific research, Ann is on extremely weak ground in her arguments to support the teaching of intelligent design in the public schools.

Professor Jerry Coyne, a distinguished professor at the University of Chicago, has written a number of articles, available at www.talkreason.org, that deconstruct the science of Ann's attack on evolution.

"First, one has to ask whether Coulter (who, by the way, attacks me in her book) really understands the Darwinism she rejects. The answer is a resounding No! . . . the Darwinism decried by Coulter is the usual distorted cardboard cutout. All she does is parrot the intelligent design (ID) line: There are no transitional fossils; natural selection can't create true novelty; some features of organisms could not have evolved and therefore must have been designed by an unspecified supernatural agent.

"And her 'research' method consists of using quotes taken out of context, scouring biased secondary sources, and distorting what appears in the scientific literature.

"What is especially striking is Coulter's failure to tell us what she really believes about how the Earth's species got here. It's clear that she thinks God had a direct hand in it, but beyond that we remain unenlightened. IDers believe in limited amounts of evolution. Does Coulter think that mammals evolved from reptiles?

"If not, what are those curious mammal-like reptiles that appear exactly at the right time in the fossil record? Did humans evolve from ape-like primates, or did the Designer conjure us into existence all at once? How did all those annoying fossils get there, in remarkable evolutionary order? And, when faced with the real evidence that shows how strongly evolution trumps ID, she clams up completely.

"But after ranting for nearly a hundred pages about evolution, Coulter finally gives away the game on page 277: 'God exists whether or not archaeopteryx ever evolved into something better. If evolution is true, then God created evolution.' Gee. Evolution might be true after all!"

Professor Coyne published a detailed point-by-point counterattack to Ann's science in the *New Republic;* the *talkreason* website is devoted to articles debunking the challengers of evolution. You can access all of that at www.talkreason.org.

What you learn, when you read about attitudes to evolution, are two things.

First, the overwhelming majority of Americans don't believe in evolution. That's right, *don't*. They think God had something to do with it, one way or the other. The numbers, to those of us who are rationalists on this one, are downright stunning.

Only 12 percent of those surveyed think that human beings have developed over millions of years from less advanced forms of life, and God had no part in the process. Thirty percent believe that human beings developed from less advanced forms of life with God's help, and an overwhelming majority—47 percent—believe that God created human beings, pretty much in their present form at one time, within the last ten thousand years or so. Five percent had no opinion.

Second, the legit scientists are overwhelming in saying Ann is wrong and Darwin is right.

In short, Ann has got a very big audience to lie to.

But Ann didn't write this book expecting her collection of secondary sources to convince a Professor of Ecology and Evolutionary Biology at the University of Chicago. Professor Jerry Coyne is not her intended audience, any more than liberals are the intended audience for the first half of the book. My guess is that she expected to be trashed by Coyne and she couldn't really care less—or that she was happy to take it, as long as it would generate a little heat.

Her audience is the people in Kansas, who are voting, even as I write this, in a highly contentious election for the state board of education, which is being shaped entirely by the issue of how creation will be taught in Kansas's classrooms.

I wonder how many books she's sold in Kansas.

All politics is local, Tip O'Neill, the former Speaker of the U.S. House of Representatives, used to say.

And nothing is more local than the schools: Who runs them, what's taught in them, where they're built, how much we pay for them, how successful they are at what they do.

In an ideal world, schools *are* where politics begin. Their success is the measure of our success.

That is, in my judgment, precisely what Ann is trying to do in the last third of her book. She is trying to make a case that will cause people to be outraged about what is going on in the public schools, that will make them want to bring her version of ideological politics to public education, that will make it important to them who runs the schools.

She is sponsoring her own sort of grassroots movement—a movement to take over the schools.

She is putting this book in the hands of the people she wants to take over public education, and she wants them to put her values into play.

* * *

Are you going to give her the next generation?

It's that simple.

That is what it comes down to, at the end.

Her or us.

Do you let her take over, or do good people wake up and start doing politics again?

She is not the only one with a vision.

* * *

My friend Steve Barr started Green Dot Public Schools in 1999 because he wanted to change the world too—just like Ann, only completely different.

He was a cofounder of Rock the Vote and a veteran of all the political campaigns of the 1970s and 1980s. He worked with me in the Dukakis campaign before he decided that, if he was really going to make a difference as a liberal in politics, it was time to stop doing "big picture" politics and focus on what mattered to real people. He decided if he could do all the other things he'd figured out how to do, he could figure out how to build and transform schools.

And he has, by listening to the smartest educators and business people, and because he's one of the most brilliant political organizers I've ever met.

In 1999, Barr started a charter school group, Green Dot, that runs the most successful group of schools in Los Angeles, all of which dramatically outperform the public schools in the same area with the same kids.

Green Dot opened its first school, Animo Leadership Charter High School, in the fall of 2000, and it graduated its first class in June 2004. In August 2002, they opened their second high school, Animo Inglewood Charter High School; a year later they opened a third, Oscar De La Hoya Animo High School. In the fall of 2004, Green Dot opened two more schools, Animo South Los Angeles Charter High School and Animo Venice Charter High School.

The Green Dot schools now send 90 to 95 percent of their graduates to college, even though their students all come from areas where most kids can't read at a ninth-grade level.

The schools are also different in that they expect parents to sign contracts agreeing to volunteer time and supervise their kids. Everyone wears uniforms. None of the schools has more than five hundred kids. But they do have unions, and they don't get in the way.

To help him continue changing the world, Steve brought in Bain and Co., the consulting firm, to figure out what was working in the Green Dot schools, and how you would take that information and apply it to transform a big, failing pubic high school. Transformation is a term of art. It means you literally come in and transform a low-performing big public high school into a cluster of separate, smaller schools.

They came up with a plan, which is available for you to download and use at the Green Dot website, www.greendotpublicschools.org.

Here's the challenge: What you do first is target your high school.

Steve, the organization, and the board (full disclosure: I'm on the board, and proud to be) picked the worst-performing high school in Los Angeles. Now, I don't want to be nasty, but that's quite an honor: the worst-performing high school in a very, very challenged school system.

The high school we picked, Jefferson High, in an area formerly known as South Central, was, to put it nicely, an unmitigated disaster.

Adding to the challenge, neither the administration nor the union welcomed the arrival of the upstart charter school organization, which had decided it could do better. Not even a little did they welcome us. They told Steve to get lost.

So Steve organized the parents around them to demand change. He organized parents who had never been organized before to believe they had a right to a better education for their kids.

Here was this guy, ready, willing, and able to open new schools where everyone would wear uniforms and be expected to go to college, and the administration and the unions were blocking it.

He had parents sign petitions, and more than a thousand turned out to deliver them in person to the superintendent. He went to the board of education. Casey Wasserman of the Wasserman Family Foundation, a young philanthropist, in his first major donation decision since his grandfather's death, stepped up to the plate to give Green Dot a grant to finance the schools that the board didn't really want. And the fight went on throughout the spring of 2006.

Ultimately, the superintendent had to give in. And now Green Dot is opening five new schools, each of which will begin with a ninth grade class, in fall 2006, in the vicinity of the Jefferson campus.

Much to the administration's chagrin, but for understandable reasons, some of the most talented and creative teachers at Jefferson—and of course Ann is wrong about this, there are always creative and talented people trying—have seized on the opportunity to work in the new schools in an atmosphere in which they will be rewarded for their talents and encouraged to innovate and develop professionally.

As if that weren't enough, here's another idea to steal. Right now Steve Barr is in the middle of organizing a parents union in Los Angeles whose agenda is to transform the Los Angeles schools as a whole. A parents' union? Steve set up this Los Angeles Parents Union to give parents a seat at the political table and push for reform.

Steal that idea: a parents union.

You're asking, What can a parents union do?

Organize parents to transform local schools into small autonomous schools.

When I say transform, I mean it. Why not?

Everything Green Dot does is built around six basic principles—the Six Tenets, as Green Dot calls them—and you'll see why. They're the building blocks.

Here they are:

1. *Small, Safe Schools:* Schools should be small—500 to 525 students (when was the last time you saw a private school any larger than that?)—to ensure that students don't fall through the cracks and to allow students to receive the personalized attention they need to learn effectively. Students are held accountable for all of their actions and teachers and administrators can develop personal relationships with each student and his/her family. Smaller schools are safer and decrease the security risks inherent in urban schools, since problems can be recognized and mitigated earlier. In addition, it is easier to implement the other five tenets in smaller schools. Classes should be kept as small as financially possible. As part of a school transformation, small schools will operate in clusters that share services and facilities, such as athletic fields and gymnasia, which will allow for a greater variety of extracurricular activities. More important, the clusters of small schools will be able to leverage specialized services, specifically special education and English language learner programs, to meet the needs of students more effectively.

2. *High Expectations for All Students:* All stakeholders must have an unwavering belief in the potential of every student and an understanding that every student will succeed with the proper support. Every student will take a rigorous curriculum that ensures that all students who graduate high school will at least have the option to attend college if they choose. Extensive student intervention and support programs

must be offered before school, after school, and during the school day, in order to help students master a rigorous curriculum.

3. *Local Control:* Principals and teachers should be the key decision makers at the school site and need to be empowered to make all decisions related to budgeting, hiring, and curriculum. Recommendations and best practices should be provided by the central district, but the ultimate decision-making power and autonomy need to rest at the school site. Local control helps ensure that the administration, teachers, and support staff at each school site stay motivated, take responsibility for their school, and continually innovate.

4. *More Dollars into the Classroom:* Shift school revenues away from central administration and toward teachers and kids. By incorporating best practices from the private and public sector, schools should be able to increase the amount that goes into classroom from roughly 60 cents on the dollar (in Los Angeles) to 90 cents on the dollar.

5. *Parent Participation:* Demand greater parental participation by requiring the families of students dedicate at least 30 hours annually to their child's education experience. Participation can range from actually volunteering in the office on campus to reading at home with one's child.

6. *Keep Schools Open Later:* Schools need to be part of the community and made available for community as well as student use. Schools should be kept open until at least 5 P.M. daily to provide students with safe, enriching after-school programs and to enable community groups offering quality services to the neighborhood to use the facilities. Allowing community groups to use school facilities helps ensure that the neighborhood takes ownership and responsibility for the school.

The students at the schools that follow the Six Tenets score on average 120 to 160 points higher on academic performance tests than students in comparable high schools in the city. But that's just the beginning of the comparison. Eighty percent of ninth graders graduate college-eligible, compared to 20 percent for the equivalent city school; 75 percent are actually going to four-year colleges—and we're talking about kids from the toughest areas of the city.

How are they run? Like businesses, in the sense that they are very professional. They are steeped in values and driven by the data. They look at the numbers all the time: who's absent, who's not doing well, when once becomes twice. Students wear uniforms. They call people Mr. and Ms.

This is what Jennifer Anderson, the valedictorian of Animo Inglewood, had to say about her school:

> My school has provided me with teachers and counselors who have pushed me to try and to reach for the stars. Without Animo, I don't know where I would be going to college. However, I know that I would not be attending Brown in the fall. I also know that I would not feel as prepared for the future as I do now.

Delbert McFarland is going to Cal State Northridge, which, for a kid who was headed straight into gangs, is like going to Harvard. He has a Magic Johnson smile, but when he started at Animo (it means spirit) Inglewood, he was hanging out with the wrong kids, the cliques that are the precursors to the gangs, getting into fights. His first year he got all Ds and Fs, and he also got shot in the stomach in a fight. But the teachers and the principal stuck with him, they kept on top of him, called him at home, sat on him to do the work, and eventually he started turning it around. By senior year he had almost brought his grades up to the place where he was up to Cal State. Almost, but not quite. He made it onto the wait list. And then once a week, every week, for two months, he and his guidance counselor and his principal called the admissions officer at Northridge to plead his case. Eight phone calls later, he was in. Today, he's living at Northridge with two of his buddies from high school, doing college work, a long way from the hospital emergency room, from the cliques and the gangs.

Or there's Jerry Najera and his mom, Mary. Jerry had already flunked out and spent time at Juvie Hall, our local corrections facility, when his mother heard about Green Dot. At the time Jerry's only ambition in life was to be a skateboarder.

For his mother, making a thirty-hour commitment to work with her son's education was a big deal. But she did it. In his first year, her son had one of those teachers who changed his life. His name was Matt Hill. Now Jerry Najera wants to be a scientist. His mother is putting in up to fifty hours a week in the school office. The two of them speak at Green Dot events.

Does every story have a happy ending? No. Alex Franco came to this country with his dad when he was seven. His mother stayed behind in Mexico and Alex was raised by his angry father, with whom he fought. But Alex maintained a 3.5 average in high school and was accepted at the University of California Santa Barbara, to study engineering no less. And don't we need engineers? But because he is an illegal immigrant, he doesn't have access to student loans. Even though Steve and the folks at Animo raised some scholarship money for him, he and his dad still had to come up with something in the order of $3,000 a year to put him through. And it just wasn't to be. Steve has just heard that Alex dropped out during his second semester and is doing landscape work with his father in Michigan.

I know what you're thinking. Or at least I know a few of the things. . . .

What about the teachers union? How does Green Dot deal with the union?

In Los Angeles, the union is called UTLA, and it's real hard line.

Here's the deal, from Steve: "The union gets too much of the blame. It's not there to create a vision for education. It's there to represent its members, to get a better contract for teachers, get more money for them. The problem with the contract is that it eats its young. It protects seniority, lifetime tenure and lifetime benefits, and longtime teachers at the expense of young teachers."

At Green Dot, because each school is autonomous—see #3 above, Local Control—each school has its own union. Green Dot has a union contract with each of its schools. So there's a union at each school, but it's not UTLA. And the pay scale is better than UTLA, but that's also because everybody is relatively younger. Still, it speaks particularly well for management, and for the advantages of decentralized management, because the fact is that public schools generally get more money, because they have certain advantages, like not having to pay rent for their facilities. The result is they start with 35 percent more on average in funds, but Green Dot still pays better.

You want to know about tenure. There is no tenure. Tenure has been replaced by "just cause." So there is protection from arbitrary firings, but not from being fired for just cause.

Is it hard to fill positions?

For starters, consider this figure that Steve shared with me: 13 percent of the graduating class at Yale and 12 percent of the graduating class at Spellman applied for Teach for America.

So maybe that makes it less surprising that Steve had eight hundred applicants for eighty openings this year, and found himself turning away even qualified science teachers, as he put it.

That's *teachers*.

As for parents, from the beginning Green Dot has required them to be involved in the schools as a condition of their kids being accepted. Don't think that they're using that for self-selection, to get the most motivated, "best" parents in the door. From the beginning, Steve has gone out looking for the families who need Green Dot.

Outreach is a really important part of this process. For many families, it all begins at church. Steve treats it like community organizing, enlisting the local clergy so he can tell mothers about the new small school where high standards will be enforced and everyone will be expected to study for college. And the parents learn that they too will participate. At meetings, Steve always has Green Dot mothers and students with him, as well as teachers, to explain what the school is like to would be students and their parents; parents who find the whole idea of participation daunting can be walked through it slowly. By the end, there are generally twice as many applicants as there are seats for Green Dot schools, requiring raffles and waiting lists, and leaving the school with a mix of kids of varying talents and needs.

And leaving lots of kids wanting, of course.

Whose responsibility is that?

I think it's ours. Whether we have kids in the system or not.

Of course, what all of this takes, which is the hardest part, is getting people involved, being involved yourself. Passing around petitions and signing them; supporting candidates for school committees and running; attending meetings and speaking. Doing politics.

For years, so much of the passion in politics has been concentrated on the right that when I ask my students if they would know how to move a stop sign they think I mean literally "move" it.

Why do it?

My friend Steve does it because he was raised by a single mom, and he wouldn't be anybody if it weren't for the fact that in those days, California had the best public schools in the nation, and he had a chance.

He also does it for his brother, who didn't make it, but went to one of those mean high schools and ended up dropping out and overdosing.

He does it because of that new immigrant fervor for a chance for the next generation.

That's what education was for my generation.

It was the American dream.

It was the golden opportunity.

It was the ticket.

Ann describes the public schools as the temple in the church of liberalism, where we inculcate the young with our Godless faith, or something like that.

If it were as she says, she wouldn't have much to worry about: We're not doing a good enough job inculcating them with anything in the public schools the way they are now.

And her goal, if you take her seriously, and if there is any conclusion to be reached from her screed against the education system, is to take control of the schools.

To play political games, and not for the sake of the kids.

"We operate off the fervor of a new immigrant generation." That's what Steve says. The fervor is there.

But will the opportunity be?

There is so much bile and hatred in this world. Our politics is so infused with meanness, so dominated by the Ann Coulters, so utterly devoid of soul, that the first reaction of a decent person is to turn away in disgust.

But, if you and I and Steve Barr and the decent people turn away in disgust, how does Jennifer Anderson get to Brown? How does Delbert McFarland get to Northridge instead of a gang? What happens to Jerry Najera?

There are real people, these kids, in your town and mine, and across America, whose lives hang in the balance.

We can get disgusted by Ann and her clan and turn away, or we can be energized by Steve and his mission, find our own souls and hearts, and fight back.

There are more of us than there are of them.

They do not have God on their side.

We know that.

How can it be that they care more than we do?

We are not the opposition party.

They do not have a better plan.
We do.
They do not have better ideas.
We do.
So how can we let them win?

10.

IF IT WERE THAT EASY TO DESTROY HER, WHY WOULD I HAVE WRITTEN A WHOLE BOOK? OR FUN WITH FOOTNOTES AND PLAGIARISM

After *Godless* was published, you may remember hearing something about plagiarism allegations, and thinking to yourself: "Whew. We're off the hook with her."

Not so fast.

If it were that easy to bring her down, would I have written a whole book?

After arguing against her worldview, would I have saved dealing with all those damning allegations till last?

No such luck.

There was indeed a minor flurry about plagiarism allegations. People are so desperate to bring Ann down that they will cling to anything.

But it isn't that easy. She isn't that stupid. And if we were to apply some of the same standards to our own friends . . . oh, you don't want to know.

I have many friends, and even more acquaintances (who shall remain nameless), who could not survive the level of scrutiny that is applied to Ann.

Some of them are actually liberal heroes, so you have to be careful here, lest what is good for the goose be good for the gander. (I'm not, I should add, talking about myself. I certainly hope not.)

In any event, none of the accusations of plagiarism by critics came up with any major ideas stolen from anyone else.

No one else thought to call the widows "harpies."

The idea of calling us "Godless," in the particular way Ann does, belongs to her alone.

There are some sweet doozies of mistakes in the footnotes.

But first, for the sake of a few chuckles, let's check out Ann's "plagiarism."

By the way, let's be fair: No one sat down and read *Godless,* as has happened with some other books, and recognized their own work. What happened is that critics of Ann used a computer program to compare the wording in *Godless* to everything else in a database, looking for similarities. And the things that came up are the kind of things that can happen when a newspaper article, or Internet clip, states a fact that supports a point you're making, and in citing the fact you end up echoing the language.

Here are five paragraphs identified by plagiarism experts for *Godless.* (A full review of all the allegations can be found at www.tpmmuckraker .com/archives/001070.php.)

Example one: A sentence about the Furbish lousewort, pulled from a newspaper clip.

Godless, page 5: "The massive Dickey-Lincoln Dam, a $227 million hydroelectric project proposed on upper St. John River in Maine, was halted by the discovery of the Furbish lousewort, a plant previously believed to be extinct."

Alleged source: "The massive Dickey-Lincoln Dam, a $227 million hydroelectric project proposed on upper St. John River, is halted by the discovery of the Furbish lousewort, a plant believed to be extinct." From "People and events that made Maine's century," *Portland Press-Herald,* December 12, 1999, and identified by Rude Pundit and John Barrie in the *New York Post.*

Example two: Two sentences, compressed words?

Godless, page 37: ". . . the judge called it 'inconceivable' that Tiffany's injuries were caused by wrestling moves. After the trial, Tate's new lawyers admitted that the 'wrestling defense' was 'bogus.'"

Alleged source: ". . . the presiding Judge said that it was 'inconceivable' that Tiffany Eunick's injuries were caused by Lionel Tate mimicking wrestling moves. Indeed, since the trial ended, Lionel Tate's new lawyers have filed court papers in which they admit that the 'wrestling defense' was, in their words, 'bogus.'" From "Retraction to WWE and the Public," Parents Television Council, July 11, 2002, and identified by Rude Pundit.

Example three: A sentence copied from a Planned Parenthood pamphlet.

Godless, page 95: "As the president of the Mississippi Baptist Convention, Pickering presided over a meeting where the convention adopted a resolution calling for legislation to outlaw abortion."

Alleged source: "As the president of the Mississippi Baptist Convention, Judge Pickering presided over a 1984 meeting where the convention adopted a resolution calling for legislation to outlaw abortion." From "About Planned Parenthood," Planned Parenthood Federation of America pamphlet, 2004 and identified by John Barrie in the *New York Post.*

Example four: A bogus list of successful treatments achieved by adult stem cells.

Godless, page 197: "A short list of the successful treatments achieved by adult stem cells are these:

- Rebuilding livers wracked by otherwise irreversible cirrhosis
- Repairing spinal cord injuries by using stem cells from nasal and sinus regions
- Completely reversing Type 1 diabetes in mice using adult spleen cells
- Putting Crohn's disease into remission with the patient's own blood stem cells
- Putting lupus into remission using stem cells from the patient's bloodstream
- Treating sickle-cell anemia using stem cells from umbilical cord blood
- Repairing the heart muscles in patients with congestive heart failure using adult stem cells from bone marrow
- Repairing heart attack damage with the patient's own blood stem cells
- Restoring bone marrow in cancer patients using stem cells from umbilical cord blood
- Restoring weak heart muscles using immature skeletal muscle cells
- Putting leukemia into remission using umbilical cord blood

- Healing bone fractures with bone marrow cells
- Restoring sight in blind people using an ocular surface stem cell transplant and a cornea transplant
- Treating urinary incontinence using stem cells from underarm muscle
- Reversing severe combined immunodeficiency (SCID) with genetically modified adult stem cells
- Restoring blood circulation in legs with bone marrow stem cells"

Alleged source: "At the same time, a long list of successful experimental treatments have been achieved using ethical sources of stem cells. These include:

- Spinal cord injury repair (using stem cells from nasal and sinus regions)
- Complete reversal of juvenile diabetes in mice using adult spleen cells, with Harvard now preparing for human patient trials using spleen cells
- Crohn's disease put into remission (using patient's blood stem cells)
- Lupus put into remission (using stem cells from patient's bloodstream)
- Parkinson's disease put into remission (using patient's brain stem cells)
- Repair heart muscle in cases of congestive heart failure (using stem cells from bone marrow)
- Repair heart attack damage (using the patient's own blood stem cells)
- Restore bone marrow in cancer patients (using stem cells from umbilical cord blood)
- Restore weak heart muscles (using immature skeletal muscle cells)
- Put leukemia into remission (using umbilical cord blood)

- Heal bone fractures (using bone marrow cells)
- Restore a blind man's sight (using an ocular surface stem-cell transplant and a cornea transplant)
- Recovery from a stroke (using stem cells from bone marrow)
- Treat urinary incontinence (using under arm muscle stem cells)
- Reverse severe combined immunodeficiency (SCID) (using genetically modified adult stem cells)
- Restore blood circulation in legs (using bone marrow stem cells)
- Treat sickle-cell anemia (using stem cells from umbilical cord blood)"

From Illinois Right to Life Committee's "Stem Cell Research Summary," and identified by Raw Story. Note: Coulter provides a "see generally" note for this list in her book, but no citation for the source of the list.

Example five: Half a sentence about Scientology doctrine from a newspaper story about Scientology.

Godless, page 209: "It's also possible that galactic ruler Xenu brought billions of people to Earth 75 million years ago, piled them around volcanoes, and blew them up with hydrogen bombs, sending their souls flying every which way until they landed on the bodies of living humans, where they still invisibly reside today—as Scientology's L. Ron Hubbard claimed."

Alleged source: "Yes, according to Scientology doctrine, a galactic ruler named Xenu brought billions of people to Earth 75 million years ago, stacked them around volcanoes and blew them up with hydrogen bombs. Their souls then clustered together and stuck to the bodies of the living." From "Pity This Blushing Bride-to-Be," *San Francisco Chronicle,* July 3, 2005, and identified by John Barrie in the *New York Post.*

That's it. And guess what? I copied this list.

You see why I left it to the end; it's not much of an argument against her. And I'm sure they'll do the same to me. I hope my research assistants are reading this sentence. We need to be careful. But this isn't really what plagiarism is about.

Now, some fun with Ann's footnotes.

The fine folks—excuse me, why do I keep getting this wrong, the "Nazi block watchers"—at *Media Matters* put together a great list of Ann's footnote bloopers, which range from minor to major. You can be the judge.

The first two, in my judgment, are the worst and rank right up there with getting the Willie Horton story wrong, which I'm probably the only one to notice.

First Coulter attacks liberals for teaching kindergarteners about anal sex, fisting, etc. . . . Citing a *New York Times* article, Coulter writes on page 175:

> But in contrast to liberal preachiness about IQ, there would be no moralizing when it came to sex. Anal sex, oral sex, fisting, dental dams, birthing games—all that would be foisted on unsuspecting children in order to protect kindergarteners from the scourge of AIDS. As one heroine of the sex education movement told an approving *New York Times* reporter, "My job is not to teach one right value system. Parents and churches teach moral values. My job is to say: These are the facts, and to help the students, as adults, decide what is right for them."

This is far different from what was in the actual article, "At Dartmouth, A Helping Candor," which incidentally was published in November 8, 1987—*almost twenty years ago*. The article was about the sex education available *to adults*, and quoted Dr. Beverlie Conant, then director of health education at Dartmouth College, discussing the moral underpinnings of the classes for the adult students.

Then Coulter attacks evolutionists for being unable to frame a coherent argument.

On page 248 of *Godless* she writes:

> In an article in the *New York Times* on intelligent design, the design proponents quoted in the articles keep rattling off serious, scientific arguments—from Behe's examples in molecular biology to Dembski's mathematical formulas and statistical models. The *Times* reporter, who was clearly not trying to make the evolutionists sound retarded, was forced to keep describing the evolutionists' entire retort to these arguments as: Others disagree. That's it. No explanation, no specifics, just "others disagree." The high priests of evolution have not only forgotten how to do science, they've lost the ability to formulate a coherent counterargument.

The actual source, Kenneth Chang, "In Explaining Life's Complexity, Darwinists and Doubters Clash," (August 2, 2005), as *Media Matters* explains, was part of a three-part series that contained detailed explanations of evolution including how evolutionary mechanisms gave rise to Darwin's finches. The series also concluded that "Darwin's theory . . . has over the last century yielded so many solid findings that no mainstream biologist today doubts its basic tenets, though they may argue about particulars."

The words "others disagree" *do not appear* in the article.

These Ann gaffes happen to be my favorites . . . and, if this is your interest, there are plenty more. Just tap your keys to http://mediamatters .org/items/200608070002.

For me, however, there's no real good reason to nitpick Ann to death—as long as you can squash her with a well-reasoned argument.

11.

THE NEXT ANN . . .

Who could she—or he—be?

So many to choose from.

Every city and town has its own. Do you take them on, or ignore them? Change the station, or demand equal time?

Wait until they go national, or start tracking them now?

Here are my three favorites. Make your own list.

One of my favorite Anns does not have blonde hair at all. She's a brunette Ann, a Filipino-American Ann, but in every other respect Michelle Maglalang Malkin, daughter of immigrants (a doctor and a schoolteacher), brought up in New Jersey, graduate of Oberlin College, where she met her husband and had her introduction to conservative journalism, is Ann to the core.

The right-wing Asian pit bull Ann.

Consider: She goes to Oberlin, a well known, liberal, liberal arts college, to study music, decides she isn't going to make it as a concert pianist, and starts writing for the college newspaper, which is something she did in high school. Then a student named Jesse Malkin decides to form an independent conservative paper and Michelle signs up. His first assignment for her is for them to work together on a story attacking Oberlin's affirmative action program (Oberlin had been known for a century for its successes in graduating blacks; as of 1900, half of blacks in America with college degrees had gotten them from Oberlin). It was, I guess, an assignment made in heaven. Fellow minorities hated the article. Malkin was energized, and maybe in love. She told a reporter:

> That's where I first really encountered the vicious response you can get when you stand up to a political orthodoxy. It's an extremely liberal campus. Even if you tread very lightly on political sacred cows, there was a huge negative response, especially from somebody who was a minority, standing up and saying, "Well, all these self-appointed minority groups on campus don't speak for me." It was seeing the violent paroxysms it caused on the Left that really put me on my way to a career in opinion journalism. I really just came into being as a political journalist towards the end of my campus experience, and it was really after I had left and started, you know, writing on my own. It was really more social conservatism than economic conservatism that I started with for my column writing. So I was not a huge lightning rod until the end of my tenure at Oberlin.

Michelle Maglalang graduated from Oberlin in 1992 and headed to Washington, D.C., to intern at NBC. She then took her first real job as a writer and columnist for the *Los Angeles Daily News* in 1993. It was in that year that she married Jesse Malkin, then studying for a Ph.D. at Rand, and became Michelle Malkin. In 1996 the couple moved to Seattle, where Michelle became an editorial writer and columnist for the *Seattle Times* for the next three years, until her daughter was born. In 1999, the family moved to the Washington, D.C., area, following Jesse's Rand consulting job. Michelle started writing a syndicated column from home and appearing regularly on the Washington-based TV talk shows.

As one observer, H.Y. Nahm, noted in the Asian-American daily *Goldsea.com,* "Freed from the restraints of staff writing, Malkin's tone became cattier and more bombastic. . . . Tying every issue to a leering swipe at the physical appearance, personal style or intimate life of a prominent figure—especially those with a high sex appeal quotient—was becoming Malkin's trademark. Malkin was becoming skilled at supplying back-door titillation to those who liked to heap righteous indignation on supposed immorality while leering at its sexiest exponents."

"Leering at its sexiest exponents?" Now who does that sound like?

An Ann in the making.

As the headshot for her column, Michelle has posted a picture that can only be described as, well, very, very Ann: Big hair, big lips, red lipstick, red top. . . . Most headshots for newspaper columns aren't quite the same. . . .

And what does she write about? Michelle is one of the most reliable spouters of the daily right-wing talking points. But she always does it with her own unique spin.

She is the author of three books about . . . Guess? Internment, immigration, and liberals, of course. She is for internment and against immigration. And against liberals, of course.

Her book *In Defense of Internment: The Case for Racial Profiling in World War II and the War on Terror* argues that the roundup of Japanese Americans during World War II was justified by national security concerns. It wasn't racism, it wasn't about race. And if that doesn't sound positively Ann I don't know what does.

Michelle's next one, *Invasion: How America Still Welcomes Terrorists, Criminals, and Other Foreign Menaces to Our Shores,* argues that bad guys are coming in. What else would you expect from a fortunate first-generation American, whose father's medical training was sponsored by an employer—one of the lucky ones who grows up believing it's all about merit.

After that it was *Unhinged: Exposing Liberals Gone Wild,* which really doesn't. It's mostly a collection of columns. But it does have the word "Liberal" in the title.

The internment book is the one that attracted the most attention. It was thoroughly interred in an eleven-part blog series by Professors Eric Muller of the University of North Carolina Law School and Greg Robinson of the University of Quebec. As with Ann's McCarthy book, you have to ask—not what she was arguing for, but why she would choose that, of all subjects, to write about.

Who, but someone who aspires to Ann's crown, would write a book defending internment?

Even the late Chief Justice Rehnquist had made his peace with the idea that the Court just got that one wrong. Not Michelle.

Ann's got Joe McCarthy. Michelle's got internment. No one was tougher on poor Norm Mineta, the longtime transportation secretary (2001–2006), whose own World War II evacuation, she says, "has absolutely clouded his view of what needs to be done now." Not tough enough rounding up Muslims, it seems. She is for racial profiling in the war against terror, just as she would have been for it in World War II.

Michelle can be plenty mean. Whose writing does this make you think about?

"Skulking in the campaign background is a ticking time bombette with a volatile temper and acid tongue who makes [Howard] Dean look like Mr. Rogers on Prozac," Michelle wrote of Teresa Heinz Kerry in a column titled, "Howard Dean in a Dress."

Malkin on "Hysterical Women for Kerry": "Get a grip, girls. You are an embarrassment to a nation at war."

One of her most famous altercations was the one that took place with Chris Matthews on *Hardball* on the subject of John Kerry's injuries. Taking her cue from the Swift Boat veterans, Malkin claimed: "They are legitimate questions about whether or not it was a self-inflicted wound."

Watch as she defends her claim that John Kerry may have inflicted his own wounds. Chris Matthews plays incredulous, as does Willie Brown, the former mayor of San Francisco, who was also on the show:

> **BROWN:** He volunteered twice. He volunteered twice in Vietnam. He literally got shot. There's no question about any of those things. So what else is there to discuss? How much he got shot, how deep, how much shrapnel?
>
> **MALKIN:** Well, yes. Why don't people ask him more specific questions about the shrapnel in his leg. They are legitimate questions about whether or not it was a self-inflicted wound. (Crosstalk)
>
> **MATTHEWS:** What do you mean by self-inflicted? Are you saying he shot himself on purpose? Is that what you're saying?

Chris is sputtering as he says this.

> **MALKIN:** Did you read the book. . . .

Who does she think she is talking to?

> **MATTHEWS:** I'm asking a simple question. Are you saying that he shot himself on purpose.

You don't want to be near his line of sputter in a moment like this . . .

> **MALKIN:** I'm saying some of these soldiers . . .
> **MATTHEWS:** And I'm asking question.

Forget pronouns, articles, excessive parts of speech . . .

> **MALKIN:** And I'm answering it.
> **MATTHEWS:** Did he shoot himself on purpose?

MALKIN: Some of the soldiers have made allegations that these were self-inflicted wounds.

MATTHEWS: No one has ever accused him of shooting himself on purpose.

Why didn't I go to law school? he's thinking. . . .

MALKIN: That these were self-inflicted wounds.

MATTHEWS: You're saying there are—he shot himself on purpose, that's a criminal act?

MALKIN: I'm saying that I've read the book and some of the . . . (Crosstalk)

MATTHEWS: I want an answer—yes or no, Michelle.

By now I could be up there with Breyer . . .

MALKIN: Some of the veterans say . . .

MATTHEWS: No. No one has every accused him of shooting himself on purpose.

What did they say about Shana Alexander?

MALKIN: Yes. Some of them say that.

MATTHEWS: Tell me where that . . .

MALKIN: Self-inflicted wounds—in February 1969.

MATTHEWS: This is not a show for this kind of talk. Are you accusing him of shooting himself on purpose to avoid combat or to get credit?

Not a show for this kind of talk. Not until I repeat it, that is . . .

MALKIN: I'm saying that's what some of these . . .

MATTHEWS: Give me a name.

MALKIN: Patrick Runyon and William Zaladonis.

MATTHEWS: They said—Patrick Runyon . . .

MALKIN: These people have . . .

MATTHEWS: And they said he shot himself on purpose to avoid combat or take credit for a wound?

MALKIN: These people have cast a lot of doubt on whether or not . . .

MATTHEWS: That's "cast a lot of doubt." That's complete nonsense.

MALKIN: Did you read the section in the book . . .

MATTHEWS: I want a statement from you on this program, say to me right now, that you believe he shot himself to get credit for a purple heart.

He's got her . . .

MALKIN: I'm not sure. I'm saying . . .

And off she goes . . .

MATTHEWS: Why did you say?

MALKIN: I'm talking about what's in the book.

MATTHEWS: What is in the book. Is there—is there a direct accusation in any book you've ever read in your life that says John Kerry ever shot himself on purpose to get credit for a purple heart? On purpose?

MALKIN: On . . .

MATTHEWS: On purpose? Yes or no, Michelle.

MALKIN: In the February 1969—in the February 1969 event.

MATTHEWS: Did he say it on purpose.

MALKIN: There are doubts about whether or not it was intense rifle fire or not. And I wish you would ask these questions of John Kerry instead of me.

MATTHEWS: I have never heard anyone say he shot himself on purpose. I haven't heard you say it.

MALKIN: Have you tried to ask—have you tried to ask John Kerry these questions?

MATTHEWS: If he shot himself on purpose? No. I have not asked him that.

MALKIN: Don't you wonder?

MATTHEWS: No, I don't. It's never occurred to me.

Another favorite spin of mine is Michelle on the subject of Hispanic politicians. For reasons that certainly have nothing to do with qualifications, Michelle seems to be viewed as an expert on minority politicians, especially Hispanic politicians. It's a kind of reverse affirmative action from which she certainly profits, though in principle she would disapprove of it. By my count, she spent three years, max, in Southern California as a junior editorial writer for the *Daily News* in Los Angeles before moving to Seattle and then Maryland. Maybe I missed something in her resume, some qualifying experience where she studied the history of Hispanic politics, or worked at something that would allow her to form some expertise, but here she is on the subject.

According to Michelle Malkin, "the vast majority of mainstream Hispanic politicians" believe that "the American southwest belongs to Mexico." Folks like Antonio Villaraigosa, the mayor of Los Angeles, who was originally planning to be at the NFL talks the day of the big immigration march here—she accuses him, by name, of being a "Latino supremacist." It would almost be funny if this stuff didn't go out all over the country.

Consider this segment from the *O'Reilly Factor,* and then this clip from her March 29, 2006 column:

O'REILLY: Joining us now from Edmonton, Canada, Dr. Raul Hinojosa, who teaches international development at UCLA, and from Raleigh, North Carolina, syndicated columnist Michelle Malkin, the author of the book *Invasion: How America Still Welcomes Terrorists, Criminals, and Other Foreign Menaces to Our Shores.* All right, Michelle, begin with you. The rhetoric is getting ratcheted up. Now, Ms. [*Nation* editor Katrina] vanden Heuvel, who you saw, or heard, on the ABC News program, is an extreme left-wing person. But you know, the personal attacks fast and furious—and then there's the Mexican flag. What say you?

MALKIN: Well, Katrina vanden Heuvel is a shameless smear merchant, and she's also very clueless and blind. She underscores something that I've noted for a long time about the far left, and that is their own blindness towards racism and ethnic separatism on the part of politically incorrect minorities within their own ranks. While she was smearing Congressman [Tom] Tancredo [R-Colo.], who has done nothing—nothing more than insist that we enforce our borders and that the federal government fulfill its obligation to provide for the common defense, while she was doing that, take a look at what was happening in Los Angeles. Just open your eyes, Ms. vanden Heuvel. *It was the far left, the open-borders activists, who were the ones who are the extremists, who were the ones advocating militant ethnic separatism. "This is our stolen land." "Chicano power." You had folks with Aztlan T-shirts mugging for the cameras in front of city hall. These are people who believe that the American southwest belongs to Mexico, that we don't have a right to enforce our borders, and who do nothing more than try to sabotage our sovereignty* (emphasis added).

O'REILLY: We are going to be as fair as humanly possible here on this whole issue. But what did the Mexican flag say to you, Michelle?

MALKIN: Well, first of all, do not buy Dr. Hinojosa's spin. He sounds very reasonable. He sounds very benign, *but the kind of quote-unquote "pride" that a lot of these illegal alien activists are touting now goes much further than just being proud about one's heritage and one's roots. The idea, the intellectual underpinnings of reconquista are embraced by the vast majority of mainstream Hispanic politicians, as well as the international—(emphasis added)*

How does she know? How in the world would she know?

> **O'REILLY:** How do you know that, Michelle? How do you know that?

Good question, Bill.

> **MALKIN:** Because I've read—because I've read the history. And look at it—can I—
> **HINOJOSA:** Not true.

Then look at Malkin's March 29 column, where she writes: "Apologists are quick to argue that *Latino supremacists* are just a small fringe faction of the pro-illegal immigration movement (*Never mind that their ranks include former and current Hispanic politicians, from LA mayor Antonio Villaraigosa to former California Democratic gubernatorial candidate Cruz Bustamante*)" (emphasis added).

Where does she get this stuff?

And that's just one of the pit bull Anns.

* * *

Then there's another Ann you may not have heard of: San Francisco talk show host Melanie Morgan.

What kind of a mouth does she have?

Well, start with this item from summer 2006, relating to the *New York Times* disclosure (shared by the *Wall Street Journal* and *Los Angeles Times*) of the program to review international banking transactions for possible connections to terrorist activity.

Here's what Keith Olbermann on MSNBC's *Countdown* had to say: "Not only has [Morgan] suggested seriously that the *New York Times* executive editor Bill Keller be jailed for treason—'I see it as treason, plain and simple'—but now she tells the *San Francisco Chronicle,* quote, 'If he were to be tried and convicted . . . I would have no problem with him being sent to the gas chamber.' Hey, somebody want to check Ms. Morgan for light bulbs? Melanie Morgan: Today's 'Worst Person in the World.'"

The gas chamber?

Ann had this to say in response to Morgan: "I prefer a firing squad, but I'm open to a debate on the method of execution." Maybe these two can run on the same ticket.

You might be thinking that since Melanie Morgan is on the radio, maybe she's not really an Ann.

Worry not. In some of her photos she's wearing a turtleneck, and looks like a veritable matron from Marin. But not in the poster you can get of "Melanie Morgan: USA Rocks," where she's sitting on the seat of a motorcycle, all cleavage and leather.

Ann dresses like a tasteful maiden lady from Connecticut compared to this getup.

Melanie Morgan started out as a radio reporter at KGO in the early 1980s, and stayed there until 1990, when her husband's job took them to Seattle. That is where, according to a CBS documentary, she developed an awful gambling problem. "I ended up going into labor early," she said. "Of course, I was in a terrible environment, smoke-filled room, hardly taking care of myself. Yeah, I was gambling right up until an hour before I gave birth." Her gambling addiction even led her to neglect the child, resulting in an informal intervention by

Child Protective Services. With the help of Gamblers Anonymous, she says, she was able to stop gambling in 1992. In the mid-1990s she and her family returned to San Francisco, and she went to work for KSFO as a right-wing talk show host.

Morgan's first big splash was as the "mother of the recall" that brought down Gray Davis and brought Arnold Schwarzenegger to the governorship of California. She then formed something called Move America Forward, which does things like run ads calling the United Nations "a corrupt body that hates the United States."

But until she got into this latest fight about the gas chamber, the best of Morgan was the summer of 2005, when she and other conservative talk show hosts went on the "Voices of Soldiers Truth Tour" to "report the good news on Operation Iraqi Freedom you're not hearing from the old-line news media."

Good news that we weren't hearing. Maybe because all those journalists in Iraq were hanging out on their hotel balconies or something instead of reporting the war. Remember that conservative line. Don't hear it that much anymore, do we?

The good news was supposed to include the "facts" that Saddam harbored four thousand terrorists "related to Al Qaeda," that "they are in the last gasps of their insurgency," and that Iraqi forces had achieved "60 percent" readiness.

When she came back she went on *Hardball* in August 2005, to bring David Gregory—standing in for host Chris Matthews—and Democratic strategist Hilary Rosen up to speed:

ROSEN: In fact, 40 percent of the people fighting in Iraq are, in theory, part-time volunteers who have been there over a year beyond when they were supposed to be. So, it is exactly because we have a volunteer army that soldiers and their families need to understand the truth. They deserve the truth. What is an exit strategy? What will satisfy the president? What does success look like? That is not happening. We're not getting that from the president—

Is this depressing? Look at the dates. 2005 . . . 2006 . . . Does it make a difference? You could be saying the same thing. . . .

GREGORY: Melanie—Melanie, is there something else at work here, despite what you said about Mrs. [Cindy] Sheehan? Is there not a kind of tipping point here, where a majority—and, certainly, the polls bear this out—of Americans are starting to raise their hands and say, wait a minute, this is not what we bargained for; this is not what the president said would happen; it's not even matching what the president is saying is happening on the ground?

MORGAN: Well, this is what is so terribly frustrating, David, because I have been to Iraq. I have been on the ground. I have seen what's going on. And *it is not being reported accurately in the media* (emphasis added). I can tell you for a fact that the soldiers there are saying that *we are winning the war,* precisely because the insurgency miscalculated back in January that the elections would be as successful as they were. They made a terrible mistake, and now they know that they have to derail the upcoming elections, constitutional referendum elections, that are this month and again in December. *And that's why they're fighting as viciously as they are, and that's why they are in the last gasps of their insurgency, because if we win—and, by winning, I mean those democratic elections—that means that we can start drawing down and coming home. And that's what the troops told me, and that's what the top brass told me.* I agree that the president has done a very poor job of articulating why we are there. And that's why I

went to Iraq, along with half a dozen of my fellow talk show
hosts, to get the message out.

Gregory: Right.

Actually, wrong.

Morgan: The reason why there's a disconnect is because the
media is not reporting the story as accurately as it is being experienced by our troops.

Right. Sure.

Gregory: All right. We are going to have to leave it there.

A few days earlier, on the same program, she had tried a similar line
on Matthews:

Matthews: Do you believe there's a—to me—I'm not over there.
I haven't been over there. The question I want to know is, who
is going to win this war based on fighting zeal? We saw for
years, as you described and everybody else knows, for years, the
minority in that country were the bullies of that country. They
ran it because they were good, smart, vicious bullies. How do
we know that those bullies won't eventually grab control again
the minute we leave, Melanie?

Morgan: We have no idea what's going to happen. I'm not a psy-
chic. I can't read the future. But what I can tell you is that,
when I talked to the Iraqi general in charge of training troops
over there, he was telling us some very good news. *They're at 60
percent troop strength now in terms of where they are trying to at-
tain a goal of 100 percent readiness. They're at 60 percent* (emphasis added). They're making progress every day.

Not exactly.

But Melanie Morgan doesn't back off. She kept giving interviews about her proposed gas-chamber punishment for *New York Times* editor Bill Keller, and complaining about how her trip to Iraq was covered. The poor victim!

Now if that doesn't qualify her as an Ann, what does?

On her website, she writes:

> If the Left ever wonders why so many conservatives are outraged by what they read from Liberal publications (such as *The American Prospect*) one need not meander any further than Greg Sargent's interview with me last Thursday.
>
> No, I am NOT backing away from any of the comments I made in the "Horse's Mouth" blog.

You gotta love the name.

> But I am pointing out that the summarization of my comments is completely misleading, and totally in character for people who despise those of us who work ceaselessly to stand-up for our troops in time of war, and who are outraged when others refuse to do the same.

So let's repeat it . . .

> First, folks, to the headline:
>
> TALK SHOW HOST MELANIE MORGAN SAYS "ANY NEWSPAPER EDITOR" WHO PUBLISHES CLASSIFIED INFO SHOULD BE "LOCKED IN A STEEL CAGE," MURDERED BY FAMILY MEMBERS OF SLAIN TROOPS, AND SENT TO THE "HOTTEST CORNER OF HELL."
>
> The truth: I pointed out in my comments that if a person is *tried and convicted* of committing treason then obviously they should face the punishment for that crime.

Oh, first they're tried and convicted, then they're put in the steel cage with the families members of the slain troops. . . .

That includes the death penalty.

I never suggested murdering Bill Keller of the *New York Times* or anyone else. Period. Look up the definition of murder. It's in *Wikipedia*, by the way.

Of course. She suggested execution, not murder . . .

The protest by *The American Prospect* and other anti-war liberals in the blogosphere over my statements shows either a naiveté concerning the law, or more likely it demonstrates once again that those in the "Blame America First" crowd are rabidly against the war on terrorism, and are blinded by all logic and reason.

Against executing newspaper editors? Blame America First. But of course.

And then there was this by Mr. Sargent: "Now she's basically said that any editor printing classified national security information should be murdered, maybe it's time to check in with the corporate owners of her local station."

Again—a complete mischaracterization of my quotes. A more accurate summary should have read, "Any editor who is responsible for leaking classified information and results in the deaths of American soldiers at a time of war should face the ultimate punishment for that crime, including the death penalty."

Ann didn't say the Jersey Girls enjoyed watching their husbands die, just their being dead. . . . Remember?

The exact quote to Mr. Sargent is, "Let me answer your question with a question. If by leaking classified information that resulted in the deaths of American soldiers—let's just say that a terrorist purchased all the ingredients necessary for an IED and detonated it against a convoy of 18, 19, 20-something Marines, killing them—do you honestly think I would give a rat's rear-end how the editor who leaked that information dies? . . . NO. I DO NOT CARE."

Once I was on one of these shows, and one of the Anns recommended a treason prosecution for someone else (it happens so often I can barely remember) and I paused to point out that our Founding Fathers actually had some views about treason. It was a sensitive subject for them, and they were careful to protect against the overuse of the charge, an abuse with which they were familiar. What makes treason unique is that the extraordinary requirements for its proof are written into the Constitution, reflecting the Founding Fathers determination that the charge not be—well, not be what the Anns use it for. Thus, the Constitution provides: "No person shall be convicted of treason unless on the testimony of two witnesses to the same overt act, or on confession in open court." Needless to say, Melanie Morgan has not had anything to say about the Constitutional requirements for treason, much less why this is an appropriate case to overcome the Founding Fathers' well-recognized (by everyone but her) admonition to use the charge sparingly. . . .

Because, after all, he or she is receiving the ultimate penalty for the charge of treason.

My WISH list for traitors who undertake to subvert national security interests that results in the deaths of American Soldiers is "to be locked in a steel cage with the family members of slain troop members who would happily deliver the ultimate punishment of death, and then sent to the hottest corner of hell."

Now that we've got that straight . . .

As a journalist of over 30 years experience covering the Mideast, the uprising for Democracy at Tiananmen Square in China, the return of hostages from the hijacking of a jetliner, I have a bit of experience in observing media convention, classified secrets, and the rule of law. And apparently Richard Valeriani, a long time former NBC reporter agrees by saying that the *New York Times* decision to publish is akin to "giving Anne Frank's address to the Nazi's [*sic*]."

I'm not just an Ann . . .

I might also point out to Mr. Sargent that his squealing over my comments most likely would evaporate if one of his friend's or loved one's [sic] were to suffer harm at the hands of the terrorists as a result of the repeated attempts to undermine the war effort by deliberately leaking/publishing classified material, and in doing so provided aid and comfort to the enemy.

One other thing. The people within the United States government who actually leaked to the NYTimes, WaPo, LAT, and Wall Street Journal such a successful, worthy program as the SWIFT database should join the folks I have suggested in taking up residence in the hottest corner of hell.

Finally, I'm delighted to report that your efforts to have me blackballed from Hardball with Chris Matthews on MSNBC were entirely unsuccessful. And my radio station KSFO AM in San Francisco, owned by ABC/Disney, has no intention of firing me.

After all, there is a First Amendment. And it works both ways. Much as the Left hates that.

Actually, we don't. We're in favor of the First Amendment working both ways. That's how it's supposed to work. Even if it brings us Melanie Morgan. . . .

* * *

So there's the Asian terrier Ann, the leather-and-hog Ann, but really, the award for Most Likely to Emerge as the Next Ann must go to radio host Glenn Beck.

Isn't that the guy with the show on *Headline News?*

That guy.

Proof that if you're a white male, who is almost as clever and vicious as Ann Coulter, it takes a little longer, and you may have to do radio every day, but guess what?

You get a much better deal. You get your own show.

And you don't have to write five bestsellers, as Ann might be the first to point out.

Consider some of Beck's best spits-in-the-face—the ones that win him "The Next Ann" crown.

Cindy Sheehan is "pimping out the tragedy of [her] son's death."

"Who's the bigger prostitute: Heidi Fleiss or Howard Dean? No, not even Howard Dean. John Kerry. Who's the bigger prostitute? Who'll do anything for money or power? I mean, at least Heidi Fleiss—this is saying something—at least Heidi Fleiss will admit to being a prostitute. You know what I mean? At least she'll say, 'Hey, I'm doing it for cash.' . . . Cindy Sheehan. That's a pretty big prostitute there, you know what I mean?"

So much for Ann's point that victims are beyond criticism.

The Katrina victims he called "scumbags," and here he is on the 9/11 victims: "But the second thought I had when I saw these people, and they had to shut down the Astrodome and lock it down I thought: I didn't think I could hate victims faster than the 9/11 victims."

On Michael Moore: "I'm thinking about killing Michael Moore, and I'm wondering if I could kill him myself, or if I would need to hire somebody to do it. No I think I could. I think he could be looking me in the eye, you know, and I could just be choking the life out—is this wrong?"

Who is this guy?

He was born February 10, 1964, and started in radio as a kid in Seattle, Washington, after winning a local contest. He became a successful

Top 40 DJ in Hamden, Connecticut, at a Clear Channel station while in his twenties—until he was brought down by alcoholism and drug addiction. His first marriage, from which he has two daughters, fell apart. He was baptized as a Mormon in 2000 after recovering from drug and alcohol addictions with the help of AA, and then launched a new career as a talk show host in 2001 in Tampa, Florida. He got picked up by a syndicate in 2002 and was hired by CNN in January 2006. He has remarried and had a new baby in the spring of 2006. His eldest daughter, born with cerebral palsy, was told she would never walk or feed herself, but now runs cross-country for her school. Beck mentions her as one of the reasons for his recovery.

But if Beck's recovery is due in any part to AA, he must have missed the meeting where the fellowship shared about the need to rid oneself of resentments.

To him, Jimmy Carter is a "waste of skin," Hillary Clinton the "antichrist."

He's thanked a purported torturer on air for his service, refers to many of his opponents as "scumbags," and regularly lampoons the difficult pronunciation of Arabic names by gagging through them.

Criticizing Al Gore, he looks at a map and says, "Oh yeah, I see that's what happening here. The ice is starting to melt in Greenland. I mean, they just don't get it, do they?"

And Glenn truly does, as the following comment from his radio show will prove. First he plays an audio clip of Gore—"The Arctic is experiencing faster melting. If this were to go, the sea level worldwide would go up twenty feet. This is what would happen in Florida. Around Shanghai, home to forty million people. The area around Calcutta [India], sixty million." And then he comments: "Stop. Just a second, stop. *This is what would happen to Shanghai. Does anybody really care? I mean, come on. Shanghai is under water. Oh, no! Who's gonna make those little umbrellas for those tropical drinks?*" (emphasis added).

In 2004, Beck called Michael Berg, whose son had been beheaded in Iraq, "despicable" and a "scumbag" because the elder Berg criticized George W. Bush in the wake of his son's death.

And despite this type of throwaway hate, Beck's radio show was the third highest ranked in the coveted 25–54 demographic group nationally at the time he was hired by *Headline News.*

He responds to those who criticize his harsh rhetoric by saying that his quotes are being taken out of context. Asked about the "I'm thinking about killing Michael Moore" quote, Beck explained: "The words reported were technically accurate, but they neglected to note the whole setup of the conversation and how it was all part of a comedy monologue. They didn't include my obvious joking with a caller and commenting that 'this whole conversation is all so wrong.' If you want to take comedy out of context and put it into a sterile room labeled 'Talk radio,' it's going to look terrible in print. . . . The problem is, the folks who were protesting are just not paying attention. The people writing in to newspapers and complaining the most, were people who don't even listen to the show."

Good for them.

* * *

Ann's crown? What does that really mean?

The one who will push the standards of tolerance and decency down another notch?

The one who will succeed in being so offensive that the sheer offensiveness of it is the news?

The one who will challenge media organizations to define whether they have any standards beneath which they will not go not in terms of words, but in terms of meaning?

Or is it a Christian crown, the one that will be won at those voter registration booths in church parking lots, where people clutch *Godless* in one hand and the Bible in the other?

There I was driving today and flipping stations, and I caught a minister quoting the Old Testament, about speaking evil of others, and I just burst out laughing . . . he went on and on about Solomon saying how wrong it was to speak evil of others, and gossip and evil were condemned in both the Old and New Testaments, and I thought how fitting it was that I turned the radio to that station that day.

In the end, I think it has to be a gold crown. It's the only kind Ann would wear after all.

So why not? Just bang it on her blonde head.

12.

SOULLESS

In a recent column, only half in jest, Ann bemoaned the fate of the traveling author:

> Dear Readers: I hope you're enjoying your summer so far. How I wish I could join you at the beach, by the pool, or out at the ranch clearing brush. Unfortunately my summer has been spent promoting my new book *Godless: The Church of Liberalism.*
>
> If you've ever wondered what it would be like to be on tour promoting a book—and, honestly, who hasn't?—it's like being on a long, low-budget vacation with all of the good parts taken out.

As for intellectual stimulation, she claimed to have found none.

Q: Have you encountered anyone on the left who has read *Godless* carefully and was willing to debate its points with you? How did it go? Have any critics addressed the content rationally? If so, what did you think? If not, do you find it amusing?

A: Only one: Michael Eric Dyson. The rest just want to talk about why my skirts are so short and why I'm "mean." It's almost as if my critics are avoiding the issues I write about in the book.

We know better. *She's* the one who avoids *them*.

As for the serious Michael Eric Dyson exchange, I'm still looking, but all Google and Lexis-Nexis have are hundreds of references to her reference to it.

Meanwhile, from everything else I can find, it does appear that someone placed a gun to her head and forced Ann to appear repeatedly in short skirts with high heels and say mean things about various people from the 9/11 widows to gays in order to keep herself in the news. Meanwhile, she is passing on various opportunities to engage on the substance of her book. Ann's column deals with other concerns:

Q: How would your career be different if you looked like Molly Ivins?

A: I'd be a lot uglier.

And would she and the other Anns get the attention they do? And would they occupy, as they sometimes do, a woman's place on the spectrum?

Q: Does Hillary Clinton have a good chance in 2008? What are her strengths and weaknesses? What did her reaction to your "Jersey girls" comments tell you about her as a potential candidate?

A: Good chance of what? Coming out of the closet? I'd say that's about even money.

Once you start dropping a few gay jokes, I guess lesbian jokes come with the territory.

* * *

And so the Machine percolates. Call it what you will.

Reverend Dobson is out there registering his millions.

The RNC continues to raise money to feed a technological machine that far surpasses the divided Democrats.

Ann is out there selling her millions of books.

A hundred talk radio hosts around the country are pitching her book.

And what do we have to counter this? Cindy Sheehan and Michael Moore scare more people than they draw, I am sorry to say. Calling the president a fascist doesn't help the cause; calling him a terrorist doesn't either. As in Ann's case, you can think it, but you don't have to say everything you think.

What's the answer? you ask.

Look to your left. Look to your right. Look in the mirror. The networks aren't going to take Ann off unless her ratings fall, or a large segment of the public starts complaining about her—unless there is a real backlash—and advertisers get nervous, and her brand of ugly trash talk is considered to go out of style with the public.

The networks aren't in the business of leadership, after all; they're just in business. Changing public discourse will have to come from the bottom up, not the top down. *You* control the media.

The ultimate question with the Anns is how you use them.

What buttons do they push in you? What do they inspire you to do? Stand Up or Sit Down?

There is a wonderful paperback book from Earth Works Action entitled *50 Simple Things You Can Do to Fight the Right.* And they're great. I'm one of these people who goes around the country giving speeches to women about how to use the power they didn't know they had, and I wish I'd come up with some of the goodies on this list.

Number 20 in their book is Take Back the Churches. In terms of "things" you do, the book says to do the same things they do: go to church, meet people, organize around issues, use the facilities, get the credibility, co-opt the forum. . . . Same stuff. What it doesn't say is to take over the school board as part of spreading the message of the church. That's the difference.

But maybe we should do it anyway. Not to spread the Lord's word. But to do the Lord's work. If you know what I mean. Godless? Says who?

It's easy to lose your political soul in this culture of Coulter and Beck.

The time I've spent inside her head writing this book has not been fun. The hair extensions were fun. The brain games aren't.

Nothing means anything, in her world, and everything means nothing. You hear the whackballs screaming, you see the negative ads on television, you watch people being ridiculed and destroyed, you see the crash of crazed absolutes, and the easiest thing to do is to turn it all off, except you can't.

It is the clash between right and wrong, and it is not one you can sit out, leave for others, spend the game on the sidelines watching. . . .

Never before has it been more important for people to be involved in politics.

Iraq teeters on the brink of civil war as I write this, even as it becomes increasingly clear how seriously this administration mishandled this war.

And what is the response of the Anns?

To call us traitors if we dare to criticize the war effort. To impugn the patriotism of those who dare to disagree with them. To silence their opponents, rather than engage in discourse with them. Precisely the tactic Ann accuses her opponents of using against her.

Does this tell you something about why you must be involved?

Does this tell you how they fight?

On this point, the only response, the *only* response, is to recognize how pitiful they are—and return to the appropriate criticism of the moment.

But the war is not the only issue that requires political involvement. Pick your issue. Pick your passion.

It is clear that we are facing a period where the government is seeking to exercise Executive powers once thought beyond the scope of the Congressional enactments which are now said to justify them. That in the name of National Security, we are entering an era of new challenges to privacy the likes of which we have not seen in decades, and could not have seen then because of the changes in technology. These people are actually serious when they accuse the editor of the *New York Times* of "treason."

It is also clear that the government is seeking to exercise prosecutorial powers once thought utterly implausible against Muslims in the name of national security. What was that joke? Move over, Mohammed . . .

I had not practiced criminal defense law in thirteen years, deciding, around the time one of Mike Tyson's lawyers came calling, that everyone may need a lawyer but they don't all need me. I have now reversed that decision because a case was brought to me that literally shocked me—that the government would prosecute someone for pure speech that took place a decade ago because the man is a Muslim and the speech is about jihad. This is a measure of the threat we face as well.

But pick your own issue—the environment, education, your list, not Ann's or mine, healthcare or education or children's rights, Social Security, Medicare. For my generation, wait till you're caring for an aging parent, and then tell me about smaller government. How can you afford to sit out?

At one level, religion is just an organizing principle for Ann—the spine for this year's bestselling attack on liberalism, the gimmick to collect the different pieces of her onslaught on abortion rights and gay rights and race into a presentable whole by calling it the "religion" of liberalism.

The joke is that "religion" is the last thing we liberals would call our activities in the civic arena. We're the ones who worship the establishment clause, after all. We may occasionally use the term "civic religion" to refer to constitutionalism, but it is not intended in the same category as the others on the block.

But of course it's more than that. By invoking religion, putting God in play as she does, Ann aims both to do her politics from a higher plane and to tap into the passion that defines Americans as religious people.

It makes this book a more passionate work than her others, not necessarily for her, but for her readers.

Dan Wakefield articulately bemoans that the church of his fathers has been hijacked by the religious right. His new book, *The Hijacking of Jesus,* is an examination of the politicization of the religious right. But, viewed from the outside, no one was taken against their will. The hijackers look like heroes to the flocks.

What is wrong with registering new voters?

Is there something wrong with Christians participating in politics?

The government's answer is that it has to be separate from church activities, or they could lose their tax-exempt status. The IRS is actually investigating a church, a liberal one, for crossing the line. That's not my problem. My problem isn't their buses but their agendas. It's when they start insisting on teaching creationism instead of Darwin and tearing the school board apart to get their way, using it as a forum for ideological politics, that it starts to be a problem.

Who would do something like that?

* * *

Reverend Dobson and I think alike.

We both understand a few things.

For one thing, that politics begins with voting.

We both want to bring millions of new voters to the polls.

He wants to use churches.

I want to use kids.

I had this great idea back in 2000, but it never quite got off the ground, and now I invite you to borrow it, appropriate it, run with it, etc.

TAKE A PARENT (or adult) TO VOTE.

Enlist the teachers union—yes, that teachers union—as your partner. That's how I was going to do it.

You go into any elementary school classroom and ask those kids how many of them would vote if they could and every hand goes up.

So fine. Take advantage of it. On the first day of school, give each of them a voter registration card and ask them to find someone in their family or neighborhood who is eligible to vote but hasn't registered and bring it back; and on Election Day . . .

The kids take a parent to vote.

And maybe even get a free ice cream, hamburger, little prize, extra recess. . . .

I remember my daughter telling me for years how she hated the phony elections in school that didn't count for anything. The value of this idea is that, in a totally non-partisan way, you enlist the kids in the real election, voting for their future.

You register one of the most underrepresented groups, demographically speaking, in the electorate: Young parents, single parents, especially inner city and poor parents.

An alternative army. An alternative band.

Just the start of an idea.

Teaching kids to start caring about politics, and figuring out how to participate in this system.

Of course voting is just the first step.

I teach undergraduates, and we joke about the range of experiences of politics kids bring to college. Some of them—okay, a very small number of them, many of whom end up in my classes—are what we call political junkies. They love the game, feel passionately about issues, and are using college as a time to perfect their skills as players around such critical issues as the rules for participation of the Greeks in the Dorm Council, or whatever.

That is, after all, what college government is for. It's not because campus rules are so important, but because in learning how to form clubs, make rules, hold elections, resolve disputes—yes, even take on the administration—young people learn the skills that are supposed to teach them how to negotiate, resolve disputes, and live together when it counts.

Of course it doesn't always work that way. I don't mind when things get hot on campus. It's when they turn ice-cold that it bothers me.

There's another group of kids whom I rarely see in class, but who occasionally visit me in the office. They're the would-be pundits from broadcast journalism. Most kids who go into broadcast journalism want to be reporters or producers or regular professionals. But every once in a while someone will come see me and will tell me that he or she wants to be "just like me," or "just like me only conservative." When I inquire what just like me actually means, it means they want to be a television pundit, but they want to "skip right to that part," as opposed to the three campaigns, and the twenty years of teaching, and all that.

What they really want, they often tell me, is to be like Ann.

When I ask them whether they think they're qualified, they invariably smile. Like Ann, they are certain that they are better looking than the rest of us. It has always given them a certain power.

Ironically, while invoking Christianity, Ann's approach to politics, as understood by the generation that seeks to emulate her, is peculiarly soulless.

* * *

Everyone expects war in 2008. Open battles for the nomination on both sides. Not since 1952 has there been no incumbent vice president on either side standing in the ready.

And then there's Hillary.

The religious right is spoiling to play a major role on the Republican side. Will McCain sell his soul? Will Giuliani?

If Hillary is the nominee, can she generate enough enthusiasm on the left to make up for the impact she will have in energizing the right?

And Hillary is not about to give up the faithful to the right. She is as comfortable in a church as they are. She is Methodist to the core. Yes, Ann, it is a real religion. Imagine a true battle of the faithful.

* * *

Sometimes people come up to me and tell me they agree with everything I say, and I politely thank them and tell them that means they're as crazy as I am. What I mean is that politics is a bit of a floating craps game, where the action is always moving around there somewhere, and no two people are really likely to land in exactly the same place, but thanks.

Of course you're guided by principle, but for most of us it's personal principle, shaped by personal experience, shaped on occasion by personal contacts, tactical judgments, and the like. And sometimes, you later decide, you were wrong. Even I come to disagree with myself some of the time. I move as best as I can with the game, trying to win more often than I lose, and trying to find things to care passionately enough about to invest in.

There's nothing inevitable about where I end up. Or where anyone else does. It's that we end up somewhere, ultimately, that counts.

That's what politics is. Messy and sloppy, it's how we live together. Codified as rules, it's called law. Enforced by judges, it's the rule of law.

What makes us unique is the relative civility and stability with which we do it. Legally, that is based in a constitutional system, which works for the simple reason that we make it work, no more complicated than that.

Which makes it both as sturdy and as fragile as it is.

Opposites are alike, my smart friend Maureen says: "People for whom it means nothing and people for whom it means everything. The ones who believe in nothing and the ones who believe in absolutes. Both are ultimately impossible to deal with."

Which is Ann? I ask, but I know the answer. Both, of course.

Politics is how we live in the middle.

NOTES

INTRODUCTION

p. 2   Ann makes it a practice not to "name names" and I think it is a good one, although I should add that it might be because there is no one who believes the version of liberalism she describes, and there's certainly something to that, too.

p. 2   "we're being divided for sport . . ." "Abortion," The Gallup Poll, April 1975 to May 2006 results (2006), http://poll.gallup.com/content/default.aspx?ci=1576; *see also*, "Single U.S. Public Opinion Polls: Same Sex Marriages and Civil Unions," Religious Tolerance.Org survey of public opinion polls from Gallop, ICR, Harris, and several other organizations, 2006, http://www.religioustolerance.org/hom_marp.htm.

CHAPTER 1: GODLESSNESS

p. 5   "My book makes a stark assertion . . ." Ann Coulter, "Party of Rapist Proud to be Godless," AnnCoulter.com, June 14, 2006, http://www.anncoulter.com/cgi-local/article.cgi?article=134 (last visited on August 29, 2006).

p. 6   "Most of what I say . . ." John Cloud, "Ms. Right," *Time*, April 25, 2005.

p. 6   "there is no culture war . . ." Morris Fiorina, with Samuel Abrams and Jeremy Pope, *Culture War?* 2d ed. (Pearson Education Inc., 2006).

p. 6   "Sir, my concern is not . . ." Abraham Lincoln, ThinkExist.com, http://en.thinkexist.com/quotation/sir-my_concern_is_not_whether_god_is_on_our_side/164075.html (last visited on August 29, 2006).

p. 7   "Liberalism is a comprehensive . . ." Ann Coulter, *Godless: The Church of Liberalism* (Crown Forum, 2006), 3.

p. 7   "is barely even a church . . ." ibid., 5.

p. 7   "Everything liberals believe . . ." ibid., 4.

p. 7   "Of course liberalism is a religion . . ." ibid., 1.

p. 8   "We believe in populating . . ." ibid., 4.

p. 9   "Their rage against us . . ." ibid., 22.

p. 9   "religion holds that . . ." ibid., 3.

p. 9   "love to boast . . ." ibid., 1.

p. 9   "Americans tell pollsters they are very religious . . ." "How Important Would You Say Religion Is in Your Own Life?" The Gallup Poll, May 2006 Results, http://www.galluppoll.com/content/default.aspx?ci =1690&t=TwAuIUSZDyf2OQvCD3TvgT-hGX2gpNAd7U3iD7kl 99gvYH3WQHb-cfoJ7%2fyB4AG-eGx1DImZDwvFseiv2fnXgyzNh l09%2fDk9fNIAdxM6k1zWfQ97ATW2e-Fzb6Ijg2VLuw-Dc%2f UUChg7jn1ctsfYWU98djOXkC5YVWuotBUMx4a (last visited on August 29, 2006); *see also* "How Often Do You Attend Church or Synagogue?" The Gallup Poll, May 2006 Results, http://www.gallup-poll.com/content/default.aspx?ci=1690&t=TwAuIUSZDyf2OQvC D3TvgT-hGX-2gpNAd7U3iD7kl99gvYH3WQHb-cfoJ7%2fy B4AG-eGx1DImZDwvFseiv2fnXgyzNhl09%2fDk9fNIAdxM6k1z WfQ97ATW2e-Fzb6Ijg2VLuw-Dc%2fUUChg7jn1ctsfYWU98dj OXkC5YVWuotBUMx4a (last visited on August 29, 2006).

p. 10   "Nazi block watchers . . ." On *The O'Reilly Factor,* Coulter called several websites "little Nazi block watchers," stating: "They tattle on their parents, turn them into Nazis," MediaMatters.org, December 2, 2005, http://mediamatters.org/items/200512020005 (last visited on August 29, 2006).

p. 10   "really bad people..." On *The O'Reilly Factor,* O'Reilly agreed with Coulter that liberals are "bad people," MediaMatters.org, December 2, 2005, http://mediamatters.org/items/200512020005 (last visited on August 29, 2006).

p. 11   James Downard, "Secondary Addiction: Ann Coulter on Evolution, Parts I–III," TalkReason.org, 2006, http://www.talkreason.org/articles /coulter1.cfm (last visited on August 29, 2006); Ian Musgrave "Ann Coulter: Clueless" ThePandasThumb.org, June 18, 2006, http://www .pandasthumb.org/archives/2006/06/anne_coulter_cl_1.html (last visited on August 29, 2006).

p. 12   "As a matter of faith..." Coulter, *Godless,* 2.

p. 12   "They exchanged the truth..." Romans 1:25–26, ibid., 1.

p. 13   "core of environmentalism..." Coulter, *Godless,* 4.

p. 13   "swoon in pagan admiration..." ibid., 3.

p. 14   "not a Christian..." ibid., 17.

p. 14   "Led by born again..." Jon Krakauer, "Under the Banner of Heaven: A Story of Violent Faith," as quoted in Coulter, *Godless,* 16.

p. 14   "If liberals are on Red Alert..." ibid., 17.

p. 15   "not particularly welcoming..." ibid., 21.

p. 19   "Look how Chris Matthews..." *Hardball with Chris Matthews,* MSNBC, July 27, 2006.

CHAPTER 2: WHO IS ANN COULTER?

p. 21   "So she leaked to the press..." Joe Conason and Gene Lyons, "Impeachment's little elves," Salon.com, March 4, 2000, http://www.salon .com/news/feature/2000/03/04/willey (last visited on August 29, 2006).

p. 21   "Who is this woman..." *Today,* MSNBC, June 6, 2006.

p. 21   "In print, she calls people pie-wagons..." Ann Coulter, "Put the Speakers in a Cage," WorldNetDaily.com, July 26, 2004, http:// www.worldnetdaily.com/news/article.asp?ARTICLE_ID=39644 (last visited on August 25, 2006); *see also* "Women like Pamela Harriman . . ." Christina Valhouli, "The Modern Courtesan," Salon.com, November 16, 2000, http://dir.salon.com/story/sex/feature/2000 /11/16 /courtesan_2index.html (last visited on September 7, 2006).

p. 22   "In an interview . . ." George Gurley, "Coulter 2005," *New York Observer,* January 10, 2005, 2.

p. 22   "His version of the group . . ." Charles Taylor, "When Right-Wing Fembots Attack," Salon.com, June 27, 2002, http://archive.salon .com/books/feature/2002/06/27/coulter/index.html (last visited on August 25, 2006).

p. 22   "Originally I was the only female . . ." Vincent Morris, "Wanna Be a Political Pundit? Being Blonde and Beautiful Helps," CapitolHillBlue.com, June 6, 2000, http://www.capitolhillblue.com /article.asp?ID=912 (last visited on August 25, 2006).

p. 22   "Taylor describes them . . ." Taylor, "When Right-Wing Fembots Attack," Salon.com.

p. 23   "My father was a lawyer . . ." Jonathan Freedland, "Coulterisms: An Appalling Magic," *Guardian Unlimited,* May 17, 2003, 14.

p. 23   "According to the *New York Observer* . . ." George Gurley, "Ann Coulter Ecstatic," *New York Observer,* July 3, 2006, 1.

p. 23   "She went on to Michigan Law School . . ." "My Life," AnnCoulter .com, http://www.anncoulter.com/cgi-local/content.cgi?name=bio (last visited on August 29, 2006).

p. 23   "Such as this unfortunate gaffe . . ." *Countdown for January 21, 2005,* MSNBC, February 3, 2005.

p. 24   "No one does smug . . ." Taylor, "When Right-Wing Fembots Attack," Salon.com.

p. 25   "Other than her year as a law clerk . . ." "My Life," AnnCoulter.com.

p. 25   "Ann owns condos in New York . . ." Adam Lisberg, "Her Disputed Elex Ballot Sparks Probe in Florida," New York *Daily News,* June 8, 2005, 5.

p. 25 "She likes to ski . . ." Booknotes.org, August 11, 2002, http://www
.booknotes.org/Transcript/?ProgramID=1688, accessed on August 25,
2006.

p. 25 "I do what comes naturally . . ." Jonathan Pitts, "She's the Hammer;
Liberals Her Nail," *Baltimore Sun,* July 30, 2005, 3C.

p. 26 "The judge ended up dismissing . . ." Peter Baker, "Judge Dismisses
Jones v. Clinton Law Suit," *Washington Post,* April 2, 1998, A1.

p. 26 "Her technique of choice . . ." Ann Couter, *Liberal Lies About the
American Right* (Crown Publishers, 2002) 15, 167.

p. 26 "In *Slander,* Ann accuses liberals . . ." ibid., 6.

p. 26 "Political 'debate' in this country . . ." ibid., 1.

p. 27 "It may have been the case . . ." Alessandra Stanley, "Battle of Wits,
And No Clear Win" *New York Times,* June 16, 2006, E1.

p. 28 "I am emboldened by my looks . . ." "The Wisdom of Ann Coulter,"
Washington Monthly, October 2001, http://www.washingtonmonthly
.com/features/2001/0111.coulterwisdom.html (last visited on August 29, 2006).

p. 28 "Anorexics never have boyfriends . . ." ibid.

p. 28 "She has had a number of very public boyfriends . . ." ibid.

p. 28 "She believes Republican women are attractive . . ." "*USA Today* Drops
Ann Coulter," CBSnews.com, July 26, 2004, http://www.cbsnews.com
/stories/2004/07/26/politics/main631949.shtml (last visited on August
29, 2006).

p. 28 "I don't think I've ever encountered an attractive liberal woman . . ."
Freedland, "Coulterisms: An Apalling Magic," *Guardian Unlimited.*

p. 28 "My allies are the ones wearing crosses . . ." Ann Coulter, "Put
the Speakers in a Cage," WorldNetDaily.com, July 26, 2004,
http://www.worldnetdaily.com/news/article.asp?ARTICLE_ID=39644
(last visited on August 25, 2006).

p. 29 "This from the woman . . ." Coulter, *Slander,* 8.

p. 30   "My feet are the size of the Atlantic Ocean . . ." *Hannity & Colmes,* Fox News Channel, April 20, 2005.

p. 30   "Her mother, who is fighting cancer . . ." John Cloud, "Ms. Right; She is quite possibly the most divisive figure in the public eye. But love her or hate her, you don't know Ann Coulter," *Time,* April 25, 2005, 32.

p. 30   "Women like Pamela Harriman . . ." Christina Valhouli, "The Modern Courtesan," Salon.com, November 16, 2000, http://dir.salon.com/story/sex/feature/2000/11/16/courtesan_2/index.html (last visited on August 29, 2006).

p. 30   "Today's worship of physical perfection . . ." Ann Coulter, *Godless: The Church of Liberalism* (Crown Forum, 2006), 9.

p. 30   "The only sort of authority . . ." ibid., 128.

p. 30   "Asked about the seeming inconsistencies . . ." John Cloud, "Ann Coulter Fires Back," *Time,* June 8, 2006.

p. 30   "The celebrity culture . . ." ibid.

p. 31   "When she can't take cheap shots . . ." Tim Grieve, "Ann Coulter: Someone Should Poison Justice Stevens," Salon.com, January 27, 2006, http://www.salon.com/politics/war_room/2006/01/27/coulter/index.html (last visited on August 25, 2006); *see also* Freedland, "Coulterisms: An Apalling Magic," *Guardian Unlimited.*

p. 31   "are not only traitors . . ." Ann Coulter, "New Idea for Abortion Party: Aid the Enemy," AnnCoulter.com, http://www.anncoulter.com/cgi-local/article.cgi?article=88, November 23, 2005 (last visited on August 25, 2006).

p. 31   "New Yorkers are cowards . . ." *Hannity & Colmes,* Fox News Channel, August 25, 2005.

p. 31   "Environmentalists can be dismissed as . . ." Coulter, *Godless,* 23.

p. 31   "the affable Eva Braun . . ." ibid., 230.

p. 31   "Reporters have all the venom . . ." ibid., 119.

p. 31   "deeply ridiculous figure . . ." ibid., 48–49, 64.

p. 31   "If you were a Democrat . . ." Pitts, "She's the Hammer, Liberals Her Nail," *Baltimore Sun.*

p. 31   "If I were a Democrat . . ." ibid.

p. 32   "somebody to put rat poisoning . . ." Tim Grieve, "Ann Coulter: Someone Should Poison Justice Stevens," Salon.com, January 27, 2006, http://www.salon.com/politics/war_room/2006/01/27/coulter /index.html (last visited on August 25, 2006).

p. 32   "She could never decide . . ." Freedland, "Coulterisms: An Apalling Magic," *Guardian Unlimited.*

p. 32   "Congresswoman Maxine Waters . . ." Ann Coulter, "Big Foot, Scoop Jackson Democrats, And Other Myths," AnnCoulter.com, August 9, 2006, http://www.anncoulter.com/cgi-local/article.cgi?article=142 (last visited on August 25, 2006).

p. 32   "Her children knew she's sleeping . . ." MSNBC, September 12, 1997.

p. 33   "Still just a right wing congressional aide . . ." Eric Alterman, "What Liberal Media? Bias, Slander and BS," AmericanProgress.org, http://www.americanprogress.org/site/pp.asp?c=biJRJ8OVF&b=35123 (last visited on August 29, 2006).

p. 33   "Ann was ultimately fired . . ." ibid.

p. 33   "Coulter's column in the *National Review Online* . . ." Ann Coulter, "This is War, We should invade their countries," *National Review On-line,* September 13, 2001, http://www.nationalreview.com/coulter /coulter.shtml (last visited on August 29, 2006).

p. 33   "Congress could pass a law tomorrow . . ." "The Wisdom of Ann Coulter," *Washington Monthly.*

p. 33   "We ended the relationship . . ." Jonah Goldberg, "L'Affaire Coulter, Goodbye to all of that," *National Review Online,* October 3, 2001, http://www.nationalreview.com/nr_comment/nr_comment100301. shtml (last visited on August 29, 2006).

p. 33   "girly boys . . ." "The Wisdom of Ann Coulter," *Washington Monthly*.

p. 33   "She earned the ire of many veterans . . ." A.Z., "The world according to Coulter," MediaMatters.com, October 4, 2004, http://mediamatters .org/items/200410040009 (last visited on August 29, 2006).

p. 34   "You know she used to go out with Bob Guccione Jr. . . ." John Cloud, "Ms. Right; She is quite possibly the most divisive figure in the public eye. But love her or hate her, you don't know Ann Coulter," *Time*, April 25, 2005, 32.

p. 35   "Let's say I go out every night . . ." *Rivera Live*, CNBC, June 7, 2000.

p. 35   "There are entire websites . . ." "Political Humor," http://politicalhumor .about.com/library/images/blpic-coulteradamsapple.htm (last visited on August 29, 2006).

CHAPTER 3: COULTER CULTURE

p. 37   "Even Islamic terrorists . . ." Ann Coulter, *Slander: Liberal Lies about the American Right* (Crown Publishers, 2002).

p. 37   "Her latest one was to call Al Gore gay," "On MSNBC, Coulter Called Gore a 'Total Fag,' While Matthews Said 'We'd Love to Have Her Back,'" MediaMatters.org July 27, 2006, http://mediamatters.org /items/200607280001 (last visited on August 29, 2006).

p. 37   "Bill Clinton . . . homosexual," ibid.

p. 37   "college liberals . . . death penalty'" "Ann Coulter," MediaMatters.org, http://mediamatters.org/items/200507290007 (last visited on August 29, 2006).

p. 38   "I say to amuse myself . . ." "Things Fall Apart (Part 3)!: Cloud Has Mastered a Standard Script—With Coulter It's Just Good Solid Fun," DailyHowler.com April 21, 2005, http://www.dailyhowler.com /dh042105.shtml (last visited on August 29, 2006).

p. 38   "If the primary effect of the media . . ." Neal Gabler, *Life: The Movie* (Vintage Books, 2000).

p. 39   "George Soros can compare Bush to Hitler . . ." "Soros Likens Bush to Nazi," NewsMax.com, November 11, 2003, http://www.newsmax .com/archives/ic/2003/11/11/102820.shtml (last visited on August 29, 2006).

p. 40   "*Los Angeles Times* columnist Tim Rutten . . ." *Larry King Live,* CNN, June 12, 2006.

p. 41   "A word to those of you . . ." Ann Coulter, "Godless Causes Liberals to Pray . . . For a Book Burning," Townhall.com, July 21, 2006, http://www.townhall.com/columnists/AnnCoulter/2006/06/21/godless _causes_liberals_to_pray for_a_book_burning (last visited on August 29, 2006).

p. 42   "These broads are millionaires . . ." Coulter, *Godless,* 103.

p. 43   "Beginning with an interview with Matt Lauer on *Today. . .*" *Today,* NBC, June 6, 2006.

p. 43   "Three quarters of the respondents . . ." "Do You Approve of the Personal Attacks Used in Ann Coulter's New Book?" *O'Reilly Poll Results,* https://www.billoreilly.com/surveyarchive?action=viewResults &surveyID=3711, premium membership needed to access link (last viewed on August 29, 2006).

p. 45   "not just her one shot . . ." Ann Coulter, "This Is War," AnnCoulter.com, September 13, 2001, http://www.nationalreview .com/coulter/coulter.shtml (last visited on August 29, 2006).

p. 45   "Bumper sticker idea . . ." Ann Coulter, "*Newsweek* Dissembled, Muslims Dismembered!" AnnCoulter.com, May 18, 2005, http://www .anncoulter.com/cgi-local/article.cgi?article=55 (last visited on August 29, 2006).

p. 45   "The rioting Muslims claim they are upset . . ." Ann Coulter, "Calvin and Hobbes—And Mohammed," AnnCoulter.com, February 8, 2006, http://www.townhall.com/columnists/AnnCoulter/2006/02 /08/calvin_and_hobbes_—_and_muhammad (last visited on August 29, 2006).

p. 45 "indoor plumbing . . ." ibid.

p. 45 "not a car-burning cult . . ." ibid.

p. 45 "Grow up, would you?'" Ann Coulter, "Muslim Bites Dog," AnnCoulter.com, February 15, 2006, http://www.anncoulter.com /cgi-local/article.cgi?article=100 (last visited on August 29, 2006).

p. 45 "Islamic fascists kill people . . ." Ann Coulter, "Terrorists Win: De- odorant Banned from Airplanes," AnnCoulter.com, August 16, 2006, http://www.anncoulter.com/cgi-local/article.cgi?article=143 (last vis- ited on August 29, 2006).

p. 46 "but that's still millions of people . . ." Jonathan Freedland, "An Ap- palling Magic," *Guardian Unlimited*, May 17, 2003, http://www .guardian.co.uk/usa/story/0,12271,957670,00.html (last visited on August 29, 2006).

p. 46 "white paraplegics in wheelchairs . . ." ibid.

p. 46 "Not so fast, Mohammed . . ." ibid.

p. 47 "women as part of the plot . . ." "Pakistan Link in British Terrorist Plot," CBS News, August 11, 2006, http://www.cbsnews.com/stories /2006/08/10/world/main1880791.shtml (last visited on August 29, 2006).

p. 47 "The recent arrests in Britain . . ." Steve Bates, "Concern and Relief Mixed with Fear and Cynicism," *Guardian Unlimited*, August 11, 2006, http://www.guardian.co.uk/terrorism/story/0,,1842278,00.html (last visited on August 29, 2006).

p. 48 "Paula Jones case . . ." "Ann Coulter," SourceWatch.org, August 9, 2006, http://sourcewatch.org/index.php?title=Ann_Coulter (last vis- ited on August 29, 2006).

p. 48 "Senate Judiciary Committee . . ." ibid.

p. 48   "most of them are in the middle . . ." Morris P. Fiorina with Samuel
         Abrams and Jeremy Pope, *Culture War?* 2d ed. (Pearson Education,
         Inc., 2006).

p. 49   "Avowed liberal . . . avowed conservatives . . ." ibid., 47.

p. 50   "you still need those 4s to win . . ." "Political Ideology," General So-
         cial Surveys, The National Opinion Research Center at the Univer-
         sity of Chicago, 1998, latest data available at http://webapp.icpsr
         .umich.edu/GSS (last visited on August 29, 2006).

p. 50   "Not moral values . . ." "The 2005 Political Typology: Beyond
         Blue v. Red," Pew Research Center, May 2005, http://people-
         press.org/reports/pdf/242.pdf (last visited on August 29, 2006);
         see also "Americans Continue to Say Iraq is the Nation's Top Prob-
         lem," The Gallup Poll, July 2006 Results, http://poll
         .gallup.com/content/default.aspx?ci=23761&pg=1 (last visited on
         August 29, 2006); *see also* "Keys to the Midterm Election: Part II,"
         The Gallup Poll, December 2002 Results, http://poll.gallup
         .com/content/default.aspx?ci=7465 (last visited on August 29,
         2006).

p. 50   "most Americans tend to be tolerant, moderate . . ." "Abortion,"
         The Gallup Poll, April 1975 to May 2006 results, http://
         poll.gallup.comcontent/default.aspx?ci=1576; *see also* "Civil Liber-
         ties: Gays and Lesbians," General Social Surveys, 1998 Results, lat-
         est data available at http://webapp.icpsr.umich.edu/GSS (last
         visited on August 29, 2006).

p. 50   "IQ above a toaster . . ." *Beyond the News,* Fox News Channel, June
         4, 2000.

p. 51   "the only group smaller than hers . . ." "Political Ideology," General
         Social Surveys, The National Opinion Research Center at the Uni-
         versity of Chicago, 1998, latest data available at http://webapp.icpsr
         .umich.edu/GSS (last visited on August 29, 2006).

p. 51   "No liberal has to have security . . ." *The O'Reilly Factor,* Fox News Channel, December 1, 2005.

CHAPTER 4: THE INTERVIEW

p. 54   "Ann Coulter, good morning . . ." NBC *Today Show* Interview: http://youtube.com/watch?v=4xv05FK69KU (last visited on August 29, 2006).

p. 66   "keep this party going . . ." George Gurley, "Ann Coulter Ecstatic: Enemies Stoke Sales—'They're Like My Pets,'" *New York Observer,* July 3, 2006, http://www.observer.com/printpage.asp?iid=13036&ic =New+York+World (last accessed on August 29, 2006).

CHAPTER 5: THE AFTERMATH

p. 67   "I'm a huge Ann Coulter fan . . ." *Michael Graham Show,* WTKK FM, Boston, MA, June 6, 2006.

p. 67   "The core of Coulter's point . . ." Tim Grieve, "Ann Coulter and those 'millionaire broads' from 9/11," "War Room," Salon.com, June 6, 2006.

p. 68   "Like an insecure child . . ." Rep. Anthony D. Weiner (D-9th District, NY), official Press Release, June 6, 2006, http://www.house .gov/list/press/ny09_weiner/911widows.html (last visited on August 29, 2006).

p. 68   "I want to focus in on . . ." *The Situation with Tucker Carlson,* CNN, June 6, 2006.

p. 69   "The next morning . . ." "Coulter the Cruel," New York *Daily News,* June 7, 2006.

p. 69   "Having my husband burn alive . . ." Adam Lisberg, "Massive Chip on her Coulter," New York *Daily News,* June 6, 2006, http://www

.nydailynews.com/front/story/424405p-358034c.html (last visited on August 29, 2006).

p. 69   "seriously deranged . . ." *Howard Stern Show,* Sirius Satellite Radio, June 7, 2006.

p. 70   "Ann Coulter Lambasts 9/11 Widows in New Book' " *Associated Press,* June 6, 2006.

p. 70   "Vicious, mean-spirited . . ." Delvin Barrett, "Sen. Clinton: Coulter's Remarks 'Vicious,' " ABC NEWS, June 7, 2006, http://www .abcnews.go.com/GMA/wireStory?id=2051534 (last visited on August 29, 2006).

p. 70   "If she's worried about . . ." Ann Coulter, as reported on DrudgeReport .com, www.drudgereport.com, June 7, 2006.

p. 71   "a leech trying to turn a profit . . ." Official Press Release of NJ Assemblywomen Joan Quigley and Linda Stender, "Quigley/Stender Call on NJ Merchants to Boycott 'Vicious' Coulter Book," June 7, 2006.

p. 71   "I was really stunned . . ." "Ann Coulter Attacks 9/11 Widows," *Associated Press,* June 7, 2006, http://www.cbsnews.com/stories/2006 /06/07/entertainment/main1690954.shtml (last visited on August 29, 2006).

p. 71   "went beyond all limits . . ." Carl McGowan, "Coulter Host Takes Heat for Author's Visit," *Newsday,* June 9, 2006, Rep. Peter King (R-3rd District, NY): http://peteking.house.gov/index.cfm? ContentID=270&ParentID=0&SectionID=41&SectionTree=41&lnk =b&ItemID=266 (last visited on August 29, 2006).

p. 71   "It crosses the line into incivility . . ." *World News Tonight,* ABC, June 7, 2006. Also *see* MediaMatters.org, http://mediamatters.org/items /200606130001, June 12, 2006 (last visited on August 29, 2006).

p. 71   "It's the ugliness of the charge . . ." NBC *Nightly News,* NBC, June 7, 2006.

p. 71   "I think Ann Coulter is getting . . ." *Hardball with Chris Matthews,* MSNBC, June 7, 2006.

p. 72   "Stop Ann Coulter before . . ." Bill O'Reilly, "Stop Ann Coulter Before She Bombs Again," FoxNews.com, June 8, 2006: http://www .foxnews.com/story/0,2933,198687,00.html (last visited on August 29, 2006).

p. 72   "I think this kind of stuff . . ." Bill O'Reilly as reported by Jackson Thoreau on OpEdNews.com, June 9, 2006, http://www.opednews .com/articles/opedne_jackson__060609_liberal_and_proud_3a_l.htm (last visited on August 29, 2006).

p. 72   "drag-queen-fascist-impersonator . . ." Andrew Sullivan, "Ann or Adolf?" *The Daily Dish,* http://time.blogs.com/daily_dish/2006/06 /ann_or_adolf.html (last visited on August 29, 2006).

p. 72   "Clinton Calls Comments on Widows . . ." Raymond Hernandez, "Clinton Calls Comments on Widows Mean-Spirited," *New York Times,* June 8, 2006.

p. 73   "What did you make of . . ." *Imus in the Morning,* MSNBC, June 9, 2006.

p. 75   "I'm attacking the whole technique . . ." *The Radio Factor with Bill O'Reilly,* Westwood One, June 8, 2006.

p. 75   "You are basically . . ." *Lou Dobbs Tonight,* CNN, June 8, 2006.

p. 75   "Well, Ann Coulter is a national treasure . . ." *The O'Reilly Factor,* Fox News Channel, June 8, 2006.

p. 76   "Do you think for a one second . . ." *Hannity & Colmes,* Fox News Channel, June 8, 2006.

p. 76   Jessica Heslam, "Liberal Dose of Outrage from 'Merry' 9/11 Widows; They Rip Controversial Conservative Coulter," *Boston Herald,* June 8, 2006.

p. 77   Adam Lisberg, "Blather Sells, So Big Mouth Keeps Shoveling," New York *Daily News,* June 9, 2006, http://www.nydailynews.com/news /gossip/story/424996p-358516c.html (last visited on August 29, 2006).

p. 77 "The *Daily News* story . . ." Jonathan Lemire and Adam Lisberg, "Oh, Please, Tell Me How Bad I Am," New York *Daily News,* June 8, 2006, http://www.nydailynews.com/news/gossip/story/424617p-358242c.html (last visited on August 29, 2006).

p. 77 "Ann Coulter owes an apology . . ." DailyKos.com, http://www .dailykos.com/storyonly/2006/6/12/222826/449 (last visited on August 29, 2006).

p. 77 "If she really believes this . . ." Cliff Kincaid, "The Coulter Fallout," NewsWithViews.com, June 24, 2006, http://www.newswithviews .com/Kincaid/cliff102.htm (last visited on August 29, 2006).

p. 77 "It seems to me that there are so many . . ." *Scarborough Country,* MSNBC, June 12, 2006.

p. 77 "And Mickey Kaus . . ." Mickey Kaus, "Kos Defends Coulter," Slate.com, July 11, 2006, http://www.slate.com/id/2145017 (last visited on August 29, 2006).

p. 77 "If you read some of what . . ." *The O'Reilly Factor,* Fox News Channel, June 7, 2006.

p. 77 "The woman isn't a pariah . . ." Meghan Daum, "Coulter's a satirist— really?" *Los Angeles Times,* June 24, 2006, http://www.latimes.com/news /opinion/commentary/la-oe-daum24jun24,1,4525785.column (last visited on August 29, 2006).

p. 78 "She's my heroine . . ." L. Ryan, letter, *Washington Times,* June 8, 2006.

p. 78 "Ann Coulter is tough as nails . . ." "Q: What is Your Opinion of Ann Coulter?" TheHill.com, June 20, 2006, http://thehill.com /thehill/export/TheHill/Features/CapitalLiving/062006_q.html (last visited on August 29, 2006).

p. 78 "Ann is an intelligent . . ." ibid.

p. 78 "Simply put, it is about decency . . ." ibid.

p. 78 "I don't spend much time thinking . . ." ibid.

p. 78 "I've never met her . . ." ibid.

p. 78 "I wrote the book to get a reaction . . ." *Your World with Neil Cavuto,* Fox News Channel, June 8, 2006.

p. 78 "Harpies and witches is what I think . . ." John Cloud, interview with Ann Coulter, "Ann Coulter Fires Back," *Time,* June 8, 2006, http://www.time.com/time/nation/article/0,8599,1202110,00.html (last visited on August 29, 2006).

p. 79 "Well, because, unfortunately . . ." *Larry King Live,* CNN, June 12, 2006.

p. 80 "When the staff of *Today* . . ." Howard Kurtz, "The Coulter Conundrum," *Washington Post,* June 12, 2006, http://www.washingtonpost .com/wp-dyn/content/article/2006/06/11/AR2006061100945_pf.html (last visited on August 29, 2006).

p. 80 "Have you no shame?" *NBC Nightly News,* NBC, June 7, 2006.

p. 81 "This is of course exactly what she wants . . ." Gaby Wood quoting Joe Klein, "Lethally Blonde," *The Observer,* June 11, 2006, http://observer .guardian.co.uk/review/story/0,,1794552,00.html (last visited on August 29, 2006).

p. 82 "I do want to pause to enjoy . . ." *Kudlow and Company,* CNBC, June 15, 2006.

p. 82 "The fact that Ann's book . . ." *Hannity & Colmes,* Fox News Channel, June 16, 2006.

p. 86 "It is the part of the chapter . . ." *Lou Dobbs Tonight,* CNN June 8, 2006.

p. 86 "All right. The book's title . . ." *The Tonight Show with Jay Leno,* NBC June 14, 2006.

p. 87 "Always fascinating . . ." ibid.

p. 87 "Always fun . . ." *Today,* NBC, June 6, 2006.

p. 87 "Have you no shame?'" Brian Williams, *NBC Nightly News,* NBC, June 7, 2006.

p. 88 "She made news . . ." Howard Kurtz, "The Coulter Conundrum," *Washington Post,* June 12, 2006.

CHAPTER 6: THE WILLIE HORTON STORY AND RACE POLITICS

p. 92   "Is Ann teaching history . . ." Lev Grossman, "10 Questions for Ann Coulter," *Time,* July 7, 2003, http://www.time.com/time/magazine /article/0,9171,1101030714-463080,00.html (last visited on August 29, 2006).

p. 92   "The 'backbone of the Democratic Party . . ." Morrie Friendly, ed., "The Wit and Wisdom of Ann Coulter," AmericanPolitics.com, September 4, 2004, http://www.americanpolitics.com/20020205Coulter .html (last visited on August 29, 2006).

p. 94   "Upwards of 80 percent of Americans . . ." Kavan Peterson, "Death Penalty: Lethal Injection on Trial," Stateline.org, March 23, 3006, http://www.stateline.org/live/details/story?contentId=98349 (last visited on August 29, 2006).

p. 97   "He 'confessed' in 1983 . . ." "Earl Washington," InnocenceProject .org, http://innocenceproject.org/case/display_profile.php?id=80 (last visited on August 28, 2006).

p. 98   "The only reason the Democrats cried racism . . ." Ann Coulter, *Godless: The Church of Liberalism* (Crown Forum, 2006), 71.

p. 98   "That's why he was the one . . ." Stewart Fleming, "Dukakis to Focus on Class and Race in Run-Up to Poll," *Financial Times,* October 24, 1988, at Sec. I, American News, 8.

p. 99   "This is how the *Financial Times* . . ." ibid.

p. 100   "Ann argues that Willie Horton wasn't a 'metaphor . . ." Coulter, *Godless,* 61.

p. 100   "She says it wasn't the age-old 'image . . ." ibid.

p. 100   "The Bush campaign surely wished . . ." ibid.

p. 102   "There is nothing more painful to me . . ." Mike Royko, "Politically Incorrect but Right on Target," *Chicago Tribune,* November 30, 1993, at NEWS, 3, Zone N.

p. 102   "As of 2001, I found reports..." U.S. Department of Justice, "Prevalence of Imprisonment in the U.S. Population," Bureau of Justice Statistics, Special Report, August 2003, NCJ 197976, http://www.ojp.usdoj.gov/bjs/abstract/piusp01.htm (last visited on August 28, 2006).

p. 102   "Some criminals happen to be black..." Coulter, *Godless,* 71.

p. 104   "If black people kill black people..." Terry Eastland, "Redeeming the race card—Pres Clinton's relations with African Americans," *National Review,* September 2, 1996, http://www.findarticles.com /p/articles/mi_m1282/is_n16_v48/ai_18614088/pg_1 (last visited on August 28, 2006).

p. 105   "Whether it is building prisons..." Coulter, *Godless,* 43.

p. 106   "Four years later, during the New Hampshire..." Sharon LaFraniere, "Governor's Camp Feels His Record on Crime Can Stand the Heat," *Washington Post,* October 5, 1992, A6.

p. 110   "The same chancellor..." "Black Student Enrollment at UCLA Plunges," National Public Radio, July 26, 2006, http:// ethnicmajority.com/blog/more.php?ID=101 (last accessed on August 26, 2006).

CHAPTER 7: THE MORAL MAJORITY IS US

p. 113   "No liberal cause is defended with more dishonesty than abortion..." Ann Coulter, *Godless: The Church of Liberalism* (Crown Forum, 2006), 78, 85.

p. 114   "Partial birth abortion..." Gail Schoettler, "Slogans Frame Political Debate," DenverPost.com, July 8, 2006, http://www.denverpost.com /schoettler/ci_4021192 (last accessed on August 15, 2006).

p. 114   "It's the only issue she can win..." "Abortion and Birth Control," PollingReport.com survey of state and national polls from Harris and other organizations on partial birth abortion from 1998 to 2006, http://www.pollingreport.com/abortion.htm (last visited on August 29, 2006).

p. 117 "a little higher than the national average . . ." Morris P. Fiorina with Samuel Abrams and Jeremy Pope, *Culture War?* 2d ed. (Pearson Education, Inc., 2006), 84–85.

p. 117 "80–90 percent . . ." ibid, 84.

p. 117 "abortion is murder . . ." Clark D. Forsythe, "An Unnecessary Evil," First Things, February 2003, http://www.firstthings.com/ftissues /ft0302/opinion/forsythe.html (last visited on August 29, 2006).

p. 117 "support the United States Supreme Court . . ." "Would you like to see the Supreme Court overturn its 1973 *Roe v. Wade* decision concerning abortion, or not?" The Gallup Poll, 1/22/2006, http://brain .gallup.com/documents/question.aspx?question=155843&Advanced =0&SearchConType=1&SearchTypeAll=roe%20v.%20wade (last visited on August 29, 2006).

p. 117 "and that Republicans and Democrats . . ." Fiorina, et al., *Culture War?* 2d ed. 85–88.

p. 117 "The fact that the differences among Americans . . ." ibid.

p. 118 "Able to get an abortion if her health is endangered . . ." "Abortion," The Gallup Poll, April 1975 to May 2006 results, http://poll.gallup .com/content/default.aspx?ci=1576 (last visited on August 29, 2006).

p. 118 "If you ask, should a woman . . ." ibid.

p. 118 "If Ann starts going on . . ." ibid.

p. 118 "They won't . . ." ibid.

p. 118 "On the issue of abortion . . ." ibid.

p. 118 "Surprise: it is the small minority . . ." ibid.; *see also* "Abortion Issue a Minefield in Battleground States?" The Gallup Poll, April 2004, http://poll.gallup.com/content/default.aspx?ci=11221&pg=1 (last visited on August 29, 2006).

p. 119   "middle class situations . . ." "Abortion," The Gallup Poll, April 1975 to May 2006 results, http://poll.gallup.com/content/default.aspx?ci=1576 (last visited on August 29, 2006).

p. 119   "Remember those numbers. . ." Nick Castronovo, "Kerry Losing Ground with Key Demographics," *Northwestern Chronicle,* October 8, 2004, http://www.chron.org/tools/viewart.php?artid=1057 (last visited on August 29, 2006).

p. 120   "Abortion is not a voting issue . . ." "Abortion Issue a Minefield in Battleground States?" The Gallup Poll, April 2004.

p. 120   "The Supreme Court describes the abortion question . . ." *Planned Parenthood of Southeastern Pennsylvania v. Casey,* 505 U.S. 833 (1992).

p. 120   "see abortion as murder but support *Roe* . . ." "Abortion," The Gallup Poll, April 1975 to May 2006 results.

p. 121   "But liberals are right . . ." Gale Schoettler, "Slogans Frame Political Debate," DenverPost.com, July 8, 2006, http://www.denverpost.com/schoettler/ci_4021192 (last visited on August 29, 2006).

p. 122   "She goes on . . ." Coulter, *Godless,* 80.

p. 123   "The advocates of the laws tend to argue . . ." Natalie E. Roche, M.D., "Surgical Management of Abortion," emedicine.com, June 16, 2006, http://www.emedicine.com/med/topic3312 .htm (last visited on August 29, 2006).

p. 123   "Opponents argue . . ." Lyle Denniston, "Ban Voted on a Form of Abortion," *Boston Globe,* http://www.boston.com/news/nation/articles/2003/10/22/ban_voted_on_a_form_of_abortion (last visited on August 29, 2006).

p. 123   "The vagueness of the language . . ." *Stenberg v. Carhart,* 530 U.S. 914 (2000).

p. 123   "The other reason . . ." ibid.

p. 123   "They have done this even though . . ." ibid.

p. 124   "case coming before the court . . ." *Gonzales v. Carhart,* 126 S. Ct. 1607 (2006).

p. 124   "harder to gain *access* to abortion . . ." "Parental Consent Abortion Law Struck Down in Arizona," *Feminist Majority Foundation,* June 10, 1999, http://www.feminist.org/news/newsbyte/uswirestory.asp?id=503, last accessed on August 25, 2006; *see also* J. Lewis and Jon O. Shimabukurro, "Abortion Law Development," *Almanac of Policy Issues,* January 28, 2001, http://www.policyalmanac.org/culture/archive /crs_abortion_overview.shtml (last visited on August 29, 2006).

p. 125   "Coulter herself speculates . . ." Coulter, *Godless,* 90-91.

p. 125   "In the meantime . . ." "The Last Abortion Clinic," *Frontline* of *PBS,* http://www.pbs.org/wgbh/pages/frontline/clinic/view (last visited on August 29, 2006).

p. 125   "That number is up . . ." Tom Strode, "Life Digest: Closing of Abortion Clinics Continue," BPnews.com, August 21, 2006, http://bpnews .net/bpnews.asp?ID=23824 (last visited on August 29, 2006).

p. 125   "Excerpt from testimony delivered to the Texas State Legislature . . ." *Uncommon Misconception,* testimony available at http:// uncommonmisconception.typepad.com/home/2005/04/out_of_the _dark.html (last visited on August 29, 2006).

p. 131   "In 1979, in *Bellotti v. Baird* . . ." *Bellotti v. Baird,* 444 U.S. 887 (1979).

p. 131   "The thinking, at least . . ." ibid.

p. 131   "The Court also said . . ." ibid.

p. 131   "So the Court wrote a road map . . ." ibid.

p. 132   "The Senate voted to make that ride . . ." Carl Huse, "Senate Removes Abortion Option for Young Girls," *New York Times,* July 26, 2006, A1.

p. 132   "It was all part of another pre-midterm effort . . ." ibid.

p. 132   "Senator Diane Feinstein . . ." "A Planned Parenthood Report on the Administration and Congress," PlannedParenthood.org,

http://72.14.209.104/search?q=cache:fVpg0Gs0W9AJ:www.planned
parenthood.org/library/facts/030114_waronwomen.html+senator+
diane+feinstein+introduces+amendment+to+abortion+legislation+
exempting+grandparents,+clergy&hl=en&gl=us&ct=clnk&cd=2
(last visited on August 29, 2006).

p. 133   "There will still be five votes for the 'Kennedy' position . . ." *Planned
Parenthood of Southeastern Pennsylvania v. Casey,* 505 U.S. 833 (1992).

p. 133   "Third, note that overruling *Roe* . . ." ibid.

p. 134   "Talk about Plan B . . ." Jyoti Thottam, "Why Wal-Mart Agreed to
Plan B," *Time,* March 3, 2006, http://www.time.com/time/business
/article/0,8599,1169740,00.html (last visited on August 29, 2006).

p. 134   "The kind that said that they feared the anti-abortion people . . ." ibid.

p. 134   "So even though they stocked birth control . . ." ibid.

p. 134   "Planned Parenthood announced a boycott . . ." "Wal-Mart's Refusal
to Stock the 'Morning-After' Pill," ReligiousTolerance.org, http://
www.religioustolerance.org/abo_walm.htm (last visited on August 29,
2006).

p. 134   "Wal-Mart to stock Plan B . . ." Jyoti Thottam, "Why Wal-Mart
Agreed to Plan B," *Time,* March 3, 2006.

p. 134   "The vote on embryonic stem cell research . . ." Sheryl Gay Stolberg,
"Senate Appears Poised for a Showdown with the President," New
York Times, July 16, 2006, Section 1.

p. 135   "The bill was drafted by a Republican . . ." ibid.

p. 135   "It didn't apply to any of the controversial issues . . ." ibid.

p. 135   "It only dealt with frozen embryos . . ." ibid.

p. 135   "All the bill said . . ." ibid.

p. 135   "Polls taken before the vote . . ." "Stem Cell Research," PollingReport
.com, http://www.pollingreport.com/science.htm (last visited on August 29, 2006).

p. 135   "A majority of both Houses of Congress . . ." Sheryl Gay Stolberg, "Senate Appears Poised for a Showdown with the President," *New York Times,* July 16, 2006.

p. 135   "The president, surrounded by his choice of victims . . ." Sheryl Gay Stolberg, "First Bush Veto Maintains Limit on Stem Cell Use," *New York Times,* July 20, 2006, A1.

p. 135   "Democrats, not to be outdone . . ." Jodi Rudoren, "Stem Cell Work Gets States' Aid after Bush Veto," *New York Times,* July 25, 2006, A1.

p. 135   "Meanwhile Ann had her own list . . ." Coulter, *Godless,* 197.

p. 135   "which she actually 'copied' . . ." "Complete List of Ann Coulter Plagiarism Allegations," TMPMuckraker.com, July 7, 2006, http://www.tpmmuckraker.com/archives/001070.php.

p. 136   "I'll be damned . . ." Lev Grossman, "10 Questions for Ann Coulter," *Time,* July 7, 2003, http://www.time.com/time/magazine/article/0,9171,1101030714-463080,00.html?cnn=yes (last visited on August 29, 2006).

p. 136   "The consensus in the country today is against gay marriage . . ." "Single U.S. Public Opinion Polls: Same Sex Marriage and Civil Unions," Tolerance.org, 2006, http://www.religioustolerance.org/hom_marp.htm (last visited on August 15, 2006).

p. 136   "a substantial majority of Americans don't think the issue is important enough . . ." Shailagh Murray, "Gay Marriage Amendment Fails in Senate," *Washington Post,* June 8, 2006, http://www.washingtonpost.com/wp-dyn/content/article/2006/06/07/AR2006060700830.html (last visited on August 29, 2006).

p. 136   "There is today a growing consensus . . ." "Civil Liberties: Gays and Lesbians," *General Social Surveys,* 1998 (latest data available), http://webapp.icpsr.umich.edu/GSS (last visited on August 1, 2006).

p. 136   "the United States Supreme Court ruled in *Bowers v. Hardwick . . .*" *Bowers v. Hardwick,* 478 U.S. 186 (1986).

p. 136   "Finally, in June 2003 . . ." *Lawrence v. Texas,* 539 U.S. 558 (2003).

p. 136   "The Christian Right declared it . . ." "News from the Right 2003–2004," *People for the American Way,* June 2003, http://www .pfaw.org/pfaw/general/default.aspx?oid=10852 (last visited on August 29, 2006).

p. 136   "As the Reverend Lou Sheldon . . ." ibid.

p. 137   "Or as my friend, conservative Moral Majority Reverend Cal Thomas . . ." Cal Thomas, "End of the Constitution?" Jewish WorldReview.com, July 1, 2003, http://www.jewishworldreview .com/cols/thomas070103.asp (last visited on August 29, 2006).

p. 137   "One poll found . . ." Fiorina, et al., *Culture War?,* 110.

p. 137   "Most Americans, according to the most recent polls . . ." "Gallup Poll Social Series—Values and Beliefs, Question qn39p-Form A," *The Gallup Poll,* May 2, 2005, http://brain.gallup.com/documents /question.aspx?question=153023&Advanced=0&SearchConType=1 &SearchTypeAll=same%20sex%20wrong (last visited on August 29, 2006).

p. 137   "In fact, solid and growing majorities . . ." "Civil Liberties: Gays and Lesbians," *General Social Surveys,* 1998.

p. 137   "Indeed, a majority of Americans . . ." ibid.

p. 137   "there are very small differences . . ." Fiorina, et al., *Culture War?,* 110.

p. 137   "Moreover, the regional differences . . ." ibid.

p. 137   "Indeed, even 40 percent of weekly churchgoers . . ." ibid.

p. 137   "What all of this suggests . . ." ibid.

p. 138   "Fight about the basics . . ." ibid.

p. 138   "I look for serious commentary . . ." "MSNBC Hyped Coulter Interview in Which She Attacked Pres. Clinton as a 'Latent Homosexual,'"

MediaMatters.org, July 26, 2006, http://mediamatters.org/items /200607260007 (last visited on August 29, 2006).

p. 138   "Everyone else . . ." Fiorina, et al., *Culture War?*, 110.

p. 138   "or as she calls it, 'Queer Theory.'" Coulter, *Godless*, 178.

p. 138   "What she chooses to address . . ." ibid, 180.

p. 139   "The campaign against heterosexual AIDS . . ." Micheal Fumento, *The Myth of Heterosexual AIDS: How a Tragedy Has Been Distorted by the Media and Partisan Politics* (Regnery, 1993).

p. 139   "It was thoroughly exposed . . ." ibid.

p. 139   "she should have been 'distributing condoms' . . ." Coulter, *Godless*, 179.

p. 139   "she called Bill Clinton gay . . ." "MSNBC Hyped Coulter Interview in Which She Attacked Pres. Clinton as a 'Latent Homosexual,'" MediaMatters.org, July 26, 2006, http://mediamatters.org/items /200607260007 (last visited on August 29, 2006).

p. 141   "Was this, as it was described by one writer . . ." "Coulter: Clinton a Latent Homosexual," *Riehl World View*, July 25, 2006, http://www .riehlworldview.com/carnivorous_conservative/2006/07/coulter_clinton .html (last visited on August 29, 2006).

p. 141   "Here is the follow-up to the Donny Deutsch interview . . ." *Kudlow and Company*, CNBC, July 28, 2006.

p. 142   "Slate.com's Mickey Kaus . . ." "Hillary Spins the *Times*," Slate.com, August 8, 2006, http://www.slate.com/id/2146861 (last visited on August 29, 2006).

p. 143   "I wonder if tortured gay teenagers . . ." *CNN Headline News*, CNN, June 13, 2003.

p. 145   "In another follow-up . . ." "On MSNBC, Coulter Called Gore a 'Total Fag,' While Chris Matthews Said 'We'd Love to Have Her Back,'" MediaMatters.org, July 27, 2006, http://mediamatters.org/items /200607280001 (last visited on August 29, 2006).

p. 145 "It was a joke . . ." *Hardball with Chris Matthews,* MSNBC, July 27, 2006.

p. 146 "She ridiculed her too . . ." "Ann Coulter's 'Godless' Triumph," FoxNews.com, June 16, 2006, http://www.foxnews.com/story /0,2933,199824,00.html (last visited on August 29, 2006).

p. 146 "No one is quite sure how many gay and lesbian voters there are pe-riod . . ." Andrew Lavallee, "Log Cabin Republicans Fault Platform Withholding Bush Endorsement, for Now at Least, Group Releases Critical TV Ad," GayCityNews.com, September 2–9, 2004, http://www.gaycitynews.com/gcn_336/logcabin.html (last visited on August 29, 2006).

CHAPTER 8: SEX

p. 147 "If you don't hate Clinton . . .'" "The wisdom of Ann Coulter (con-servative commentator)," *Washington Monthly,* November 1, 2001, No. 11, Vol. 33, 18.

p. 147 "We're now at the point . . ." *Equal Time,* CNBC, August 19, 1998.

p. 147 "He was a very good . . ." George Gurley, "Coulter 2005," *New York Observer,* January 10, 2005, Media & Society, NY World, 2.

p. 148 "I have always been unabashedly anti-murder' . . . " Ann Coulter, "Lie down with strippers, wake up with pleas," AnnCoulter.com, April 19, 2006, http://www.anncoulter.com/cgi-local/article.cgi? article=109 (last visited on August 29, 2006).

p. 152 "The *Los Angeles Times* described the case . . ." Bradley Olson and Andrea F. Siegel, "Naval Academy Football Player Not Guilty of Rape; A court-martial jury finds him guilty of two lesser charges in the case, which involved a fellow midshipman," *Los Angeles Times,* July 21, 2006, A19.

p. 154 "Ann is arguing for . . ." *Hannity & Colmes,* Fox News Channel, May 19, 2006.

p. 158 "However the Duke lacrosse rape . . .'" Ann Coulter, "Lie down with strippers, wake up with pleas," AnnCoulter.com, April 19, 2006.

p. 159   "There was an important Pennsylvania..." *Commonwealth v. Berkowitz,* 641 A.2d 1161 (PA 1994).

p. 163   "She writes: 'In addition to...'" Ann Coulter, "Party of Rapist Proud to Be Godless," AnnCoulter.com, June 19, 2006, http://www.anncoulter .org/cgi-local/welcome.cgi (last visited on August 29, 2006).

CHAPTER 9: PUBLIC SCHOOLS: THE NEXT BATTLEGROUND

p. 165   "Most Americans do not believe in teaching..." "Gallup Poll Social Series—Work and Education," Questions 35a–c, The Gallup Poll, August 8, 2005, http://brain.gallup.com/documents/question .aspx?question=154000&Advanced=0&SearchConType=1&Search TypeAll=creationism (last visited on August 21, 2006).

p. 167   "Most public schools are..." Ann Coulter, *Godless: The Church of Liberalism* (Crown Forum 2006), 169.

p. 168   "that 'reducing class size'..." ibid.

p. 168   "there's nothing the matter with teachers..." ibid., 171.

p. 169   "First, one has to ask whether..." Jerry Coyne, "Ann Coulter and Charles Darwin: Coultergeist," TalkReason.org, http://www.talkreason .org/articles/coultergeist.cfm (last visited on August 25, 2006).

p. 170   "the overwhelming majority of Americans don't believe..." "Would you say that you believe more in: the theory of creationism or the theory of evolution to explain the theory of the origin of human beings, or are you unsure?" The Gallup Poll, Feburary 19, 2001, http://brain.gallup.com/documents/question.aspx?question=69868 &Advanced=0&SearchConType=1&SearchTypeAll=believe%20in %20evolution (last visited on August 25, 2006).

p. 170   "Second, the legit scientists..." Jerry Coyne, "Ann Coulter and Charles Darwin: Coultergeist," TalkReason.org, http://www.talkreason .org/articles/coultergeist.cfm (last visited on August 25, 2006).

p. 170   "Her audience is the people in Kansas..." "Skeptics Lose Majority of Kansas Board of Education," CNN.com, August 2, 2006, http://www.cnn.com/2006/POLITICS/08/02/kansasevolution.ap (last visited on August 25, 2006).

p. 172 "Green Dot opened its first school" "About Us," Green DotPublicSchools.org, http://www.greendotpublicschools.org/aboutus (last visited on August 29, 2006).

p. 172 "In the fall of 2004, Green dot opened two more schools . . ." ibid.

p. 172 "The Green Dot schools now send . . ." "Results, Green Dot Public Schools," GreenDotPublicSchools.org, http://www.greendotpublicschools .org/results (last visited on August 29, 2006).

p. 172 "The schools are different also in that . . ." "School Model," GreenDotPublicSchools.org, http://www.greendotpublicschools.org /schoolmodel (last visited on August 29, 2006).

p. 172 "None of the schools has more than . . ." ibid.

p. 173 "Casey Wasserman of the Wasserman Family Foundation . . ." "Wasserman Foundation Gifts $6 Million to Green Dot Public Schools for High School Transformation Plan," GreenDotPublicSchools .org, http://www.greendotpublicschools.org/news/wassermangift.html (last visited on August 29, 2006).

p. 173 "Right now Steve Barr . . ." "Parents Union," GreenDotPublicSchools .org, http://www.smallschools.org (last visited on August 29, 2006).

p. 175 "The students at the schools that follow the six tenets . . ." "Results," GreenDotPublicSchools.org, http://www.greendotpublicschools.org /results (last visited on August 29, 2006).

p. 175 "Eighty percent of ninth graders . . ." ibid.

p. 180 "Ann describes the public schools as . . ." Coulter, Godless, 152.

CHAPTER 11: THE NEXT ANNS

p. 191 "She's a brunette Ann . . ." Michelle Malkin, "Just a Yellow Woman Doing a White Man's Job," MichelleMalkin.com, November 19,

2005, http://michellemalkin.com/archives/003955.htm (last visited on August 29, 2006).

p. 191   "The right-wing Asian pit bull . . ." H. Y. Nahm, "Michelle Malkin: The Radical Right's Asian Pitbull," Goldsea.com, http://goldsea.com /Personalities/Malkin/malkin.html (last visited on August 29, 2006).

p. 191   "Then, a student named Jesse Malkin decides . . ." Malkin, "Just a Yellow Woman Doing a White Man's Job," MichelleMalkin.com.

p. 192   "She told a reporter . . ." Nahm, "Michelle Malkin: The Radical Right's Asian Pitbull," Goldsea.com.

p. 192   "In 1999, the family moved . . ." MichelleMalkin.com, http:// michellemalkin.com/about.htm (last visited on August 29, 2006).

p. 193   "Freed from the restraints of staff writing . . ." Nahm, "Michelle Malkin: The Radical Right's Asian Pitbull." Goldsea.com.

p. 193   "As the headshot for her column . . ." Malkin, "MichelleMalkin.com.

p. 193   "It wasn't racism . . ." Michelle Malkin, *In Defense of Internment: The Case for 'Racial Profiling' in World War II and the War on Terror* (Regnery Publishing, 2003).

p. 193   "What else would you expect . . ." Michelle Malkin, *Invasion: How America Still Welcomes Terrorists, Criminals, and Other Foreign Menaces to Our Shores* (Regnery Publishing, 2002).

p. 194   "It's mostly a collection of columns . . ." Michelle Malkin, *Unhinged: Exposing Liberals Gone Wild* (Regnery Publishing 2005).

p. 194   "It was thoroughly interred . . ." "Muller and Robinson on Malkin," IsThatLegal.org, August 2004, http://www.isthatlegal.org /Muller_and_Robinson_on_Malkin.html (last visited on August 29, 2006).

p. 194   "As with Ann's McCarthy book," Ann Coulter, *Slander: Liberal Lies about the American Right* (Crown Publishers, 2002).

p. 194   "Even the late Chief Justice Rehnquist . . ." *Hamdi v. Rumsfeld,* 542 U.S. 507 (2004).

p. 194 "No one was rougher on poor Norm Mineta" "Michelle Malkin Defended WWII Internment, Racial Profiling Today; and Mineta's View 'Clouded' by His Internment," MediaMatters.org, August 11, 2004, http://mediamatters.org/items/200408110001 (last visited on August 29, 2006).

p. 194 "Skulking in the campaign background . . ." Michelle Malkin, "Howard Dean in a Dress," WorldNetDaily.com, January 28, 2004, http://www.worldnetdaily.com/news/article.asp?ARTICLE_ID=368 12 (last visited on August 29, 2006).

p. 194 "Malkin on 'Hysterical Women for Kerry' . . ." Michelle Malkin, "Hysterical Women for Kerry," WorldNetDaily.com, http://www .wnd.com/news/article.asp?ARTICLE_ID=41005 (last visited on August 29, 2006).

p. 194 "They are legitimate questions . . ." *Hardball with Chris Matthews,* MSNBC, August 19, 2004.

p. 195 "Chris Matthews plays incredulous . . ." ibid.

p. 198 "It's kind of a reverse affirmative action she profits from . . ." "About," MichelleMalkin.com.

p. 198 "Maybe I missed something in her resume . . ." *The O'Reilly Factor,* Fox News Channel, March 30, 2006.

p. 198 "she accuses him, by name . . ." ibid.

p. 198 "Consider this segment . . ." ibid.

p. 201 "Here's what Keith Olbermann on MSNBC's *Countdown . . .*" "Frequent MSNBC Guest Melanie Morgan: If *NYT*'s Keller Convicted of Treason, 'I Would Have No Problem With Him Being Sent to the Gas Chamber,'" MediaMatters.org, June 29, 2006, http://mediamatters.org/items/printable/200606290007 (last visited on August 29, 2006).

p. 201 "Ann had this to say . . ." "Coulter: 'I Prefer a Firing Squad' for *NY Times* Keller," MediaMatters.org, July 13, 2006, http://mediamatters .org/items/200607130003 (last visited on August 29, 2006).

p. 201   "In some of her photos she's wearing a turtleneck . . ." "Shopping,"
MelanieMorgan.com, http://www.melaniemorganrocks.com/shopping
.html (last visited on August 29, 2006).

p. 202   "With the help of Gamblers Anonymous . . ." *48 Hours,* CBS,
May 25, 2000.

p. 202   "Morgan's first big splash . . ." "Melanie Morgan," Sourcewatch
.com, http://www.sourcewatch.org/index.php?title=Melanie_Morgan.

p. 202   "She then formed something called . . ." ibid.

p. 202   "But until she got into the latest fight about the gas chamber . . ."
"The   Truth   Tour,"   MoveAmericaForward.org,   http://www
.moveamericaforward.org/index.php/MAF/CurrentProject/the_truth
_tour_live_from_baghdad (last visited on August 29, 2006).

p. 202   "Maybe because all those journalists in Iraq . . ." *Today,* NBC, March
21, 2006.

p. 202   "The good news was supposed to include . . ." "Truth Tour's Morgan
Falsely Suggests that Iraqi Forces Have Achieved 60 Percent Readiness," MediaMatters.org, August 3, 2005, http://mediamatters.org
/items/printable/200508030003 (last visited on August 29, 2006).

p. 202   "When she came back she went on *Hardball* . . ." *Hardball with
Chris Matthews,* MSNBC, August 11, 2005.

p. 204   "A few days earlier, on the same program . . ." *Hardball with Chris
Matthews,* MSNBC, August 1, 2005.

p. 205   "She kept giving interviews about her proposed gas-chamber punishment . . ." "Radio Host Morgan: Iraqi General Told 'Truth Tour' Par-
ticipants that Saddam Harbored 4,000 Terrorists Related to Al Qaeda,"
MediaMatters.org, August 18, 2005, http://www.mediamatters.org
/items/200508180004 (last visited on August 29, 2006).

p. 205   "On her website, she writes . . ." Greg Sargent, "Melanie Morgan
Clarifies: Only Editors *Convicted of Treason* Deserve Death
Penalty," *Horse's Mouth,* http://www.prospect.org/horsesmouth/
2006/07/post_210.html (last visited on August 29, 2006).

p. 207   "Thus, the Constitution provides . . ." Constitution of the United States of America, Article III, Section III.

p. 209   "Cindy Sheehan is . . ." "Recent CNN fire back on Cindy Sheehan: 'That's a pretty big prostitute,'" MediaMatters.org, January 19, 2006, http://mediamatters.org/items/200601190005 (last visited on August 29, 2006).

p. 209   "That's a pretty big prostitute there . . ." ibid.

p. 209   "So much for Ann's point . . ." Ann Coulter, *Godless: The Church of Liberalism* (Crown Forum, 2006), 101.

p. 209   "The Katrina victims he called 'scumbags . . ." "Beck Defended with Falsehoods His Earlier Remarks that New Orleans Katrina Victims Were 'Scumbags,' He Hated 9/11 Victims' Families," MediaMatters .org, May 5, 2006, http://mediamatters.org/items/20060550012 (last visited on August 29, 2006).

p. 209   "On Michael Moore . . ." "Radio Host Glenn Beck 'Thinking about Killing Michael Moore,'" MediaMatters.org, May 18, 2005, http:// mediamatters.org/items/200505180008 (last visited on August 29, 2006).

p. 210   "Beck mentions her as one of the reasons for his recovery," "About the Glenn Beck Program," GlennBeck.com, http://www.glennbeck .com/about/about-glennbeck.shtml (last visited on August 29, 2006).

p. 210   "To him, Jimmy Carter is . . ." "More Clinton-bashing on *Glenn Beck*," MediaMatters.org, August 11, 2006, http://mediamatters.org/items /200608110002 (last visited on August 29, 2006).

p. 210   "He's thanked a purported torturer . . ." "Beck to Purported Torturer: 'I Appreciate Your Service,'" MediaMatters.org, October 7, 2005, http://mediamatters.org/items/200510070011 (last visited on August 29, 2006).

p. 210   "Criticizing Al Gore . . ." "Beck: Bush Alone in Fighting 'World War III,' While Gore Worries That 'The Ice is Starting to Melt in Greenland,'" MediaMatters.org, July 13, 2006, http://mediamatters.org/items/200607130006 (last visited on August 29, 2006).

p. 210 "And Glenn truly does . . ." "Beck Responded to *An Inconvenient Truth: If 'Shanghai is Under Water,' 'Does Anybody Really Care?' . . . ,*" MediaMatters.org, June 15, 2006, http://mediamatters.org/items/200606150002 (last visited on August 29, 2006).

p. 211 "In 2004, Beck called Michael Berg . . ." "Clear Channel Radio Host Railed Against Nick Berg's Father, Called Him a Scumbag," MediaMatters.org, May 17, 2004, http://mediamatters.org/items/200405170002 (last visited on August 29, 2006).

p. 211 "And despite this type of throwaway hate . . ." "Premiere Radar Networks Maintain Strong Competitive Stance in Radar 87," PremiereRadio.com, December 19, 2005, http://www.premiereradio.com/news/view/92.html (last visited on August 29, 2006).

p. 211 "He responds to those who criticize . . ." "Glenn Beck: Criticism," Wikipedia.org, http://en.wikipedia.org/wiki/Glenn_Beck (last visited on August 29, 2006).

CHAPTER 12: SOULLESS

p. 213 "all of the good parts taken out . . ." Ann Coulter, "What I Did on My Summer Vacation," WorldNetDaily.com, http://www.worldnetdaily.com/news/article.asp?ARTICLE_ID=51356 (last visited on August 29, 2006).

p. 214 Ibid.

p. 215 *50 Simple Things You Can Do to Fight the Right,* Earth Works Press, 2006.